ne

SUNY Series in Philosophy
Robert Cummings Neville, Editor

The Reality of Time

Errol E. Harris

State University
of New York
Press

Published by
State University of New York Press, Albany

© 1988   State University of New York

For information, address State University of New York Press,
State University Plaza, Albany, N.Y., 12246

Library of Congress Cataloging-in-Publication Data

Harris, Errol E.
   The Reality of Time.

   (SUNY series in philosophy)
   "An expanded version of the Gilbert Ryle lectures, delivered at
Trent University, Peterborough, Ontario, in Canada, in 1984"—Pref.
   1. Time.   I. Title.   II. Series.
BD638.H277   1988   115   88-2136
ISBN 0-88706-860-X
ISBN 0-88706-861-8 (pbk.)

10 9 8 7 6 5 4 3 2 1

'Die Zeit ist der Begriff der da ist…'

Hegel
Phänomenologie des Geistes, VIII.

Contents

Preface

This book is an expanded version of the Gilbert Ryle Lectures, delivered at Trent University, in Peterborough, Ontario, in 1984. To the four lectures originally delivered, I have added here an introductory chapter, which seemed desirable in order to anticipate objections to indulging in metaphysics when so many professional philosophers still frown upon it. This chapter is a modified and expanded version of a paper read to the International Society for Metaphysics at Montreal in the previous year. The third of the Ryle Lectures (now Chapter IV) has been extended to include new material, and the original final section augmented to form the present Chapter V on Psychological Time. The last chapter was originally delivered to the Teilhard Centre in London, England, later in 1984, and was published in the *Teilhard Review*, to the editor of which I am indebted for permission to reprint it here, with some changes and additions, as a fitting conclusion to the book, in that it addresses the crucial question left unanswered in the preceding chapters.

My sincere thanks are due to Professor Lionel Rubinoff of Trent University, and his committee, for inviting me to give the Ryle Lectures, in what had already become a distinguished series, associating my name with others more eminent and deserving; and for the warm hospitality that I enjoyed at the University. I am also most appreciative of the generous reception given to the lectures when they were delivered by an unflagging audience. Likewise, I am indebted to the Ryle Lecture Committee for permitting publication in the revised and expanded version.

The central metaphysical questions about time, which seem at first sight so easy to answer (Just what is the passing moment? How do we identify the present? What constitutes the passage of time?), remain enigmatical. That they are the mere consequence of linguistic ineptitude is, I am convinced, altogether untrue, because they are rooted in the nature of our experience, which makes such alleged linguistic misuse unavoidable in one form or another. I cannot see that so-called advances in tense logic do anything to mitigate the problems, because tense logic must inevitably presuppose the experiences which give rise to the puzzlement. What this is I have tried to set out and make as plain as I can in Chapter II. The problems remain a source of a continuing bewilderment, which my best efforts have been unable to remove. What I have attempted, however, is to clarify, as far as I know how, the interrelation of permanence and change, which, we learn from Kant, are both indispensable to the experience of time, for only the permanent can change, and only what changes can be permanent. How far this, along with other characteristics of time, is true of the physical world, as well as of our experience, I have attempted to show. I have also sought to demonstrate the connection between physical time and the time involved in biological processes, and the inseparability of these from psychological time. This led onto the way in which the succession of human actions that we recognize as historical events ought to be viewed. What can be meant by the phrase, so frequently on the lips of religious persons and of theologians, "the end of time," is difficult to understand, for it seems to involve a contradiction. But the final chapter is intended to throw some light on this question.

Twice before I have written, if only briefly, on the subject of time, and while it has not been altogether possible to avoid repeating here what I had previously argued, I have done my best to reduce such repetition to a minimum. Still, I am acutely aware that far more needs saying about the topics discussed in the short compass of this book, although, at the present time, I do not feel competent to go further. I hope that brevity may not be considered too serious a fault, where prolixity was certainly to be deprecated.

In four short lectures it was not possible even to attempt an exhaustive commentary on the existing literature on Time; and in the short compass of this book, even as an expanded version of the lectures, I have not set out to remedy this defect anything like sufficiently, much as I might have wished to do so, and desirable though it may well be. Famous names and theories have been omitted or barely mentioned: Bergson, Peirce, Dewey, and William James have not been discussed as they should have been. My excuse is that I wanted mainly to pursue my own investigation, referring to others only if and when their views seemed too serious an obstacle to my own. Where they agree with mine or support my case, I have not felt it necessary to enlarge upon the fact. Josiah Royce, for instance, in *The World and the Individual*, argues powerfully for many points crucial to my case, but as I believe myself to be in full agreement with him, I have made reference to his discussion only in footnotes. Further, I have tried, as far as possible, to discuss the subject chiefly in the light of contemporary philosophy, without undue reference to theories which are well known and less current.

I cannot claim even to have stated adequately all the curiously intractable philosophical problems attending the nature of time and our experience of it, let alone to have offered any final and convincing solution. I have merely sought to express the thoughts that have occurred to me in my efforts to wrestle with questions that have perplexed me repeatedly throughout my philosophical pilgrimage, questions by which my mind has often been, even distressfully, exercised.

The irretrievability of the past, the inexorable passage of the present, the inevitable approach of the future, must at some time have given pause to every thinking person—a progression that, whatever its content, is ceaseless and unremitting, yet one the movement of which is virtually unintelligible, is not literally motion at all, and, for the most part, seems irrelevant to the nature of the events by whose sequence it is constituted and measured. If we are not habitually puzzled by all this, it is only through indifference bred of perpetual familiarity. But who has not felt sentimental regrets for the past just because it is past and gone? Who does not resist and resent change merely because it is change? And who does not at times fear the juggernaut approach of the future, irrespective of what it may bring? What is it that underlies such emotions?

My own reflection has led me to the conclusions, provisional though they must remain, that the necessary character of the finite is temporal, and that our own subjection to time is the consequence of our finite nature. It is possible that our very awareness of its passage results from the finite nature of our consciousness. But however that may be, it is only through transcendence of the finite that temporal matters ever become coherently intelligible, and that transcendence is *ipso facto* a transcendence of time—yet, equally, because of our finite nature, it should be a transcendence of the limits of our understanding.

Nevertheless, we can still say, with Spinoza, that we feel ourselves to be eternal, so that we have access, in some measure at least, to what exceeds and encompasses our finite bounds. Nor can we ever consistently entertain the belief that this premonition may be only an illusion, because the very judgement that it is so would be evidence that our finitude did not constitute an ultimate confinement, and that we are still capable of assessing our own limitations from a point of view that lies beyond them.

This book is offered as a somewhat tentative effort—which can at best give only partial satisfaction—to reflect upon questions such as these. My own discontent with the result has been gratifyingly mitigated by the consistent and flattering approval of what I had to say expressed by the audiences who originally heard the lectures, in Montreal, Peterborough, and London. But it is still apparent that much remains to be done to clarify the issues discussed and to disentangle their complexities. Whether I shall ever be able to undertake this work myself is dubious. Perhaps, therefore, I have sufficient justification for acquiescing in the publication now of these somewhat condensed, incomplete, and inconclusive reflections.

It remains only for me to express my thanks to those who read earlier drafts of the book, and made helpful and constructive suggestions for its improvement. They are in no way responsible for what I have written, or for any mistakes I may have made, but without their criticism I should have omitted much that would have left the book deficient. They are Dr. Robert Neville, the editor of the Series in which the book appears, Dr. Charles Sherover, Dr. George Kline, and Fr. Norris Clark. I am sincerely grateful to them for pointing out to me much that I had overlooked, some of which I have since tried, however inadequately, to supply. If I have failed to do more it is, at least in part, because, in actual fact, time is running out, and the human limitations, on which I have dwelt in the text to apply to, and are taking their toll of, its author.

E. E. H.
High Wray

Introduction

The Nature and Vindication
of Metaphysics

Time you old gypsy-man,
    Will you not stay
Put up your caravan,
    Just for one day.
        — Ralph Hodgson

How many have not felt sympathy with the poet's desire to arrest time, the old gypsy? But the very question and the appeal to tarry just for one day entails a contradiction. If time could stop for a day, that would mean that nothing would happen for twenty-four hours; yet the time of cessation is still assumed to have been measured, so that time would not have been stayed. Without time, contemporary physicists assure us, there would be no space; without either, there would be no energy and no motion; without energy no matter, and without matter no physical world. Even if there could be a physical world without time or motion, there would be no life in it; for life is a metabolic process, the self-maintenance of a dynamic system, a perpetual renewal and persistent regeneration of organic relationships through time, the cessation of which is death. So without time there could be no world such as we know it.

Nevertheless, the very nature of the world, in its physical and biological aspects, compels us to postulate something other than continuous change, in contrast to which alone that change is possible, something other than time, on which time itself is dependent, or of which it is a necessary aspect, yet which is not and cannot be in process. Further, as the paradox exhibited above reveals, process and time are distinct, so that when the first ceases the second does not, though they seem inseparable in our conceiving. How are they related?

This puzzling question, difficult as it is, is but the first of many into which reflection on the nature of time leads. It is clearly a metaphysical question, as are those that subsequently arise: for example, what is it about time that creates in our minds the illusion (for, as we shall presently see, it is an illusion) of motion, or flow, where none in fact occurs?

The central metaphysical problem seems to me to be how we identify the present moment; and if a solution to it could be found, it might well be the key to solving all the rest. But I have to confess that I am unable to solve it. And if the relation of time to process, with which it is so commonly confused, remains enigmatical, that of process and time to eternity is a further question to which, perhaps, at least some partial answer may be possible. The one I shall suggest depends on the logical structure of a whole, such as we are compelled by the findings of contemporary science (especially physics) to believe the world to be. This logical structure I have examined in some detail in *Formal, Transcendental, and Dialectical Thinking*. It demands, as correlatively necessary, both unity and diversity—the latter inevitably involving process—in ways to be explained in the body of this essay.

We shall confront these questions in the next chapter; but I have deemed it prudent first to consider the legitimacy of raising metaphysical questions at all, whether about time or any other matter.

Prevalent Repudiation of Metaphysics

Nowadays metaphysics is frowned upon by a large body of philosophers and, in some quarters, has become almost a term of abuse. Before presenting to the public a book the contents of which are plainly and unashamedly metaphysical, therefore, it may well be advisable to make some provision against the possibility that the reader may take Hume's advice summarily to consign it to the flames, as containing nothing but sophistry and illusion. Accordingly, the arguments which have been advanced against the practice of metaphysics must be faced before embarking upon the main theme.

At the recent XVIIth World Congress of Philosophy, I was privileged to hear two distinguished speakers, both of whom, in quick succession, declared that metaphysics was impossible. They did not say by what reasons they were persuaded to this conclusion, but I presume it was the prevalent belief that metaphysics is the philosophical quest for "foundations," and that it is inevitably a futile quest—like that of Locke's Indian who believed that the earth was supported on the back of a giant elephant and the elephant on the shell of an outsize tortoise, but could not reveal any ground on which the tortoise might stand. If every "foundation" discoverable commits us to the search for another, more fundamental still, we are swept into an infinite regress without prospect of rest or fulfillment.

Some such anxiety seems to lie behind the polemics of Richard Rorty's recent book, *Philosophy and the Mirror of Nature*. His repudiation of philosophy seems clearly to be simply the natural sceptical and relativistic fruit—probably the logically final product—of analytic philosophy. This is apparent from his own admission that it is through the vocabulary of that philosophy and its treatment of philosophical issues that he has come to the position (or lack of one) that he presents in his book. He professes to be pressing further the aim of undermining our confidence in philosophy as establishing "foundations" for knowledge and culture. Presumably, if he is to succeed, we must accept his judgements concerning philosophy and its history as true and well founded; but where are we to get assurance either of truth or foundation, if not from some metaphysical theory of truth and knowledge pre-supposed by Rorty's explicit claims? This dilemma is sometimes smoothed over by the allegation that Rorty does not expect us to take him (or any other philosopher) seriously; and if we do not, of course, there is no need for us to heed his strictures against metaphysics.

May it not be that the difficulty with "foundations" is due to the imagery entertained by both metaphysician and critic alike, itself suggested by a repressed metaphysic? If we envisage the world in crudely material form, we are apt to require substantial support for its contents. But such imagery *is* crude, and, like so many of the doctrines criticized by Rorty, long outdated and abandoned by reputable philosophers. Perhaps there may be more coherent conceptions that do not succumb to his critique.

Similarly, we tend to feel that theories subject and vulnerable to adverse criticism should be reinforced by the support of principles more basic and secure than they themselves establish. This is the pursuit of certainty that has enthralled philosophers at least since Descartes (if we overlook Plato and his successors). It is a pursuit which more recent philosophers have come to regard as futile and frustrating, besides being altogether unnecessary, because, they say, no knowledge ever is or need be certain, as long as it is sufficiently well supported by good evidence and sound reasons. But then, again, we must wonder how we are to assess the evidence and the soundness of the reasoning.

Contentions of this sort seldom confine "good reasons" to purely formal arguments, and, so far as they do, they overlook (or deny) the metaphysical presuppositions of the very formal logic they employ, if they are ever aware of the suggestion that there are any such. I have tried to demonstrate in some detail elsewhere[1] that formal logic does involve metaphysical presuppositions, and it would be tedious to repeat that argument here; but I have claimed that they include the empiricist presumption that knowledge is originally acquired through immediate sense-perception, which is the source of the belief that uninterpreted observation is sufficient to constitute "good evidence." So that too tacitly presupposes a metaphysic, and one that I have on numerous occasions striven to expose as incoherent, self-refuting, and false.[2] Moreover, those who declare that all knowledge (apart from tautologies revered as logical truths) is merely probable, ignore the fact that probability, which they admit is a matter of degree, is an approximation to truth, the necessity of which, as certainty, they deny, while, at the same time, they insist that if anything is to rank as knowledge at all, it must be absolutely warranted. It would seem, then, that some definition of truth is indispensable to any coherent thinking, and that the search for a criterion is not altogether uncalled for.

Empiricist presuppositions also account for the fact that critics of metaphysics seldom adopt an attitude of scepticism towards the natural sciences. These, they would claim, have a firm basis in observational evidence; and even though some of them are acclaimed philosophers of science, their convictions seem to remain unshaken despite the widespread acknowledgment, since the writings of N.R. Hanson and Thomas Kuhn, that all observation is theory-laden, which plays havoc with the primary assumption of philosophical Empiricism. Moreover, the objectivity of science itself has come under attack from a variety of sources. Karl Popper has classified scientific hypotheses as mere conjectures and declared verifiability to be logically impossible;[3] Kuhn has pronouced all scientific theories to be esoteric to a closed community of investigators working under the aegis of a "paradigm" of their own making, their theories being incommensurable with any other standard, or any with the least claim to objectivity;[4] Feyerabend has hailed science as a form of imaginative art and welcomed a profusion of hypotheses without any pretence of factual support as a sign of intellectual fruitfulness.[5] From a different quarter, Husserl has maintained that the sciences are secondarily derived from a more radical form of consciousness inalienably subjective,[6] and has been followed by Heidegger with a kindred argument and one not dissimilar from that of Kuhn.[7] So if metaphysics is suspect, empirical science, according to these estimates, is in no better shape.

For years I have been under the impression that all the stock arguments against metaphysics, from Kant to Wittgenstein, had long since been exposed as self-refuting; and that so far from being impossible, metaphysics is indispensable and unavoidable, always inescapably presupposed in whatever philosophical position is adopted—even one that repudiates it—as, in mid-century, the followers of the Vienna Circle, having first repudiated metaphysics as devoid of sense, later discovered for themselves.

But, having made the discovery, instead of acting upon it by examining the implied metaphysic of their own position (along with that of others) and correcting its errors in the endeavor to make it coherent and self-sustaining, they concluded that metaphysics and its progeny were all the consequences of the misuse and misapplication of ordinary language, which could only be remedied by a therapeutic course in a sort of linguistic psychoanalysis to make the speaker (the metaphysician) aware of his mislocutions. They saw that Wittgenstein's search for an ideal logical language which would "show forth the form of the fact" was inspired by a belief in logical atomism, and that that was metaphysical. So they concluded that there was no such language, and that, of the possible alternative forms of symbolization, none could be in this way ideal. One could, therefore, only examine the "logical grammar" of one's linguistic habits in order to purge them of the confusions which occasion philosophical puzzlement. It did not occur to these therapists that their theory and practice itself made tacit metaphysical presuppositions about the nature and function of language, its relation to the actual world and our experience of it, and about what these (the world and our experience) were like.

Nevertheless, the erstwhile "queen of the sciences" seems in this century to have become a mere historical relic of no scientific validity and of little philosophical interest, except (to change the metaphor) as a whipping boy. Attacks made upon it, for different reasons and from different angles, by Positivists, Logical Empiricists, Historicists, Phenomenologists, and Existentialists, seem to have relegated metaphysics to the limbo of abandoned superstitions. Such contempt of the discipline—although more recently it may have been somewhat mollified—has affected the whole tradition of philosophizing, so that in these times of dominant technology, it appears largely to have been superseded by symbolic logic and computer science.

But attacks on metaphysics are not peculiar to the present day. They have been launched throughout the history of speculative thinking. If we overlook those of Epicurus and Lucretius as directed more against superstition than metaphysics, we cannot ignore those made by Hume and Kant, by Nietzsche and Marx, long before Carnap or Wittgenstein entered the fray. Yet, somehow, or in some form, metaphysics has always survived, and its survival is to be expected as inevitable because it is the product, indeed the most characteristic and essential expression, of that self-reflective capacity which is definitive of human thinking and without which there could be no science or technology. In fact, the very attacks that have been made on metaphysics are the outcome of the same self-reflection which gives rise to metaphysics, and they are all made, if not (like Kant's) in the cause of metaphysics itself, yet in the interests of some, even if unacknowledged, metaphysic tacitly presupposed. Every attack presupposes a metaphysic of its own. For this reason metaphysics is ineradicable from any critical and reflective thinking.

The most strident denunciation of metaphysics in this century was that of the Logical Positivists led by Rudolph Carnap and the early Wittgenstein. Their weapon was the Verification Principle, and, while their critique initially had devastating effects and far-reaching consequences, in many ways still very potent, it soon became apparent, even to the exponents of the doctrine themselves, that the weapon was double-edged. The Verification Principle was, by its own criterion, unverifiable, and stood revealed as a metaphysical principle. Moreover, it was derivative from an acknowledged Empiricism which gave rise to a metaphysical theory explicitly stated by Bertrand Russell, as well as by Wittgenstein, in his *Tractatus Logico-Philosophicus*: that of logical and ontological atomism. So the later Wittgenstein, while professedly abandoning atomism, modified his central position; and some of his followers became more tolerant of metaphysics, both "descriptive" and "revisionary," as conceded by Strawson, tied though it was to linguistic analysis (the metaphysical grounds for which were not investigated).

The Marxist attack was not so much on metaphysics as such as upon the alleged "idealism" of Hegel and his predecessors; for Marx and his followers openly espoused historical and dialectical materialism,[8] which, though they claimed for it scientific status, was in fact a metaphysic, for which empirical evidence was neither sought nor available, and the internal inconsistencies of which remained unnoticed.

In the early decades of the twentieth century Constantin Brunner castigated "metaphysics" as a form of superstition.[9] But the kind of metaphysics he opposed was rather pseudometaphysics than genuine philosophical thinking, the older metaphysic which Kant, Fichte and Hegel rejected as "dogmatism." Brunner criticized Kant's notion of the *Ding-an-sich* as metaphysical and is here in agreement with Hegel; but he is himself an idealist of a sort, not unlike F. H. Bradley, and as much a metaphysical thinker as Spinoza, whom he admired and closely followed, basing his own system on Spinoza's (although he does not always interpret Spinoza correctly).

The followers of Husserl have defended him and themselves against positivist attacks by claiming that Phenomenology is neutral to all metaphysical disputes, and while it seeks to provide a new route and new access to the traditional problems, is not primarily concerned (if at all) with the ultimate nature of reality or of the consciousness the phenomenal disclosure of which it describes. Husserl's first aim was to establish philosophy on firm ground and give it a rigorous method.[10] In consequence, metaphysics might come to be defined afresh and to be seen in a new light. This is a much gentler renunciation than that of the Positivists, but the claim to neutrality can hardly be sustained. The reader of Husserl's *Cartesian Meditations* is left in little doubt of the metaphysical position from which his proposed methods flow. Its central and fundamental tenet is the indubitable existence and originary activity of the transcendental subject, whose constitutive performance is indispensable to the nature of its intentional objects.

Subsequent thinkers have made strenuous and heroic efforts to repudiate and evade this metaphysical underpinning of Phenomenology. Heidegger (Husserl's sometime pupil) strove to replace it with the direct existential experience of "being-in-the-world"; but that, we shall see in a later chapter, did not absolve him from the implication of a subject, transcendental at least in the same way as Kant's "unity of apperception," despite his failure to acknowledge it. Much the same sort of move was made by Merleau-Ponty, who sought to replace the transcendental *ego* by the organizing effects upon perception of the sensory-motor skills of the "lived body." The apparent success of this stratagem, however, depends upon an ambiguity in the use of the word "lived," which, when detected and clarified, should reinstate the conscious subject with similar implications of transcendental idealism to those of Husserl (see Chap. V, below).

Related to Phenomenology, and in part derived from it, there is today an influential school of Hermeneutics, whose approach, motivated similarly by an aversion to Husserl's transcendental "*Sinngebung*," is also antimetaphysical. Its contribution to epistemology, like that of Phenomenology, is nevertheless important and often profound. It is antimetaphysical so far as it rejects the conception of any ultimate or independent reality that is objective to knowledge and the existence of which can be established *a priori*. Hermeneutics is in essence historicist in its attitude, and is a reaction against the Rankian notion that "*the facts*" can be ascertained as they were (or are) in themselves—"as they really happened"—free from all interpretive bias or historically conditioned prejudice. Heidegger castigated such alleged "objectivity" as (on the contrary) an eminent example of subjectivism, just as Husserl had criticized the contemporary scientific outlook as "objectivation" through imposition of artificial restrictions on direct experience. If no such "objective" reality can be isolated and identified, it follows that our views of the world are all interpretations, and philosophy becomes analogous to, and in large measure actually is, the interpretation of written texts, in which the author's meaning has to be recovered by the application of a methodological technique—a hermeneutic—in which due weight must be given to the interpreter's own thinking, conditioned as it is by cultural and historical circumstances and customary linguistic usage.

This approach obviously owes much to Nietzsche's insistence on "exegesis" as a condition of all knowledge and even of all existence, with consequently ineliminable perspective bias. "There is no set of facts"; he writes, "everything is fluid, evasive, receding; our opinions are the most enduring things of all." But just as this view of Nietzsche's implies a metaphysical theory of the nature of man and of human cognition (not to mention that his other attacks on metaphysics consort ill with his addiction to the belief in eternal recurrence), even if he does not work out these metaphysical ideas systematically, so Hermeneutics rests on metaphysical presumptions about the reality and nature of history as a process, as well as others about the nature of human society, human intercourse, human cognition and reflection, and their relation to their objects. All this, again, implies some conception of the relation of man to nature, as the background and underpinning of society and of the hermeneutical activity itself.

The problem of objectivity is central and crucial to any theory whatsoever, be it hermeneutical or other; for unless some satisfactory and self-sustaining criterion of truth can be established, there can be no such thing as knowledge. Hermeneutics itself requires a standard of sound interpretation, which if it were radically unstable would be constantly dissolving, so as to make all interpretation invalid and all hermeneutics futile. But the establishment of a standard of objectivity is impossible if it does not bear some relation to the real world as well as to the nature of the knowing mind, of either of which any conception will of necessity be metaphysical.

A still more radical revolt against transcendentalism has appeared in the endeavor of Structuralism to dispense with not only the knowing subject but even with meaning itself, claiming (in the words of Hubert Dreyfus and Paul Rabinow) to find "objective laws which govern all human activity."[11] To whom they would be "objective" once the subject had been abolished is difficult to imagine, and without meaning it is not clear how they would operate, or how the structuralist would discover them. Of course, "meaning" here may be intended to refer only to the understanding of human beings whose activity is said to be governed by objective laws. They need not be, and are seldom if ever, aware of such laws—at least, until they begin, as structuralist sociologists, to reflect upon their own activity. Yet if they are to do that, they must once again be viewed as subjects cognizant of meanings, a status they may not deny to other human beings, whose social conduct they theorize upon, any more than they can exempt themselves from the restrictions they place upon others (which would make the pursuit of their discipline impossible). Nor, if we are dealing with human action, can objective laws be wholly indifferent to human awareness of the environment and circumstances in which, as persons, they act; and that again requires the presumption that every agent is a subject of consciousness.

Simply as a holistic approach to the social sciences, Structuralism has much to recommend it; and that is how it is described and defended by Jean Piaget in his book of that name.[12] But, as such, it has definite metaphysical implications, not unlike those unfolded in my ensuing discussion of time. Merely as an attempt to exclude the postulation of a subject of experience, and of an interpretable meaning inspiring human behavior, however, it is (as we shall discover more fully anon) a self-defeating form of positivism, that in the last resort is both incoherent and false.

Michel Foucault, strongly influenced by Structuralism although he disavows allegiance to its doctrines, has repudiated interpretation altogether, refusing to seek for what lies below the surface of the spoken and written word. His so-called archeology of knowledge is starkly antimetaphysical, and in fact is not strictly philosophical at all. At most, it seems to be the suggestion of a method, not altogether new, for historiography, eschewing philosophical reflection in any recognizable form. But once one allows oneself to reflect upon the presuppositions of its requirements (e.g., the account Foucault himself gives of statement and discourse), a more penetrating philosophy of history becomes inescapable, disclosing metaphysical implications. To these I shall return in the proper place.[13] Here I must make clearer the position that I myself wish to espouse.

What is Metaphysics?

So far I have been taking for granted that everybody knows what metaphysics is and does, and I must now make some attempt to justify this assumption. It would be tedious and, for the purpose of this introduction, it would hardly be appropriate for me to expatiate upon the meaning and use by Aristotle of the phrase, *meta ta phusika*, or to thread my way through the labyrinths of the traditional *metaphysica generalis* and *metaphysica specialis*. It was against the tortuous reasonings and the obscure abstractions of these disciplines that the protest of Hume was levelled and the critiques of Kant, Fichte, and Hegel were directed. What I shall try to do is to grasp afresh and to define the nature and function of metaphysical thinking, and to indicate what I think its appropriate role should be at the present time, in the hope that this may give some excuse for what I have to offer in succeeding chapters and some justification of the manner in which I have treated my subject.

As I hinted earler, self-reflective and self-determining thought is the predominant characteristic of humanity, cursed though we may also be with other more irrational traits consequent upon the finite conditions of human existence. For without self-consciousness in some degree, and some capacity for self-reflection, we could not even recognize our own shortcomings and finitude, nor could anyone properly be described as more than animal. Even when this restriction seems to give rise to moral and ethical problems, as it does in some circumstances, we have to recognize that unless it were appropriate those very ethical perplexities would not arise.

Self-awareness and reflection go hand in hand with an insistent demand for self-knowledge, for understanding of ourselves and our place in the world; and that demand carries with it the inevitable need to unify and systematize our experience of that world and of ourselves. As Kant unerringly taught us, the center and source of this systematization, or (as he called it) "synthesis," is the undeniable and inescapable unity of the apperceptive subject, always aware of itself as "I" and of its objects as "mine." Accordingly, the experience of each one of us, necessarily related as it is to a single subject, is a unified experience of interrelated and interconnected elements constituting an organized whole. The demand, in consequence, is to grasp—to conceive (*begreifen*)—all of it as a whole, to understand each of its elements and phases as exemplifying the principle of order which unifies the whole. This is what we mean (or should mean) by explanation; and it is in response to this demand that we seek to systematize our experience in the sciences and in philosophy, so as to see it, in the final outcome, as a single systematic unity. That is the task of metaphysics.

The sciences are steps along the way, and the various branches of philosophy are specific and overlapping phases of the self-exposition of this unity. Thus it has been well said that all philosophy is, or participates in, metaphysics; and every branch of philosophy involves every other, each being interdependent with the rest. Metaphysics is the comprehension of the whole and the exposition of the principle of structure by which it is pervaded.

It is this endeavor to comprehend the world of our experience as a whole and to grasp the universal and fundamental principle of its unity that lies behind Aristotle's definition of metaphysics as the science of Being *qua* Being; and, similarly, it is this to which Whitehead refers as "the endeavor to frame a coherent, logical, necessary system of general ideas in terms of which every element of our experience can be interpreted."[14] The generality on which Whitehead insists, and the ultimacy implicit in Aristotle's definition, reflect the universality of the principle of organization in terms of which the total system of our

experience and of the world which it discloses become intelligible; and
the conception and exposition of this principle is the aim of metaphysics. Let us consider a little more closely what is involved in such a
concept.

The ineluctable unity of self-consciousness guarantees that experience will be a systematic whole, which it could not be unless, as Kant
maintained, it were a system of related and connected elements
(*Vorstellungen*), without which no such thing as knowledge would ever
arise.[15] The principle of unity by which a system is integrated determines
both the nature and the interrelations of all the particular elements and
phases by which it is constituted. In both of these it will, in consequence,
be immanent, and they will exemplify it in varying degrees. No such
system is possible without diversified and interrelated contents, for no
merely blank unity is a system of any kind. Now, interrelated terms, as I
have argued elsewhere, always, of necessity, overlap, even when *prima
facie* they appear to be separated; because, to be related at all, they must
be connected by a continuous gradation of some common matrix or
quality—e.g., different colors in the color series, tones in the sonic scale,
relatives in degree of consanguinity, and likewise, whatever examples
one chooses. All terms in relation, therefore, are and must be embedded
in a qualitative or quantitative continuum (or both) of gradually diverging
phases, are necessarily interdependent, both for their place in the
continuum and for their distinctive natures, upon their mutual relations.
All this is because of the immanence in them of the universal principle of
order governing the system to which they belong.

Thus every portion or limited element in the system will imply the
whole, and the development of this implication will involve the
successive explication of the interrelations between the part and its
determinants within the system, until the entire structure has been
serially unfolded, the principle of its organization being thereby
progressively revealed. As all experience is necessarily unified in its
diversity (Kant would have said, "in synthetic unity"), each phase of this
progressive revelation is itself a whole of sorts; but according to its degree
of abstraction, the degree of its systematic integration will vary.
Knowledge, in consequence, develops itself through successive stages, in
each of which it is a whole, progressively increasing in degree of
systematic unity, beginning with the perceptual world of "the natural
attitude" (or common sense), continuing through the sciences—the
exact, the natural, and the social sciences—and culminating in

philosophy, which is a body of overlapping and intermeshing reflection upon our total experience, combining to form, and issue as, the body of metaphysical speculation.

What we have before us is, then, a series of wholes or systems of knowledge progressively differing in degree of reflective self-awareness, ranging from the crassly empirical to the comprehensively speculative, and culminating in metaphysics; so that Plato's descriptions of the dialectician are true of the metaphysician, that he "sees all things together" and becomes "a spectator of all time and all eternity."[16] As such a conspectus, metaphysics remains, or is reinstated as, the queen of the sciences.

The Restoration of Metaphysics

This restoration is taking place only gradually at the present time, but the signs of its growing influence are clearly discernible. A recent interpretation of Husserl by André de Muralt recasts the structure of Phenomenology as a dialectical system in a series of endeavors, increasing in clarity, tending towards the complete and perfect cognition of the intended object. The two poles of this process are the empirical, or "factical," and the ideal, the *eidos*. The series issues, for de Muralt, in a science very similar to what I have here described as metaphysics, though he regards it as unattainable in its full development and approachable only asymptotically.[17]

Heidegger urges the metaphysician to return to the origin of speculative thinking and to appreciate existentially the problem of the Presocratics with respect to Being—the relation to it of beings and of the *Dasein* of human awareness. In all this his precise meaning remains obscure, but what he writes strongly suggests the pervasiveness of a universal principle (Being), which manifests itself in all existences (*Seiendes*), and reveals itself as undeniably present in human self-consciousness.[18] This universal essence is the true and proper object of metaphysics.

Whitehead found such a principle in the "Primordial Nature of God," which he saw as universally ingredient into the actual entities of the world, perpetually reconstituting in themselves a microcosm of the universe out of the perished "superjects" of their predecessors, in a continuously creative process. The description of this process, in accordance with general definitive categories—that is, "a coherent, logical, necessary system of general ideas"—constitutes for him the science of metaphysics. That Whitehead's theory answers to the account I have given of the subject is not difficult to show. The Primordial Nature of God is the ordering principle of the whole; the creative process of concrescence issues as a complex series of actual entities and nexūs in increasing degress of integration, which ultimately culminate as the Consequent Nature of God—the total system displaying the universal principle of structure in complete elaboration. The growing body of process philosophy at the present time, which develops these ideas, gives further evidence of the resurgence of metaphysics.

Still more recently, developments in Hermeneutics contribute further to this revival of metaphysics, even in spite of themselves. Gadamer's plea for the recognition of a dialectical interplay between present and past in the process of interpretation, and of the necessary prevalence of the encompassing "horizon" of interrelated ideas and "prejudices" (in part prepredicative and unthematized), in terms of which we understand,[19] leads directly to the presupposition of a comprehensive totality of experience embracing both past and present, the interpretation of which requires the grasp of its principle (or principles) of structure, so that they transpire as the rules or canons of hermeneutic. The science of Hermeneutics then corresponds to what I identify as metaphysics.

One of the most interesting, and perhaps the most neglected accounts of metaphysics produced during this century is that given by R. G. Collingwood. In his *Essay on Metaphysics*[20] he maintains that the aim of the discipline is to discover and to trace the development of the absolute presuppositions of science. A presupposition he defines as a postulate, or belief, which gives rise to questions. If it is itself the answer to a prior question, he calls it a relative presupposition; but if there is no prior question which it answers, and the questions to which science seeks answers arise out of it, it is an absolute presupposition. Those ingrained prejudices which, according to Gadamer, are engendered by our cultural environment and tradition, and which condition and determine our methods of interpretation seem at least to be analogous to Collingwood's absolute presuppositions.

In Collingwood's view, it is the task of metaphysics to isolate, by a method of logical analysis, the absolute presuppositions of the sciences in any given period. If it is the science of a former day, the investigation will obviously be historical; but even the analysis of present-day scientific theories requires methods of the same kind, for the study of the present and the study of the immediate past coincide. The task set is to discover what presuppositions have actually prompted scientific questions in the minds of practising scientists and ultimately lie behind the course of their investigations.

The absolute presuppositions made by the sciences of any one historical period, Collingwood holds, form a "constellation" of theses, which ought to be, but are not always, consupponible. If they are not, they give rise to "strains," to remove which the constellation must be modified, so that constellations change and develop in the course of time. The metaphysician's task, in consequence, is not simply to reveal the presuppositions of science but also, and more significantly, to trace the process, and presumably, to detect the reasons, for their changes.[21]

In his earlier *Essay on Philosophical Method*,[22] Collingwood had very cogently argued that an historical process of this kind constitutes a scale of forms, in which each philosophical (or metaphysical) theory exemplifies, in a specific degree of adequacy, a generic essence, or universal. Each theory is a specific form of the universal, and each as superseding its predecessor and correcting its errors stands in opposition to it. Every metaphysical theory should then be a more or less adequate exemplification of a generic essence (or universal) presupposed by, and expressing itself in, every science; and the history of metaphysics should be a series of progressively more adequate expressions (in some sense of "adequate" yet to be defined) of the universal principle immanent in all experience.

Thus we reach an account of metaphysics similar to that which I have already outlined, requiring only an explanation of the sense in which successive metaphysical doctrines become more adequate. That to which they become more adequate is, of course, the universal principle of order and unification, which in origin is the unity of the self-conscious *ego* (the unity of the universal whole immanent in human cogni-tion). Hence, as we have already found, the scale is one of increasing self-awareness on the one hand, and of more coherent integral unity on the other. Degree of adequacy, accordingly, turns out to be the degree of systematic unification required by what Whitehead called "a coherent, logical, necessary system of ideas," as well as the degree of explicit self-awareness. This is the criterion of advance in all knowledge at every stage, whether explicitly it takes the form of "agreement with experience" (i.e., between theory and fact), or, as for the Pragmatist, between theory and practice. In every case, what is sought is a coherent experience eliminating conflict and contradiction.

Contradiction and conflict is the stimulus to advance, through the demand for its removal. It is this stimulus that prompts the advance from common sense to science. Common experience is notoriously flawed by contradictions—if only the ubiquitous paradoxes, exploited by Zeno, in the phenomena of movement and change. These exercised the minds of the Ancient philosophers, along with the contradictory appearances in the motion of the heavenly bodies. It was the effort to "save the appearances" and remove the contradictions that gave rise to science, and which has in the course of time burgeoned out into a system of sciences, each in itself systematically unified, and all interconnected and mutually sustaining, so that they form, if only ideally and in aspiration, a single unified system. What the metaphysician seeks is the universal principle ordering this whole and the way in which it expresses itself as the absolute presupposition of science at each stage of its development.

There is now no danger of an infinitely regressive search for "foundations," because it is not by retrogression that we reach the ultimate principle of explanation but by dialectical progression. The ordering principle of a system developing as a graded scale of forms is not what lies at its base—not the vague immediacy from which the beginning of the investigation starts—but what reveals itself at its culmination. The whole is self-complete and self-sustaining. The universal principle of order reveals itself fully only at the end of the scale as that which has been immanent from the beginning. The imagery which we rejected above of an underlying fundament is inappropriate. There is no infinite regress; but there is a circle—not, however, vicious, but simply what is necessarily involved in the return upon itself of progressively self-reflective thinking, which discovers in the final phase what has all along been implicit in the earlier. The criterion of truth and validity emerges at the end as what has throughout been the sustaining principle of order and rationality. No infinite regress is involved, there-fore, as the system closes in upon itself and maintains itself in its integral wholeness, justifiying Spinoza's claim that truth is the measure both of itself and of falsity.

To see metaphysics in this way is to dispose once and for all of the positivistic denunciation that because of its lack of empirical evidence it can have no factual meaning. In any case, the recent rediscovery (becoming, at long last, generally recognized) that empirical evidence is always theory-laden has undermined empiricism so fatally that the accusation itself has lost all plausibility. Likewise, the outworn slander that metaphysics is mere cerebration without practical significance loses all force in an age when science and technology have permeated our entire way of life, frequently to its detriment, so that the examination of the presuppositions of science can scarcely fail to have practical relevance.

The history of science thus constitutes a scale of forms in which each major epoch is dominated by a conceptual scheme, somewhat inappropriately called by Thomas Kuhn a "paradigm," and more suggestively by Collingwood a constellation of absolute presuppositions. The ultimate and most comprehensive conceptual scheme in any period is metaphysical, and the sciences operate under its aegis as long as the latent contradictions inherent in it can be overlooked—so long as they do not interfere too seriously with the solution of minor problems (what Kuhn calls "normal" science). When that does occur, as it did, for example, in the fifteenth century, the conflicts become intolerable and the conceptual scheme is modified, producing a scientific revolution and establishing a new metaphysical system in which previous contradictions have been resolved. So progress has been made from Aristotelian to Copernican, from Copernican to Newtonian, and from Newtonian to Einsteinian science—to the contemporary system of relativity and quantum physics (passing over for the moment other sciences, which are, however, not unconnected with or uninfluenced by developments in physics). At each stage a new conceptual scheme is presupposed, which, as set out by the philosophers of the day, is the appropriate metaphysical theory. But whereas the metaphysics of the Ancients, and subsequently that of the seventeenth-century Rationalists and Empiricists, each expressing the absolute presuppositions of their contemporary science, were systematically set out by the philosophers of those times, the appropriate metaphysic of the twentieth century is still in the process of gestation.

I have tried to give some indication of the way in which this is proceeding, although as yet there is considerable confusion of voices. It must be a metaphysic at once of relativity, of evolution, and of historical interpretation; and this has been developing first through the systems of Samuel Alexander, Henri Bergson, and A. N. Whitehead; then, after an interruption by the somewhat abortive efforts of Positivism to dispense with metaphysics altogether, through Phenomenology and Hermeneutics, which have taken up the trail at a different point and from a different angle. With the help of Collingwood's theories of absolute presuppositions and the scale of forms, adumbrating a universal principle of systematic wholeness (implied, if not always clearly expressed), the process may continue further.

Positivism, despite its vociferous claims, failed, with its throwback to eighteenth-century Empiricism, to provide adequate interpretation or expression of the scientific spirit of the age; and Phenomenology and Existentialism, as well as Hermeneutics, have failed to relate their metaphysical schemata to a sufficiently wide range of scientific thought. Phenomenology and Existentialism have obvious important relations to psychology, and Hermeneutics has similar important relations to the social sciences—to anthropology and history. But what is needed and still remains to be worked out is a metaphysic in the style of Alexander and Whitehead, which will comprehend the fundamental presuppositions at once of physics and biology as well as of psychology and the social sciences.

The chapters which follow can scarcely claim to offer more than a very small contribution to this task, although elsewhere I have tried to pursue it at more length. Here attention is devoted only to one central topic, that of time. I have not explicitly raised Collingwood's question as to the absolute presupposition of contemporary science with respect to time, but it will be obvious to the reader that it is the crucial issue throughout. For a return to metaphysics in an age of scepticism I make no apology. What I have written above aims at establishing its legitimacy, and the parlous condition of our contemporary society, which has been brought about largely through the overpowering domination of a technology devised by sciences, of which the absolute presuppositions have remained for the most part unexamined, is a sure indication of its necessity.

Metaphysical Problems of Time

As for man, his days are as grass; as a flower of the
field, so he flourisheth.
For the wind passeth over it, and it is gone; and the
place thereof shall know it no more.
Ps. 103:15-16

We are all creatures of time and change, and are as much
ephemerids (though we live longer) as the mayfly which expires at dusk
on the day that it was born. Yet we have immortal longings and continually question the futility of this inexorable evanescence.

We look before and after
And sigh for what is not. . . .
(Shelley)

If time involves continuous passage, and whatever comes to be inevitably
passes away, what, we ask, is the significance of this ceaseless generation
and demise? Is the meaning and importance of our experience really
affected by its flowing and its impermanence, or is there something of
permanent value that persists? On the other hand, the satisfactoriness of
changeless permanence is equally dubious. For frozen unmoving
immutability excludes activity and liveliness; yet the price we pay for the
excitement and interest of life seems inevitably to be death.

Shakespeare's Brutus reflects

That we must die we know. 'Tis but the time
And drawing days out that men stand upon.
(*Julius Caesar*, Act III, Scene 1)

And some die sooner than others. Commonly we regard premature death
as a disaster, while long life is considered a boon. What are the grounds
of this evaluation?

In this small book it is my intention to consider this ineliminable temporal aspect of our experience—the time and drawing out of days—to reflect upon some of the (at least seemingly) impenetrable puzzles it presents, to examine the various forms in which it appears to us and the degree of concern with which, in each of these forms, we ought to regard it. For along with, and inseparably from, the process of change, we are just as inescapably aware of a changeless and permanent reality to which also we feel ourselves to belong. How do these aspects of the world and of our awareness of it relate to each other, does either ultimately take precedence, and what relevance has either of them for our assessment of value, including that of our own existence?

It is because we die and life is short in comparison with the vast eons of the world's existence that we seek to understand how this fleeting life is compatible with our conscious grasp of the encompassing cosmos and its duration; and also how it is possible (or is it mere self-deception?) that, as self-conscious beings, despite our inescapable temporality, in Spinoza's words, "we feel ourselves to be eternal."

These are difficult questions and I do not pretend to be able to find definitive answers to any of them. But they are questions which, if we reflect at all, we cannot avoid raising, and there may well be interest even in considering the sources of the puzzlement which they occasion.

Passage, Movement, and Measurement

Every student knows that Augustine said of time:

> What, then, is time? If no one asks me, I know: if I wish to explain it to one that asketh, I know not...[1]

Contemporary analytic philosophers, following the later Wittgenstein, have claimed to dispose of Augustine's problems by pointing to the tenses of verbs and our use of them to refer to past, present and future events. But it does not seem to occur to them that our use of language in this way is but a sign and an acknowledgement of our awareness of the passage of time which occasions the problems, and, so far from removing, it only underlines them.

The conception of passage is central to our puzzlement, for passage is primarily a spatial concept applying to movement in space; yet we say—and it seems we cannot avoid thinking—that time passes. But how does it pass? What does it pass? In what sense does, or can, it possibly move? Any spatial motion takes time, occurs in time, as well as in space; but the passage of time itself cannot take time. There is no other time in which it could occur.[2] Nor does time move in or through space; rather every point in space "moves," in some odd metaphorical sense, through or with time. The fact that we *say* of events that they *have occurred, are occurring* now, and *will occur* later, throws no light on this problem. Time "passes," however we speak of it, even if nothing occurs (this is the essence of *ennui*), and our reference to past, present, and future by means of verbal tenses only emphasizes the continuous passage of time, it does nothing to make it intelligible. I shall return to this point later; let us meanwhile notice another difficulty about passage.

When on the highway we read the sign "NO PASSING" we know that this refers to the overtaking of one car by another. Both move in space, both take time to move a given distance, and one passes the other. But time does not move in space, nor in time, yet (as we say) it "passes" continually, although we cannot indicate anything that it passes as we can indicate the objects by the wayside, and other cars upon the road, which we pass as we drive along. It does not pass us, for we are carried along with it, but the events of our former experience have passed and are past. Yet they are our own experiences, and we cannot "pass" ourselves. Yet we constantly do just that; we leave our own past "behind" our present selves, while we still remember and carry it along with us. And though we seem somehow to pass through events and leave them behind, ourselves being carried along by time, it nevertheless seems also to pass us by: "Time and tide wait for no man." How is all this possible?

We say of our past experiences that time has "carried them away," as it will carry each and all of us away, "like an ever rolling stream." But, again, this is a spatial metaphor, nor is there anywhere to which time can "carry" events, nor can it "move" as a stream moves through space and in time. In what possible sense, then, does time move? For it never stands still, even when spatial movements cease.

If time never stands still, however, it is also the case that temporal relations never change. If event A precedes event B, nothing can ever alter that order. A may be repeated after B, but the repetition is a new and separate event coming later than either B or the original A. The temporal order of before and after is eternally fixed and cannot be changed without contradiction. This is what we mean when we say that time is irreversible; and it is a feature of time persistently overlooked by science-

fiction writers who imagine travelling back and forth in time. Nevertheless, the events themselves are all and always changes of one sort or
another. That is what makes them events. They are, as it were, markers in
the perpetual flux.

Augustine asks, How do we measure time?[3] and what do we
measure when we do? We cannot measure the past for it has gone and is
no longer subject to our manipulation or available for comparison with
anything else. Much less can we measure the future, for it does not yet
exist to be measured. The present, because of time's continuous passage,
has no duration, so how can we measure that? Yet we do measure time,
and, therefore, this question should be answerable.

We measure time by identifying some periodic sequence as
uniform and consistent as we can discover—like the earth's revolution
around the sun, or better, the vibration of the caesium atom—and we
compare with this other processes of change which occur coincidentally
with it. The uniform and constant periodic sequence which we use as our
standard thus constitutes a clock, and by counting its phases we have a
measure of the rate of change. This practice bypasses the facts that the
past has gone and the future not yet come. It simply counts the passing
moments of the current flux.

What is it, then, that moves? Bodily movements in space may be fast
or slow, and we measure velocity by comparing distances traversed
within the same time. It would be absurd, however, to allege that we can
do this with time alone. Time cannot pass more or less speedily—in spite
of Rosalind's pretention in As You Like It;—for what she distinguishes are
different rates of change within a given lapse in experience. Five minutes
cannot take more or less than five minutes to elapse, and the minutes we
regard as units of measurement. They are fixed quantities which can
change as little as the relations of precedence and simultaneity. So
conceived, time must be distinguished from change, which may occur
more or less rapidly, while time does not change, or "move," in any sense,
but is merely the metric by which the rate of change is measured.

Even so, though we recognize this distinction between change and
the metric by which it is measured, we have still not solved St. Augustine's
problem; for to establish a metric we have to know that the periodic
sequence that we use to measure is uniform and regular. But we can find
this out only by measuring its phases, by comparing them together and
finding them equal. But the phases never exist together. They cannot be
coincident and so can never be directly compared. If we compare them
with other processes, we are faced with the same difficulty over again

with respect to these. We can at best base our confidence in the regularity of our clock upon theoretical assumptions, or principles such as "same cause same effect."

Commonly the distinction between time and change is not clearly made and we tend to think of time in two different ways, which we then confuse. We think of it as clock time, which does not move or change but is only the metric with which we measure the rate of change; but we also think of the incessant process of change itself as time, as when we compare it to "an ever rolling stream," or speak of it as passing more or less rapidly. Then, again, we fail to distinguish these two senses of time. Physicists, for instance, say that time slows down when the universal rate of change decreases and affects clocks as well as all other processes, equating the metric with that which is measured. Yet, on the other hand, when they attend to the metrical aspect of time, they tend to abstract from passage and to think of time as a fourth dimension (in space). As Bergson complained, they spatialize time, regarding events as fixed and coexistent in a four-dimensional manifold, or what he (following William James) called a "block universe." We shall see later that this does not relieve us of the problem of passage, for there must still be some sense in which our experience flows from one event to the next across the intervals of space-time; and this flow is not the spatial movement represented in the manifold.

Donald Williams has emphatically rejected any notion of passage or flux,[4] because movement, being change, is itself a series of events; hence, to say that time moves implies that the happening of an event is itself another second-order kind of event, and that would require a third-order series, and so on ad infinitum. In this, he is, of course, entirely correct. He advocates, in its stead, what he calls the theory of the manifold, which is just what we have referred to above: for example, the conception of the four-dimensional framework without passage. Williams alleges that this does not spatialize time or commit us to a "block universe." But here he is wrong, for obviously it is a spatialization, as it requires the assumption that the time axis runs at right-angles to the other three spatial dimensions, and literally it cannot. It can do so only in what mathematicians call "configuration space." In short, it is a blatant spatialization. The four-dimensional manifold must be recognized as a mathematical device for interpreting physical measurements. Further, as we have stated above, and as will appear more fully anon, it does not eliminate the temporal aspect of passage, of which Williams so much wishes to be rid.

When we attend to the processive aspect of change we spatialize again and speak of it as a stream, a movement, or a flux. Spatial movement is certainly a form of change, but it is not the only one; change may also be of shape, size, or quality, as Aristotle recognized (although he still categorized change as motion). Yet, however we think of time we seem unable to avoid spatial metaphors, none of which may be understood literally though we are still unable to interpret them nonspatially.

As already noted, the alleged movement of time does not manifest itself in the change of temporal relations, before and after. It is expressed in the perpetually changing relations of past, present, and future. These, as J. M. E. McTaggart reminds us,[5] *all* belong to *every* event in time, which is successively each of them, continuously changing from distant future (notice once more the spatial metaphor!) to near future, from future to present, from present to past, and from recent past to remote past. So McTaggart analyses time into two series of events, which he calls the A-series and the B-series. The A-series is the succession of events passing from future to present and then to past; the B-series is the same succession simply related as earlier and later. The events in both series are, of course, the same, but only in the A-series does their temporal description change. One may liken the series of events to a cinematograph film on which successive frames occur one after another. This is the B-series. As they pass over the lens of the projector, they are successively (with respect to projection) future, present and past—the A-series.

Now what, in the actual passage of time, represents the lens of the projector? What identifies any event in the B-series as present—for it is that equally that determines which events are past and future? To this question, before it is raised, like St. Augustine's, we feel that we know the answer; but once it is asked we find it unanswerable.

How Do We Identify the Present?

We cannot identify the present event by giving it a date. Dates are indifferent to past, present, and future. Dates belong to the metric, they are the numbered moments which succeed each other, and every one of them is, in turn, future, present, and past. The year 1066 is now past, but in 1066 it was present, and in 55 B.C. it was future. Like events, every date is all three. It was for this reason—because, he alleged, it involved self-contradiction—that McTaggart maintained that time could not be real. His argument is far more difficult to refute than is commonly held, but I do not wish to discuss it at this point and shall return to it later. The present event has the date which it has because it belongs to the B-series, and comes after the events which have earlier dates and before those which have later dates. The dates are simply the numbers on the frames of the film. So the same problem of identifying the present event applies equally to dates. In what way does 1988 differ from any other number so as to distinguish it as present?[6]

Is it then immediate experience of events that makes them present? What is present to me is what I experience immediately—what I experience *now*. And whatever is simultaneous with that is the present. True indeed; but every experience, whenever one has it, is immediate, so that immediacy cannot distinguish between past, present, and future. The point, however, you will say, is that we distinguish between what is immmediate to us *now*, at this moment; and what is not so immediate is not present, even if other experiences were immediate to us in the past and will be in the future. That we do distinguish cannot be denied, but the question is *how* do we distinguish?—and this cannot be by means of that characteristic which is common to all experience.

Merleau-Ponty writes:

> No one of time's dimensions can be deduced from the rest. But the present (in the wide sense, along with its horizons of past and future), nevertheless enjoys a privilege because it is the zone in which being and consciousness coincide.[7]

Certainly presentness is crucial to the whole conception of time—"it enjoys a privilege," and it is true likewise that in it being and consciousness coincide. But this provides no answer to our problem, and is not what distinguishes the present; for with all consciousness, whenever it occurs, being coincides. *Cogito ergo sum* (where *cogito* means "I am conscious"); and that is undeniable whenever I am conscious and whatever I am conscious of. One may not say that I am not conscious of the past, because it exists for me only as I am conscious of it, and of its effects. Nor may one say that in the past being and consciousness did not coincide. And as I am conscious of the past in the present, that coincidence is also present. What the future will disclose, I do not precisely know, but I do have some consciousness of it in anticipation— as Merleau-Ponty says, the present has its horizons of past and future. My future consciousness will evince its coincidence with being, just as much as my present consciousness does. So in this respect there is still nothing to distinguish past and future from the present, and no distinguishing mark of the present as such.

One might argue that the being of the past does not coincide with my present consciousness; but it does whenever I think of the past. You may object that then I am not, and cannot be, aware of the past *immediately*. But through what am I mediately aware of it, if not my immediate awareness of its relation to the present, for which I have found no distinguishing mark? It is not that my present consciousness does not coincide with the being of (say) Julius Caesar; for, inasmuch as I am conscious of him and his history, it does. To say that my consciousness is present, and the history of Julius Caesar is, by definition, past, is undoubtedly true, but I am still unable to explain how I make this distinction, and by what criterion, apart from relating the periods of history in the B-series, where nothing is identified as present or past.

Moreover, the matter is complicated by the fact that, in some quite definite sense, we experience the past immediately in memory and the future in anticipation, and we do so *now*; so that immediacy cannot be the distinguishing feature. Nor can we distinguish by using the word "now," because that begs the question. It is the "now" that we seek to identify. When is now? How is it differentiated from then? We have just seen that it cannot be by the immediacy of experiencing. And the claim that we identify the present as what we experience now, in contrast to what we have experienced before and will experience later, does not help, because what we seek is the distinguishing mark of the "now"; so we cannot use *it* to distinguish the event as present. To say that we experience X *now* is simply to say that it is present. It tells us nothing about how the present now differs from past nows and future nows—for whenever they occur they are always now. You may wish to protest that they are and can be now *only* when they occur; but when is that? The only answer we can give is "the present," which leaves us where we began.

Another form of this appeal to immediacy is to equate the present with sensation as opposed to imagination and memory, as Whitehead does in effect in *The Concept of Nature* (Chap. III). The obvious failure of this suggestion, however, lies in the fact that imagining and remembering occur as much in the present as does sensation, though their objects may be future or past events. Moreover, that the objects of sensation are present when we experience them (and are not being merely imagined) is ascertainable directly only be means of sensation, if at all. The British Empiricists from Locke to Hume all tried to establish some criterion by which to distinguish between sensation and imagination (including memory) but without success, for there is no intrinsic difference which will universally discriminate between them. Images can, in certain circumstances, be as vivid as sensations, and sensations, in other circumstances, can be as dim as imaginings. And the immediate presence of the object cannot be independently perceived. As a means of distinguishing the present from the past and future, therefore, the difference between direct sensation and imagination will not serve.

The suggestion might be made that action is a sign of the present, the fact that action is going on. Alas! this proposal is no help. First, to say that action is going on is no more than to say that it is present, without offering any distinguishing criterion. Secondly, the inactivity of what is not acting is just as much present as the exertion of the active. Inertia does not disqualify the inert from being present. Further, past action is often (if not always) operative in the present (for example, the generation of energy in the sun), and present action will undoubtedly operate in the future. In fact, the continual transmission of action is universally characterisitic of temporality. Thus the distinctions between present, past, and future action remain as puzzling as before.

Adolf Grünbaum maintains that temporal becoming, involving past, present, and future, is mind-dependent, and that the distinguishing characteristic of presence is conceptual awareness of the presented event, including awareness that it is presently being perceived.[8] Such conceptual (or judgmental) awareness, however, is in no better case than immediate awareness, because every event to which tenses then apply will be one of which we must have been conceptually aware when it was present, so that conceptual awareness cannot distinguish present from past. The best we can do is to say that the past event was one of which we were (at the time), but no longer are, aware; but that presupposes that the distinction has already been made on other grounds. The statement, moreover, would strictly be self-contradictory, because one must be conceptually aware of the past in order to identify it as what one has previously experienced.

Indeed it is true that events are "now" when they occur; and if they are not occurring, they are not present. But it is just this difference that we are seeking to define. It is an empty tautology to say that past and future are not present. What we want to know is how we distinguish them as such, and the answer cannot be that we do so by identifying the present as neither past nor future (i.e., as what is now being immediately experienced).

Might we then say that what is present is what exists, for the future does not yet exist and the past exists no longer? Again we have a criterion which is either inapplicable or question-begging. If we distinguish sharply between the past (as no longer existing) and the present, and that again from the future (as not yet here), we find that the present has no duration, and so it does not exist either. "There is no such thing as nature at an instant posited by sense-perception", so Whitehead has assured us.[9]

But nature as "posited by sense-perception" invokes, by implication, the so-called specious present, and that, in principle, is once more an appeal to immediacy, for the specious present is what we are immediately aware of as present. And it is a virtual admission that what now exists consists equally of past and future. Further, it has been cogently argued by J. D. Mabbott that the specious present is of no fixed duration and may in different circumstances include considerable periods of time. It may be "this present moment," or "today," or "this week," "this semester," or "this year"—for the historian, even the current century may constitute a specious present.[10] But one may demur from this contention on the grounds that "the specious present" is a technical term in psychology meaning precisely that span of which a conscious subject is directly aware at any one time. This objection, however, does not escape the difficulty that the present then includes both past and future (Husserl's "retention" and "protention"), nor the difficulty that immediacy cannot distinguish between them. Besides all this, the specious present has still to be identified as present in distinction from what is not yet specious and what has been. At which time is it present? Which of the successive specious presents is *now*?

Further, the present cannot exist simply in its own right, but is nothing more than the inherited past which is encapsulated in it. What is now occurring is what has come to be out of what has just been, incorporating the effects of the past. And it is just as much the potential future, for unless it were it would not encapsulate the past. What is happening now is what the past has become and what is about to become what the future will disclose. Even if, as Whitehead insisted, every actual occasion introduces novelty into the world, it is not independently of the past but only by prehending and integrating anew what the past delivers to it, and it does so in virtue of a "lure" directed to the future through its (conceptual) prehensions of "eternal objects." What exists is in consequence a composite of past, present, and future, continuously accepting from the first and transmitting to the last, without giving us any clear hallmark by which we can distinguish any of them.

Could we say that what is accepted is past becoming present, and what is transmitted is present becoming future? This, clearly, reverses the proper order, for it is by accepting from the past that the future becomes present.[11] But however we describe the process, we have not yet found any distinguishing mark by which the present is identifiable—a mark by which we can point to a particular event in the B-series and say, "This is the present event."

When all is said and done, existence is also a question-begging criterion, because if only what is present exists, only what has existed is past. Existence thus characterizes the past as much as it does the present. The distinction is made only by the verb form ("has existed"); and we have already seen that the verb form presupposes the temporal distinction. Before we can know what has been, we must know what is and how the two are related temporally. We must know that existent E_1 preceded existent E and that E exists *now*. It cannot, therefore, be the fact of existence that determines being *now*, for being *then* is equally being. *Mutatis mutandis* the same applies to what will be. The very fact that we use the verb "to be" in all three tenses gives the game away.

At this point, Heideggerian existentialists may have become impatient, and may protest that I am using the word "exist" carelessly and uncritically, as it applies only to things "ready to hand," or (better) "present at hand." Temporality, they will say, is intrinsic to and is the constitutive character of *Existenz*, in which past, present, and future are projected by the authentic (or even inauthentic) understanding by *Dasein* of its *Seinkönnen*. This understanding is the awareness of possibilities, and these necessarily have reference to future being, as something "not yet" and "still to come"; and such possibilities are derivative from the acceptance by *Dasein* of its *Geworfenheit* (its "thrownness"), as "having been".[12] So the future generates the present in the process of becoming past.

Heidegger's treatment of temporality contains many pregnant insights and suggestive implications, to which I shall have occasion to return. I cannot pretend always to understand his position fully, or ever to be able to penetrate all the obscurities of his perverse and tortuous use of language, least of all, perhaps, when he speaks of the "ekstases" involved in the above-described temporality of *Dasein* and its *Sorge* (care, concern, interest?). These "ekstases" seem to be projections or extrapolations of the "anticipation" of *Seinkönnen* (potentialities for being), of its enactment (in consequence of "anticipatory resoluteness") and the "having-been-ness"of *Geworfenheit*; and they (the "ekstases") constitute the past, present, and future of everyday notions of "being-in-time" (*Innerzeitigheit*).

Projection, or extrapolation, however, presupposes a framework on which to project, a surrounding (logical) space, a structure of relationships, such as the A-series of McTaggart. This requirement is not removed by Heidegger's protestations that *Dasein's* understanding, expectation, anticipation, and so forth, are no mere succession of "nows." Moreover, he speaks of "the future, as coming towards," and outstanding possibility held out before itself by *Dasein's* "coming towards itself," as the original phenomenal character of the future.[13] This is further emphasized by his preoccupation with death and its authentic anticipation as the final extinction of *Dasein*. Here we have persistent spatial metaphors and images of motion (towards—as in a stream), an envisagement of temporality that involves all the metaphysical difficulties I have been discussing and that obviates none of them.

Michael Gelven, in his *Commentary on Heidegger's Being and Time*,[14] says that Heidegger has scrupulously avoided a formulation of "metaphysical time," that would treat time as some sort of entity or substance. In this he is undoubtedly right, for certainly time is no sort of substance moving through space as water flows along a streambed. But as soon as one speaks of *Seinkönnen* (e.g., death) as "to come," or of the future as what "I am as coming toward," or the past as what "I am as having been" (before)—and both Heidegger and his commentator use such phrases with approval—one invokes spatial metaphors and appeals to concepts of motion that immediately suggest a stream with which, or a path along which, the self comes towards itself, or a current against which we press to anticipate what comes towards us. Heidegger (so far as I can understand him) maintains that the present is a making present by *Dasein* of what it has chosen from among possibilities yet to come, as if one were to look ahead along an approaching assembly line of possibilities and to choose which of them to appropriate. This is not unlike what the lens in a film projector does with the advancing frames (except that it does not actively choose, but simply projects what the machine presents). It makes present what is to come.

So let us return to our comparison with the film projector. The lens is not part of the film, and it is the frame before the lens which is presently being projected. What determines the present here is the relation of the event (depicted in the frame) to something *outside* the series of events. But this is not conceivable in the case of the temporal B-series. First, there is nothing outside the series to which its members could be so related. It could not be empirical consciousness (mine or any other), be it expressed as "care," or "understanding," or "resolve," or just observation of what is "present-at-hand," because in any of these forms it is within the flux. As Kant constantly reminds us, time is the form of innner sense; and Heidegger insists that the very foundation and meaning of *Sorge*, which if primordially characteristic of *Dasein*, is temporality, and that this derives from the responsible, concerned activity that is the form of *Dasein's* being—it makes present the possibilities for being that it imagines. Is it in relation to this "making present" that the elements of *Dasein's* existence are "datable" (though Heidegger suggests rather that expectation is prior)? Whatever it is, it cannot for that reason be removed from the flux of "coming toward," "coming alongside," and "having been." For Heidegger, temporality, as the meaning of concern (*Sorge*), is the source and foundation (in effect) of the A-series, and the origin of all inauthentic (fallen) conceptions of time as measurable. McTaggart's whole theory might be rejected as belonging to the latter, but (as will be argued below, in Chapter V) not even an "authentic" awareness of time avoids the imputation of a moving series of events (or experiences); and the image of a film and its projector, introduced only as a simile, to try to enable us to identify the source of our difficulty in deciding what exclusively characterizes the present, is not altogether inappropriate. The criterion should, apparently, be a relation to something external to the flux of the series (whether A or B), but the "making present," the *Da* of *Dasein*, is not so external, and is itself in process of "coming towards itself" and towards its own death.

Husserl, in his *Phenomenology of Inner Time Consciousness*, shows how, by retention and protention, we constitute time in the flow of our own stream of consciousness, which, so he contends, is itself constituted by the same act. But here, of course, so far from having the means of solving our problem, we are more deeply ensnared in its toils. The "stream" of consciousness and the flow of time are just what we are seeking and failing to make intelligible.

Could it then be transcendental *ego* relation to which determines the present? For without that, no temporal relations could be cognized at all; and the transcendental *ego*, in consequence, cannot be any one term in the series of events.[15] That again is undeniable; but all terms (all events) in temporal succession are related to the transcendental *ego* in the same way. It grasps them all as terms in relation constituting the series as a single whole, and this applies equally whether the series is viewed as the A- or the B-series; so that for the transcendental *ego*, past, present, and future are coordinate in a comprehensive synthesis. They are, no doubt, distinguished, but by what criterion still remains a mystery. It certainly is not simply relation to the transcendental unity of apperception.

The problem remains unsolved and is really at the root of McTaggart's denial of the reality of time. For temporality requires change, without which, in some form or other, time is inconceivable. Change involves the A-series of past, present, and future; and without that there would be no B-series, no succession of events related as before and after, relations which do not change. Yet we cannot identify events as past, present, or future by any assignable mark, and we nevertheless attribute all three mutually exclusive relational qualities (as McTaggart rightly calls them) to each and every event.

It cannot help to point out that the three relational qualities are mutually incompatible only if they are assigned to an event *at the same time*, and are compatible if assigned to it successively; because in this case there is no way of indicating what "the same time" would be. Wherever any event falls in the B-series it must have all three relational properties with respect to other events, because it is before some and after others and simultaneous with whatever is present when it is present. And as we can find no distinguishing determinant of presence, we cannot say at which time it is neither past nor future. We know that it is neither past nor future when it is present, but we cannot explain when that is. We have been unable to discover what it is, outside the series, relation to which constitutes presence, and nothing inside the series can serve this purpose. We may say that at any moment, no matter which, whatever is present is neither past nor future in relation to that moment. But then we must equally say that it is so at the same time, even if not in relation to the same moments. Yet it cannot have all three relational qualities at once without self-contradiction; and it would not have them all at once if we could indicate precisely when it had each of them separately. But until we have a definitive mark of the present we cannot do this.

It does not seem to me that this problem is in any way affected by the use, or abuse, of the so-called nontemporal copula (e.g., twice two is four), when we say that an event *is* past, or *is* future; because the use of the temporal copula does not help us to identify the present. Nor can I see that C. D. Broad has done anything to remove the difficulty, by seeking to substitute "things," which change, for "events" which do not. We should still be at a loss to identify the present change. No more does it help to point out that the present is simultaneous with the utterance of the sentence which names it as "this."[16] For every event can be so named at any time. If "occurring now" is substituted for "this," it would still be true of every event while it is occurring, and so no clear distinguising mark would yet have been provided.

The point I have rather laboriously been trying to make is that every event in time is of equal status with respect to the criteria so far considered, whereas there is always one, the present, which is special, because it determines the relational qualities of all the rest (whether they be past or future, earlier or later). Causal relation, indeed, necessitates the precedence of cause to effect (the publication of a symphony could not precede its composition). But what determines when either should occur, or which, if either, has already happened or has yet to be awaited, is what is actually happening now; and although we have no difficulty in knowing what that is in fact, we cannot indicate the benchmark of the present that enables us to do so.

Cosmically considered, there are yet more complex considerations about the present in which the problem becomes involved. Before Einstein, the belief was that the present moment was the same for the entire universe, and that with what is happening now, simultaneous events could be identified throughout space. According to the theory of relativity, however, the "now" is confined to the "here," and the only present event is what is happening where it occurs. Elsewhere everything is absolutely past, or absolutely future, or else is indeterminately either. An observer may calculate which distant event is simultaneous with a designated observation only relatively to the velocity of motion of the frame of reference in which the observation is made, and that is indefinitely variable, depending on the relative motion of the object observed. Do we now have a distinguishing mark? Is the present solely what happens *here*? Indeed, but "here" is a relative term, not only for different observers, but is such that where any observer is will be differently assessed by each. And as it is never fixed and is only relatively assignable, it is no stable criterion. Moreover, every present, for every observer, is always here, so that the relational qualities of past, present, and future remain complexly ambiguous.

Yet more intriguing is that, astronomically, what is observed here and now, whenever it may be, is always past, and, according to the distance, is of varying antiquity, from minutes to thousands of millions of years—the time it has taken light to reach the observer. Thus the present observation may embrace all of time past up to the event-horizon in an expanding universe, beyond which light signals cannot penetrate. The present and the past are, therefore, merged, while whatever may be happening "now" in distant galaxies can, for observers elsewhere, only be future. And the question always persists: What distinguished this "now" from which the past and the future must be calculated? How does it differ from any other "now" so as to enable us, as it undoubtedly does, to experience the so-called passage of time?

We may note in passing that the difficulty with which we have been fruitlessly wrestling bears some significant relation to the wonderment with which we began, about our own transience in the world. Our lives pass and come to an end. Yet that does not seem to be the last word, for passage implies some, however mysterious, fixed marker defining the flow of that which is evanescent; and to this fixed marker what has passed still maintains a persistent, if changing, relation. If we could conceive clearly what the marker was and the precise nature of the relation, it might throw some light upon the uncertainties which occasioned our original puzzlement. Our failure to discover the hallmark of the present, however, suggests another reflection. As the present is indistinguishable from any other moment of time, it would seem to have no intrinsic value of its own, and tears shed for the past as such are indeed idle tears. To be justified, they must mourn the loss of some value independent of time (as, for instance, the destruction of the Parthenon). Only what occurs has significance and value; not time itself, only its filling. It is not then "the time and drawing days out" that is important, but only what we do and what happens in the course of that time. The best admonition, therefore, is Kipling's, to "fill the unforgiving minute with sixty seconds' worth of distance run."

Change, Permanence, and the Transcendence of Passage

Meanwhile, however, quite apart from any puzzles uncovered by Augustine, and apart also from those propounded by Zeno, we have on our hands the apparently irremediable paradox which prompted McTaggart to deny the reality of time. But it does not help us in the least to deny the reality of time, because nothing in our experience, either of ourselves or of the world, is properly intelligible without it, for reasons presently to be explained. McTaggart himself resorts to a third series, which he calls the C-series. *That* he alleges is real. The elements in it are the same as those of the other two series, but for the relations of succession he substitutes those of being-included-in and inclusion, which are said to correspond to those of before and after. All this achieves, however, is the transformation of the temporal series into a spatial one, with relations of coexistence instead of those of succession. It remains a series of distinguishable elements, and if it were not it could represent nothing intelligible. A reality without internal differences is inconceivable. Parmenides tried to conceive one; in fact, he maintained that nothing else was conceivable. Being, for him, excluded all difference and all change, but it was, in consequence, a blank and empty unity devoid of all content, and that, as Hegel has shown, is identical with nothing. Nothing real is so utterly void, and not Parmenides, nor Melissos, nor any of their successors were able, without self-refutation, to maintain the purity of Being from change and diversity.

All reality and all experience, however unified, must be at the same time and by the same token, differentiated. This is true of space as of time; so that a spatial series, like the one substituted by McTaggart for the temporal, is still a diversified whole. And what diversifies space, what distinguishes points and positions one from another, is nothing but distance, which, to be distance, must be traversed. But it can be traversed only by movement in time. It is this inescapable feature of space which underlies the contemporary theories of relativity in physics, in which distance is inseparably correlated with motion and velocity. This is why it makes no essential difference to substitute a spatial series for a temporal one. It is, in fact, no genuine substitution, and cannot solve the problem of succession. Nor would any other sort of series, so long as it remained serial; because every series is a succession of differences, and, however coexistent they are declared to be, in order to be set out as a series, that is, in order to be a series at all, the differences must be run through and told off successively. In short, any series involves time, in the sense of becoming, or process. It follows that, as all reality, to be real at all, must be differentiated, it must involve a series of changes, and time, as becoming, is indispensable and ineradicable. Heraclitus, Bergson,

Whitehead, and all who exhort us to take time seriously, are thus, all of them, vindicated. If time, *in this sense*, is not real, nothing is.

This, however, does not imply the final rout and supersession of "Father Parmenides." If change and diversity are inexpungeable, they are equally impossible apart from some permanent and unifying matrix within which they occur and of which they are the diverse accidents. The attempt to maintain diversity and change without unity is what gives rise to the paradoxes of Zeno, by which he tried to demonstrate the absurdity of pluralism and so (as he thought) establish the truth of the Eleatic doctrine. In ontology radical pluralism and atomism leads finally to sheer chaos, because it posits a sheer congeries excluding all order and system that might impose unity on the plurality; in epistemology, radical pluralism and atomism necessarily involve scepticism, consequent upon their intolerance of any kind of organizing principle, necessary connection, or universally valid laws, without which knowledge of any kind disintegrates.[17] What is intelligibly diverse must be unified and whole, and only what is whole and unified can be intelligibly diverse. At the same time, only what is diversified can be intelligibly one. This is because change requires continuity if it is to be change *of* anything at all, and the parts of what is continuous must be distinguishable or else it congeals to a dimensionless point (or instant). For reasons such as these Kant was able to assure us that only what is permanent can change and only what changes can be permanent.[18] Nothing that is can be utterly disparate—so far, indeed, Parmenides was right, and Plato tells us, in the *Sophist* that "whatever comes to be comes to be as a whole."[19] Although a whole is a single unity, it is at the same time a unified diversity. The reality of time, therefore, establishes concurrently the reality of a whole which is nontemporal.

This means more than what Parmenides was able, or what Kant intended, to convey. Kant is contending that change presupposes a continuity between what is changed and that into which it changes, that change takes place always, and only, in a continuum; and that, again, requires that the parts (or phases) of the continuum are distinguishable. Hence, only what changes can persist. But Kant was arguing for no more than a perduring substance underlying change, that need not be atemporal. Spinoza before Kant, and Hegel after him, saw that this had deeper implications: that the true "substance" must be a whole in the fullest and most genuine sense of the word, a unity transcending (in Hegelian terminology, *übergreifend*) its own self-differentiation, and thus transcending time, a whole that does not simply endure, but must be, in the Platonic sense, eternal. The reasons for this will become more apparent in the sequel.

It follows that there can be no time without eternity, and *vice versa*.[20] For every temporal series is a coherent sequence and presupposes some kind of universal principle of order which it embodies and actualizes. As a sequence it is a whole, and as a whole it does not change, nor is the universal principle determining its course an element within the temporal series. That is the Platonic *eidoes*, which is eternal and transcends the flux. Nor can the temporal series be cognized except as a whole, as an order, in which the mutual relations of the elements (in this case, events) are grasped in a single apprehension by a unitary subject. This is the essential point of Kant's transcendental deduction, and it remains incontestable. It is, moreover, not just a matter of our conceiving, or the conditions of finite thinking. Only a consecutive series of events can constitute time, and any and every series, as such, is a whole the principle of generation of which is nontemporal and the totality of which is not a member of the series. The plot of a novel or drama is a temporal series of changes; but the plot, as a whole, is not one of them, nor does it change, nor does the pattern of its unfolding. This is why Kant can so confidently assert that only what changes can be permanent and that it is the permanent that changes. Time without eternity is strictly inconceivable, for, as Hegel puts it, "*Die Zeitselbst ist in ihrem Begriffe ewig.*"[21]

The understanding of the nature of time has, in consequence, to be found, if it can be found at all, in the necessary self-manifestation of a principle of structure, or organization, in and as a succession of differences, or changes, all of them essential to the integrity of the whole, so that the whole, and the universal principle ordering its elements and governing their process, are eternal and unchangeable, yet it is nothing apart from its self-actualization in the succession of changing manifestations. This, at least, must be recognized, even if it does not provide a solution of the central problem to which attention has been drawn.

Spinoza Provides a Clue

The truth of the matter seems to have been well represented by Spinoza in his famous thirty-second letter (to Oldenburg). Here he explains what he means by "whole and part," as opposed to what is usually meant by that phrase. Commonly a collection of disparate and relatively independent entities collected into a group or somehow held together is called a whole, and the parts out of which it is made are held to be prior. To this notion Spinoza objects elsewhere, calling it an *ens rationis* or *auxilium imaginationis* corresponding to nothing real. A true whole is one in which the parts are mutually adapted to one another in their character and behavior—as, in the human blood, lymph, chyle, and other fluids and bodies are combined to form a specific organic whole, which remains the same in spite of constant changes in the quantities of these constituents—in order to maintain a fixed ratio of what Spinoza calls "motion and rest." He explains, both in this letter and in the *Ethics* (II, P. xiii, S. and Lem. vii, S.) that bodies may be simple or complex in degree according as they are contiguous and transmit motion and rest to one another in constant proportion. Such bodies are individual wholes maintaining an overall identity and structure despite internal changes among their parts, as do the bodies of animals and men. The more self-dependent they are for their self-maintenance, the more are they capable, as he says, of "doing and suffering many things together." He goes on to say that gradation of complexity proceeds continuously "to infinity," so that finally the whole physical world constitutes one individual structure, "the face of the whole universe" (*facies totius universi*), which is an infinite mode of the Attribute of Extension. This is all-inclusive, and there is nothing beyond it which can act upon it from without. Therefore it is eternal and unchangeable in its comprehensive structure, although that constantly requires change, perpetual transmission of motion and rest among its parts to maintain a constant ratio (as in the case of the blood—or, for that matter, any organic body).

> For all bodies are surrounded by others and are mutually determined to exist and act in a definite and determined relationship, always preserving together the same proportion of motion and rest, that is, in the entire universe; Hence it follows that every body, so far as it exists modified in a certain way, must be considered as part of the whole universe, as conforming to its totality and as coherent with the rest; and as the nature of the universe is not, like the nature of the blood, limited, but is absolutely infinite, therefore, by this nature of infinite power, its parts are modified in infinite ways (*modis*) and are compelled to suffer infinite changes. (Ep. XXXII).[22]

"The face of the whole universe" is the physical world, and does not, for Spinoza, exhaust the whole of Nature-or-Substance (in spite of what, in the quoted passage, must be a slip, where he says that it is "absolutely infinite"). It is one infinite mode in only one of infinite Attributes, the order and connection of modes being the same in all. The point is that the totality is infinite and eternal—an unchanging principle of structure expressing itself in and as a ceaseless progression of changes (the finite modes), the nature and interrelations of which it governs and directs. The progression of changes occurs in time and is the manifestation (what Plato calls the "image") of a constant and unchanging principle of order, of eternity.

In what follows I shall try to demonstrate this relation of "whole and parts," the necessary relation of temporal change and process to an eternal structural principle immanent in all its diverse manifestations, as it presents itself to us in the different forms and various levels of being that make up the experienced world.

Physical Time

Attempts to Eliminate Passage from Physical Time

If time were unreal despite our unremitting experience of its passage, it would be a peculiarity solely of our consciousness. Several philosophers have taken this view. Parmenides declared that all change, difference, or diversity was only appearance. This followed from his denial of the reality of nonbeing (or "what is not"), for if B differs from A it is not-A, and if what is not *is* not, then not-A cannot exist. This applies to any distinction one chooses to make, and so eliminates all differences and consequently all change—time along with it. What A symbolizes here is the Parmenidean One or Being, which, for him is the sole reality. In the hands of Plato this reality became the eternal truth and perfection of the Forms, of which spatiotemporal things were imperfect imitations appearing to our senses; so that time is a moving "image of eternity." For Spinoza, time, as we perceive it (as a chance succession of haphazard occurrences—*communis ordo naturae*), was a product of *imaginatio*, to which nothing real corresponded. For Leibniz, it was, or was characteristic of, *phenomena bene fundata*. Kant held that it was one of the *a priori* forms of intuition, empirically real but transcendentally ideal; and McTaggart, as we have seen, like F. H. Bradley, because they both found it self-contradictory (if for not quite the same reasons), declared it to be mere appearance.

In the preceding chapter we rejected any view of the unreality of time on the grounds that, whatever reality might turn out in the final analysis to be, if it is in any way determinate, it must be a differentiated whole; and differentiation of any kind implies passage or becoming. If time is real, however, it cannot be restricted to what appears in consciousness; and even if one espoused an idealistic metaphysic, one would have to regard time as a feature of the physical world. If it is, we must then ask whether physical time is the same as the time of which we are conscious, and, if not, how it differs. These questions may be answered in various ways. While attributing time to the physical world, we may deny that it involves becoming, or passage; or we may conceive physical time as having a different structure from mental time; or we may conclude that physical time and mental time are one and the same.

Philosophers are not the only nor the chief advocates of the unreality of time. Some of them, indeed, have expressed the view more explicitly than have scientists, but for centuries it has been the physicists themselves who have, in one way or another, attempted to abolish time, or, at least, becoming. They have done this in their persistent attempts to geometrize physics, in their endeavor to overcome some of the difficulties (e.g., with respect to measurement) that we noticed in the preceding chapter. They have persistently sought to formulate laws which would remain invariant despite assumed reversal of the time order, and so, in effect, to eliminate time. When irreversible processes have been demonstrated (like the continuous increase of entropy), efforts have been made to prove them cyclical, or, when theories of eternal recurrence have become unacceptable, hypotheses have been proposed of continuous creation of matter and a steady-state universe in which the total condition of the world remains the same at all times. If, in this way, "different" times become indistinguishable, time is, in effect, eliminated. Under Newton's laws of motion all dynamical processes are reversible; and as early as the late eighteenth century, Lagrange, anticipating Einstein and Minkowski, suggested that time could be treated as a fourth spatial dimension. Similarly, conservation laws, whether in physics or in chemistry, have the effect of maintaining that, despite change, nothing has really happened; so that Emile Meyerson concluded that "science in its effort to become 'rational' tends more and more to suppress variations in time."[1]

Donald Williams and Adolf Grünbaum have argued that to treat time as a fourth dimension is not to spatialize; but this argument is specious, first because to speak of dimensions is already to use a spatial term. Dimensions in geometry are represented by axes orthogonal one to another, and an axis perpendicular to other spatial axes is still spatial. Secondly, to conceive temporal events as arranged in order along an axis is to visualize them as spatially related along a line. It is of no avail to say that direction along the time axis is irreversible, for the very conception of an axis, as a line, implies reversibility.

Grünbaum, however, maintains that temporal passage is mind-dependent, analogously to secondary qualities; he holds that the present can be identified only by a conscious subject who is aware of the event being perceived as simultaneous with the act of perception. Temporal presence, therefore, requires (according to Grünbaum) conceptual awareness. As the identification of the present is prerequisite to the recognition of past and future, and as these, constituting the A-series, are the phases of temporal passage, all such passage, or becoming, is mind-dependent. Temporal becoming, accordingly, is not a feature of the physical world.[2] Time in the physical sense thus becomes simply the B-series of successively earlier and later events, ordered by relations which cannot change. As such, it can be treated as a fourth dimension and events can be regarded as points in a line, facilitating measurement and calculation.

It is not obvious how Grünbaum could reconcile this view with the prevalent notion that the direction of time's arrow is determined by the continual increase of entropy; for entropy increases only in and through processes in which energy is expended and degraded to heat— essentially a form of motion. It is this inevitable increase of entropy within the processes of our own organisms and brains that is supposed to underlie our consciousness of the passage of time, and thus our perceptions of past, present, and future. If that is so, the physical process must be prior to any conceptual awareness, and the source of the distinctions we make in the A-series must lie in the physical world itself.

But in any case the position is really inconsistent and untenable, for the reason which McTaggart saw quite clearly, that without becoming the relations of before and after disappear and the B-series is not possible. We can date event E at time t_0 and relate it (as earlier) to event E_1 at time t_1 only if, at t_1, E is past; in other words, only if the A-series is presupposed. But if the A-series does not belong to the physical world, physical events are not related as past, present, and future, and so cannot be related as earlier and later. Consequently, the representation of time as a fourth dimension necessarily represents events as cotemporaneous or coexistent, necessarily geometrizes time and seeks to conceive the world as a "block universe." Yet it fails in the last resort to eliminate becoming.

The geometrization of time in physics is nothing to be deplored or regretted. It is, in fact, a highly desirable and necessary device for precise correlation of spatiotemporal measurements, making possible the formulation of exact laws of motion. But it has to be recognized for what it is: a mathematical device, a geometrical fiction, which abstracts from and seeks to suppress the aspect of becoming or passage of physical events. The advantage for specific investigation and interpretation of suppressing this mysterious and troublesome character of "passage" in temporality is obvious. Nevertheless, it does not succeed. In a four-dimensional manifold, the existence of material things is represented by world lines traversing the space-time intervals between events in their life histories (these intervals being invariant with respect to differing frames of reference, or rotation of axes); but as events are successive, the course of the "life" or "experience" of each thing has to be imagined as a "movement" along its world line, superimposed upon the fixity of the four-dimensional manifold. In relativity physics, the transmission of light waves especially has to be thought of in this way, in order to determine the limits of absolute past and absolute future. Incidentally, the very use of these terms by physicist reveals the difficulty of excluding altogether any reference to A-relations in a description of the physical world. The notion of movement along a world-line, however, reintroduces passage into our conception of the world and demands a fifth dimension for complete geometrization with an evident threat of infinite regress.

For this reason, no doubt, Professor J. J. C. Smart has protested against talk of "light signals being transmitted from one point in Minkowski space to another,"[3] as a misuse of four-dimensional logic; but it is difficult to see how such alleged logical invalidity can be avoided (despite Professor Smart's assurance to the contrary), because, as Smart admits, causal sequence requires the distinction between earlier and later events, and that, as we have seen, requires in its turn the distinctions between future, present, and past, which in relativity physics has to be established in terms of the velocity of transmission of light. This can never be conceived as static, for there can be no such thing as a static light wave front. The generation of an electromagnetic field is brought about only by the *movement* either of a magnetic field or of an electrical charge, so Einstein assures us that there can be no such thing as an electromagnetic field at rest.[4] The inescapably processive character of the space-time continuum is well illustrated and emphasized by E. A. Milne's remark that it is the spreading light wave that creates space.[5]

The allegation that becoming is mind-dependent is made in the context of a realistic metaphysic, for it would clearly be futile to propose a distinction between the A- and the B-series on this ground if, like Berkeley, we were to contend that the existence of the entire physical world was mind-dependent. If, then, we wish to try to follow Grünbaum, we have to conceive (*per impossibile*) a physical world independent of human conceptual awareness, in which time is somehow real, in so far as it involves a B-series, although it excludes the A-series. Physical events would "occur" (in some undefined sense) one before another, but without ever being future, present, or past. "Before" and "after" are now being used in a quasi-spatial sense, like "in front" and "behind." But, again, any such use tacitly presupposes motion and direction. What is in front and behind in space depends on the position of the observer, and we come to Niagara before we come to Toronto only if we travel northward. So we can substitute the terms "before" and "after" for "in front" and "behind" only with reference to an observer, or to the direction of motion. Similarly direction can be determined in time only in terms of future, present, and past, with reference to our experience, and without that, "before" and "after," "earlier" and "later" cannot be definitively distinguished. Time t_0 can be distinguished from t_1 as earlier only if the direction of time has been established, and making time a fourth dimension does not ensure that it is unidirectional. On the contrary, apart from an observer, whatever "occurs" in the fourth dimension is as reversible as in any of the other three. If we try perversely to persist in conceiving a physical world independent of our conception, in which all events are arranged spatiotemporally in serial order, it will have to be one in which nothing ever happens, because all relations will be eternally fixed and unchanging. In short, it will be a world devoid of time altogether, notwithstanding the ascription to "events" of presumed temporal numbers (t_n). In fact, we can now see that, as direction cannot be set, no such ascription would really be possible. Professor Grünbaum's physical world, then, if it were possible at all, could only be a block universe, thoroughly spatialized throughout.

Furthermore, a physical world apart from our conceptual awareness, is equally independent of our perception; and however realistic we may wish to be, and however necessary we may feel it is to regard the physical world as independent in this way, if we protest too much, we must give up contemporary physics. For Relativity Theory in its entirety, both Special and General, requires the presumption of an observer, to whom physical measurements are relative. Attempts to avoid this presumption by substituting the frame of reference for the observer are unavailing, because there can be no frame of reference if there is no observer to refer measurements to it. No doubt a measuring instrument set on some celestial body takes its readings with reference to a particular frame; but an instrument is an artefact and pointer readings do not, of themselves, indicate physical facts unless they are *read* and interpreted by scientists. E. A. Milne clearly demonstrated that the formulation of all physical laws depends essentially on the presence of an observer.[6] So we cannot divorce the nature of the physical world from our observation and conceiving; nor should we try, for we are ourselves part of the physical world and must give an account of ourselves in terms of it, just as we can give an account of it only in terms of our own perception and conception.

Grünbaum might justifiably protest (and has done so in other contexts) that the four-dimensional world by no means excludes time. Nor indeed need it do so; what I have been stressing is simply that also it does not and cannot exclude passage. Only if the attempt is made to eliminate becoming would time be excluded. The Minkowski manifold is a mathematical device, and one essential to the precise formulation of physical laws. In fact, so far from actually excluding time, the theory based upon it temporalizes space as much as it spatializes time, for relativity infuses motion into spatial distance making them inseparable, which is the very reason for requiring a four-dimensional metrical field. Nature cannot exist at an instant if only because there is no simultaneity at a distance, and the old classical idea that the whole of space can be present at once is no longer tenable. Spatial extensity, therefore, cannot be postulated without motion, or becoming, and space itself is saturated with time. The Minkowski world is a continuous whole, but it is none the less differentiated, and no adequate account of its differentiation can be given unless we take time seriously—so seriously that not even spatial intervals can be properly conceived without the motion of transition.

Process, Order, and Chaos

If some philosophers and physicists haves sought to eliminate becoming from the physical world, others have seen it as the sole reality. Heraclitus declared that all things flow, so that one cannot step into the same river twice; and in our own day Bergson, Whitehead, and their followers have taken a similar position, maintaining that all reality is in process. It is they who accuse thinkers like those whom we have just been discussing of refusing to "take time seriously." But even if we do so, we cannot without disaster ignore its continuity and the wholeness (and permanence) of that which flows. Whitehead does not commit the error, but some philosophers, both ancient and modern, have had at least a tendency to forget the aspect of time other than that of passage.

Bergson viewed the world as the creation, or the self-exertion, of the life-force (*l' élan vital*), the physical world being no more than what life, as it were, sloughs off—its spent remnants. The creative process of the activity of the life-force is, for him, a continuous enduring generation of novelty, tirelessly evolving new and more elaborate forms. The trouble with this theory, however, is that Bergson envisages no goal or final aim for evolution. It is ceaselessly creative, but has no recognizable direction. Such a process would be one of change but not of development, for, if we are to speak properly, we may use that word only of a process moving in the direction of some recognizable maturity or fulfillment; and that is lacking in Bergson's theory. Sheer change without clear direction, though it necessarily does imply novelty, is indistinguishable from random change, lacking order. This is not, of course, Bergson's intention, but it is implicitly the effect of his doctrine.

Without order, change degenerates into mere chaos, which in the end becomes identical with uniformity, or homogeneous continuity. This may be illustrated by analogy with the motion of particles causing Brownian movement. The randomness consists in the persistent sudden changes of direction in the motion of the particles. As long as direction is conserved, the particle moves in an orderly fashion, and order can be established among the multitude; but the total elimination of order would mean that the intervals between changes of direction would be reduced to zero, and that would amount to the complete elimination of direction—in short, of movement itself, or the cessation of all change; and homogeneity would result.[7] This is the precise opposite of what Bergson wishes to maintain, although it results from pushing the logical implications of undirected change relentlessly to their conclusion. What has been overlooked in the theory is the unity of process necessary to give it direction and so to maintain the order of time. In this instance (in Bergson's doctrine) it is the unity of the living organism (which we shall be investigating in the next chapter), a unity of which Bergson was undoubtedly aware, but which he failed to stress, or to give definitive place in his conception of *durée*. It is this unity alone that can give direction, and genuine meaning, to evolution and make it truly creative.

Whitehead also postulates continuous creation of novelty, but he does not neglect the correlative and indispensable wholeness. His process is throughout one of integration, in which at each successive occasion an actual entity prehends the entire universe and fuses its multiplicity into unity. The way in which it does so is governed by its "subjective aim," and that again is dependent on its prehension of "eternal objects," constituting its "mental pole." The eternal objects are ordered relative to all actual entities in the Primordial Nature of God. Process, for Whitehead, thus tends towards unity and is directed by the spontaneous urge of the actual entity towards a "satisfaction" regulated by what is eternal and unchanging—a principle, or system of principles, of order (what he calls "definiteness") eternally structured in God's Primordial Nature.

The Paradoxes of Zeno

This indispensability of wholeness is indirectly illustrated by the famous and much discussed paradoxes of Zeno. In defense of his master's doctrine, Zeno, Parmenides' pupil, argued that those who maintained that "things are a many" became involved in absurdities if they tried to explain motion. For, if things are a many, they will consist of ultimate, indivisible, elementary parts, which will preclude motion, whether we assume that space and time are continuous and infinitely divisible, or that they consist, like material things, of discrete parts.

If we assume that the parts of space and time are discrete, then a flying arrow cannot move, because at every moment it will occupy fixed parts of space; and if at the next moment it is to occupy a new position, there will be no time in which it can move from one place to the next. The difficulty is not removed (as has been suggested by Bertrand Russell[8]) by admitting that the arrow is stationary in each instant so that its motion depends, as G. J. Whitrow explains, only on the rapidity of our perception; for that presumes change in our perception, which has yet to be elucidated, and neither explains the transition of the arrow from one part of space to the next, nor provides the time of transition between positions which is still required. No motion, however short, can be instantaneous unless the velocity of the moving object is infinite; but that is impossible and is the negation of motion, because, in effect, it requires the object to be in two places at once without transition between them. So the motion between successive positions of the arrow remains wholly inexplicable.

Another paradox arising out of the presumption of discrete parts is that of the stadium. Suppose three rows of objects, *A*, *B*, and *C*, aligned opposite one another, thus:

$$A \; \underline{1} \, \underline{2} \_ \_ \_ \_ \_$$
$$B \; \underline{1} \, \underline{2} \_ \_ \_ \_$$
$$C \; \underline{1} \_ \_ \_ \_ \_ \_$$

A remains stationary, while *B* moves to the left at the same time as *C* moves to the right. In the first instant, the first part of *B*, *B*1, will have moved one space to the left of *A*1, while *C*1 will have moved one space to the right of *A*1:

$$A \underline{1} \, \underline{2} \_ \_ \_ \_ \_$$
$$B \underline{1} \, \underline{2} \_ \_ \_ \_ \_$$
$$C \underline{1} \_ \_ \_ \_ \_ \_$$

Thus in one moment *C*1 has passed *B*1 and *B*2, which should be impossible without subdivision of the supposedly indivisible parts of space and time.[9]

If, however, in the attempt to avoid these difficulties, we presume that space and time are continuous, with infinitely divisible parts, we find ourselves in even worse case. Now it will be impossible for any movement even to begin, because before a moving object can traverse any spatial interval it must traverse the first half of that interval, and before it can do that, it must have traversed the first quarter, and then likewise before that the first eighth, and so on *ad infinitum*; thus no start could ever be made. This is known as the paradox of the dichotomy.

The fourth and best known of Zeno's paradoxes is that of Achilles and the tortoise, which claims to prove that Achilles could never overtake a tortoise in a race, if he gave his lumbering opponent a headstart, of whatever length. The principle is the same as that in the dichotomy. By the time Achilles reaches the point at which the tortoise started, the latter will always have moved some distance ahead, however small, and if space and time are infinitely divisible, these intervals, shrinking though they are ever more rapidly, can never be eliminated.

Professor Grünbaum has tried to show that in the last two cases no paradox arises so long as we adopt the "denseness postulate" for time correlatively to space.[10] This postulate asserts that between any two instants, as between any two spatial points, there is always at least one other. Strictly, this is too weak a requirement, for the implication of infinite divisibility is that between any two instants (or points) there is always an infinite number of others. Mathematically this makes it possible to fit an infinite number of subintervals into any finite interval, both of space and of time. The paradox only arises, it is alleged, because of confusion between the interval of physical space (and time) with the perceived interval, which is inevitably composed of a finite aggregate of *minima perceptibilia* and is held to be continuous simply because it exhibits no perceptible gaps.

But no such confusion is committed by Zeno, whose initial presumption for the last two paradoxes is precisely the continuity and infinite divisibility of space and time (equivalent to the denseness postulate). That indeed reinforces his conclusions and reemphasizes the dilemma. For the denseness postulate never permits any first subinterval for any given interval; thus no runner, or moving object, could ever traverse the first subinterval, which is prerequisite to proceeding further. Similarly there can be no last subinterval, which is the only one the completion of which will enable Achilles to overtake the tortoise.

The presupposition of Zeno's paradoxes—which he claims to be adopting from his opponents, in order to reduce their position to absurdity—is that space and time, even if assumed to be continuous, are nevertheless divisible into discrete, denumerable, parts (in effect, the same as Grünbaum's). His conclusion is that, whether they are finite in size or have no magnitude, no coherent account can be given of motion or becoming. Grünbaum's purported "solution" is irrelevant; and that is not surprising, because his avowed object is to eliminate becoming from the physical world while retaining time and motion. The moral of Zeno's argument is that radical pluralism is as inimical to time and change as is radical monism. In fact, neither by itself really makes sense. Process and becoming are only intelligible if they occur within a continuum, which is continuous in the sense that its parts overlap and merge into one another, while still being mutually distinguishable; for if they did not overlap they would not be continuous, and if they were not distinguishable there could be no continuum at all. And the appropriate answer to Zeno is that continuity and discreteness are inseparable and interdependent moments of every quantity.[11]

Cosmic Time

Time cannot be eliminated from the physical world, nor does modern relativity physics have this effect. The four-dimensional manifold of Einstein and Minkowski (despite geometrization) is not a solid block of coexistent quasi-events, but is the dynamic self-creation of a metrical field by the incessant pulsation of radiant energy.[12] This cannot, however, be treated as a mere fleeting succession of momentary events, because what it creates is a field, a spatial expanse, which is concomitantly a motion with definite invariant velocity. A field cannot be simply a succession of perishing particulars, but is necessarily a whole with structural integrity.

Modern physics, moreover, is not content with simple four-dimensionality. Energy and matter introduce curvature into space-time and wrap it round upon itself, so that the physical universe becomes a hypersphere with a three-dimensional surface, in which all transition is cyclical. Just as a traveller on the surface of a three-dimensional sphere meets no edge or boundary, so the cosmic hypersphere is unbounded, although it is of definite measurable extent. This is known as the closed universe, and different mathematical theories of its precise form vary according to the assumption made as to the distribution of matter. The most widely accepted are those due to Einstein, de Sitter, and Lemaître, which accord with the observational discovery of the recession of the galaxies, giving an expanding space and resulting in a velocity of recession proportional to distance. The hyperspherical universe is thus like an inflating balloon with the galaxies corresponding to spots on its surface which, as it dilates, recede from one another at a pace that accelerates as their mutual distance increases.

Now in such a universe, finite but unbounded, it might seem that time is only relative, or local, and that its cyclical character would eliminate it in any cosmical sense. First we may note that the expansion, after a certain period, produces what the theorists call an event horizon, beyond which an observer at the point of origin can never observe any event, because no light signals from beyond this limit can ever reach him. As Eddington once put it,[13] the light ray is like an athlete on a track which is expanding so that the winning post recedes as fast as he can run. Accordingly, for the designated observer (let us call him A), time at this horizon appears to come to a stop, because the interval between events which are not simultaneous becomes infinite. But this is only an apparent effect, as an observer (B) on the horizon will experience time passing normally. It would be impossible, however, for any body travelling at a speed less than that of light to reach B from A, or vice versa. In any case, it seems that the end of time is not to be reached in this way, and is not entailed by the hyperspherical conception of the physical world.

One model of the universe, due to K. Gödel,[14] obeying the laws of general relativity, has the peculiarity that, although the world-lines of fundamental particles (galaxies) are open, so that events do not recur in the experience of observers attached to them, other time-like lines exist which are closed. Thus, if P and G are events in the world-line of any particle, such that P precedes G, there is a time-like line joining them on which G precedes P. A vehicle therefore, travelling forwards in time, might overtake its own past, as imagined by H. G. Wells in his book *The Time Machine*, so that its occupant could influence events in his own previous history. This, however, entails the possibility of mutually incompatible causal connexions between P and G. Gödel, who is arguing against the physical reality of cosmic time, points out that no such time machine is practically possible, because to make the necessary circuit in time it would have to travel with a velocity approaching that of light.

Such practical difficulties do not affect the principle of cyclical time, but the very notion of Wellsian time travel through Minkowski space, which must take time other than that represented by the fourth dimension, not only seems impermissible but also implies the reality in the physical world of movement and becoming—and so does the motion of the assumed vehicle in Gödel's model. Such considerations would seem to make cyclical time physically impossible; and indeed if in the course of time an event exactly similar to some prior event were to occur (or, as we say, the same event were to recur), this would still mean that the second event was later than the first, and subsequent occurrences could never make it earlier than itself.

Meanwhile, the very conception of an expanding universe implies the continuous passage of a time which is not cyclical. Those who wish to eliminate becoming from the physical universe will, no doubt, point out that the recession of the galaxies appears in a four-dimensional manifold simply as the divergence of world-lines. The empirical equivalent of this, however, the way in which the recession is observed, is the red shift in the spectra of the galaxies, and that is a feature of the ineliminable transmission of light waves (which can never be conceived as stationary), with the persistent implication of passage and becoming.

Nevertheless, the idea of cyclical time, in the form of eternal recurrence, has been attractive to philosophers often enough in the past. Empedocles imagined a world perpetually alternating between unity and dissipation under the influence first of "Love" and then of "Hate," with constant alternate recurrence of complete uniformity and total disruption. Nietzsche entertained a similar notion of eternal recurrence; and a related, if somewhat different, notion of constant recurrence has been advocated, at least with respect to human affairs, by philosophers of history like Vico and Toynbee.

Time Reversal

Because cyclical time involves the reversal of earlier and later, it introduces the idea of possible inversion of the time order. Some writers have equated reversal of the order of events with reversal in the direction of time. David Park, for instance, in his book *The Image of Eternity*, remarks that we are led by the daily experience of water running downhill, heat flowing from hot to cooler bodies, and the like, to say that time flows always in the same direction "-or that events do—the meaning is the same."[15] But if the order of events could (*per impossibile*) be reversed, it would not reverse the order of time. Park himself, two pages earlier,[16] gives an inadvertent illustration of this fact, when he imagines the reversal of movement among gas molecules in a closed cylinder. Suppose at 9 a.m. a partition between the top one-fifth of the cylinder, filled with oxygen, and the lower four-fifths, filled with nitrogen, be removed. By 11 a.m., he tells us, the two gases will be thoroughly mixed. Now if we imagine the motions of the molecules to be reversed, he continues, the gases will again have been separated by 1 p.m. If, however, the order of *time* had been reversed with the motion of the particles, this result should have returned us to 9 a.m., but it has not. The reverse process has occupied the succeeding, not the previous, two hours. If it is argued that the reversal of *all* movement, including that of the earth and of clocks, would have returned us to 9 a.m., we could still ask how long that would have taken; and the lapse of time must have been subsequent to the time of reversal, it could not have been prior. We should have to say, for example, that two hours after the reversal we had returned to two hours before it—a contradiction in terms.

Time reversal has also been proposed in particle physics to explain away the phenomenon of pair production. Particle tracks in a Wilson cloud chamber have been observed indicating that a gamma ray suddenly splits up into an electron and a positron moving in opposite direction. The positron soon meets another electron and combines with it to reconstitute the gamma ray. The world-lines of the particles may then be represented thus:

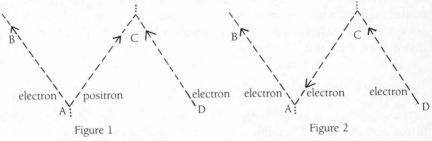

Figure 1   Figure 2

In Figure 1, the gamma ray is converted at A into the pair of oppositely charged particles, the positron is extinguished at C in combination with the second electron reproducing the gamma ray. E. C. G. Stückelberg and R. P. Feynman have suggested that the track of the positron could be regarded as that of the electron moving backwards in time, as represented in Figure 2. There would then be only one particle and no pair production or annihilation to be explained. As the whole process occurs in the minutest fraction of a second, the time reversal would only be microscopic and would not be observable on the macroscopic scale. Hans Reichenbach has therefore proposed the hypothesis that time is statistical . On the microscopic level time direction is chaotic, but asymmetrical time order arises at each moment because the longer-lived particles, like electrons and protons, preponderate.

Perhaps physicists and mathematicians know best; but this idea of time reversal, even on a microscopic scale, must seem to the layman quite incoherent. Even though electrons and protons are "longer-lived," if their motion could be reversed in time at arbitrary moments, the time order would still be chaotic. And the Stückelberg-Feynman hypothesis requires that in Figure 2 the electron would be at D and at A simultaneously (in two places at the same time). Is this not too high a price to pay for the elimination of pair production?

A particle moving backward in time would be observed to arrive at a place, B, before it had left its starting point. This would equally be true of a particle travelling faster than light, if such were possible. Physicists have found reason to speculate on the existence of such particles, and have called them "tachyons." If there were such, they could carry faster than light signals, which the theory of relativity forbids. Recently, however, it has been argued that all the theoretical reasons given for assuming the existence of such particles are untenable and involve either self-contradiction, or the violation of fundamental physical principles.[17]

On the other hand, the possibility of faster than light influences, which are not and cannot be signals, has recently been mooted, with highly significant implications. Dr. Henry P. Stapp, working from the Bohm and Aharonov version of what has come to be called the EPR paradox, claims to show, with mathematical cogency, that such influences must be assumed if the predictions of quantum theory for the experiments described are accepted as valid.

Einstein, Podolsky and Rosen (EPR), in 1935, published a paper[18] arguing that the interpretation of the quantum theory then under discussion was inconsistent with the belief that the theory gave a complete description of physical reality. That interpretation has since become generally accepted. It is held that indeterminate quantities pertaining to physical systems do not actually exist until experimentally measured, although the limits within which they will probably be found are given by the psi-formula. Einstein, Podolsky and Rosen argued that, when two systems (e.g., electrons) interact, it is possible, with the help of the Schroedinger equation, to calculate precisely the state of the combined system at any subsequent time, even after the interaction has ceased. This entails that any measurement performed on either of the systems after they have ceased to interact should determine the corresponding quantity in the other system, which must, therefore, be part of the physical reality. As this determination is instantaneous, it can involve no electromagnetic radiation; and even if it did, it could not possibly, according to relativity theory, be due to a signal radiated from one system to the other (when they are no longer in contact); and as quantum mechanics cannot predict the unmeasured quantity precisely, it cannot describe the reality completely (though the authors leave open the question whether some modification of the theory, or some other theory, could do so). Bohm and Aharonov introduced a simplified experimental arrangement, known as the "spin-correlation experiments," exhibiting all the necessary features to make the same point.

Stapp has shown that the predictions of quantum theory for such an experiment give a set of conjoint possibilities such that it is impossible, without inconsistency, to satisfy the conditions requisite to there being no faster-than-light influences. Such influences then are necessary to ensure the linkage of results of experiments performed at a space-like distance on physically related particles.[19] Although they involve no reversal of the direction of time, the occurrence of such influences would provide impressive evidence of the inseparability of physical events, the interdependence of physical phenomena, and the unity of the physical world.

Cosmic History and Cosmic Unity

The conception of an expanding universe not only implies continuous becoming but also cosmic history. Extrapolating the galactic recession backwards, physicists have calculated a time at which all the matter in the universe was compressed together in a single agglomeration, some ten thousand million years ago. According to the so-called Big Bang Theory, this mass was unstable and exploded, starting the recession that we now observe as that of the galaxies. Some think there was a stable stage in which gravitational attraction and forces of repulsion balanced each other, giving a formation corresponding to the Einstein model. Subsequently, the theory maintains, the equilibrium was upset and the current expansion proceeded. Meanwhile, galaxies, stars, and solar systems in their various dispositions evolved, as well as the range of atomic forms from nitrogen to uranium, and their combinations as we know them today. Recently, radio astronomers have claimed to detect radio signals which they believe to be caused by waves remnant from the original big bang; and physicists seek to produce conditions in a super-cyclotron replicating those that pertained during the first fractions of a second after the initial explosion. They are seeking a single primordial force, which subsequently differentiated itself into those now known as primary (strong and weak, gravitation, and electromagnetism) according to a single fundamental law.

Any such cosmic history involves a cosmical time process (measured by what Milne, in the work to which reference has been made, used to call τ-time, as opposed to the t-time of local motion). Neither can be eliminated by simple spatialization, and both are entailed by the notions of an expanding, hyperspherical world, determinate in extent but boundless in configuration. At the same time, this cosmic history transpires as the self-differentiation of a unitary and indivisible whole.

The unity of the physical universe was demonstrated, first by Eddington, who showed that the masses of, and forces acting between, the electron and the proton in the hydrogen atom were mathematically implied by the cosmical number (that of particles in the universe), the cosmological constant (which determines the velocity of recession of the galaxies) and the radius of curvature of space, which, he showed, functioned as a natural unit of length.[20] D. W. Sciama has demonstrated the single wholeness of the universe somewhat differently. He shows centrifugal and Coriolis forces on the earth to be related inseparably to the motion of the fixed stars ("that is," he writes, "relative to some suitably defined average of all the matter in the universe."[21]). "The rest of the universe" is a phrase which also bulks large in Eddington's argument and is an essential term in the calculations of E. A. Milne in his deduction of the Einsteinian and Newtonian laws of motion from a minimum of initial assumptions.[22] "The universe," writes Sciama, "is not a collection of independent objects. Its different regions strongly influence one another, as in a machine all of whose parts are closely linked together."[23] Sciama argues that a finally satisfactory physical theory of the universe should tolerate no accidental features, so that everything, the formation of galaxies, of stars, of the various atoms, the distribution of matter, the relative abundance of the elements, and all such facts, can ultimately be calculated from the fundamental laws of nature; and these, we have seen, depend upon the overall structure of space-time as a whole—*facies totius universi*.

Heisenberg, likewise, has maintained that a single equation should be discoverable from which the nature of all elementary particles and the laws governing the interacting forces among them should be derivable: a single principle of organization governing all the physical events which continuously occur in the course of time.[24] The unified field theory, which Einstein, Weyl, and Schroedinger strove to perfect, bespeaks a physical world that is all of a piece; and this idea has recently been revived by the particle physicists and has been persuasively advocated by David Bohm on the basis of new concepts. He envisages a multidimensional sea of energy (which he calls the "holomovement"), of which the perceptible world in three dimensions is a relatively stable projection. It is the "explication" of an "implicate order" that is enfolded in the "holomovement," and which unfolds in the forms that we experience. This implicate order embodies at all points the principles of structure of the continuous and indivisible whole. He writes:

> in the implicate order the totality of existence is enfolded within each region of space (and time). So, whatever part, element, or aspect we may abstract in thought, still enfolds the whole and is therefore intrinsically related to the totality from which it has been abstracted. Thus the wholeness operates all that is being discussed, from the very outset.[25]

The same thesis is very forcibly argued by Fritjof Capra in his book, *The Tao of Physics*,[26] and is also defended by Paul Davies.[27] Stapp's argument for faster-than-light influences strengthens still further the thesis that the physical universe is one indivisible whole. In fact, nowadays, it is a view very widely accepted by physicists, supported and reinforced not only by the requirements of relativity theory but also, even more, by those of quantum and particle physics.

The physical world is thus one multidimensional space-time whole, for which the principles of structure are the physical constants, and the radius of space-curvature provides the natural unit of measurement. Physical events are nothing more nor less than the infinitely various specific manifestations of the principles of order implicit in this whole— that is, of the laws of physics—and the temporal process is simply the self-differentiation of the whole. One might say, with Samuel Alexander, that time is the differentiation of space.[28] So the view of the physical world at which we have arrived is closely analogous to what Spinoza called "the face of the whole universe"—an eternal invariant whole (or *Gestalt*), the ordering principle of which determines the indefinitely various changes and the unceasing occurrence of events.

What, to my mind, is most significant about all this is that it presents us with a cosmic whole, made up of successive phases that form a scale of hierarchial forms related to one another in very special ways, rich in implications. The universe has evolved from what appears to have been a close accumulation of hydrogen atoms to separate masses that form systems of stars and galaxies containing a range of elements. Thus we get a series of forms: first energy, then matter, then complications of material structures from the lightest to the heaviest elements, from the simplest to the most complicated molecules. The successive forms, while each develops from and incorporates its predecessor, so that they overlap, are nevertheless opposed to each other—energy (waves) opposed to matter (particles), which nevertheless overlap as wave packets, proton (positive) opposed to electron (negative), each excluding yet complementary to the other. Within the atom the arrangement of electrons is again regulated, at once through exclusion and complementation, by Pauli's principle, and this determines the chemical affinities of the elements, the structure of molecules, and the shapes of crystals, with profound consequences for what succeeds as the scale continues to macromolecules and living forms.

The complex relations between the phases of such a scale I call dialectical, because they combine opposition, supplementation, gradation and sublation, or hierarchical development. Here we cannot enter in detail into the discussion of the nature of such a scale. Suffice it to say that it is typical of the self-differentiation of a structural whole, such as the physical universe is found to be, and it is the principle of all becoming and all process in time, the characteristics of which are overlapping parts that are nevertheless distinguishable and progressively developmental. This, I have tried to show elsewhere, is the proper logical structure of every systematic whole, and its serial unfolding (as time) is its necessary self-differentiation.[29] Thus, the impossibility of excluding becoming from the physical world is a natural and logical consequence of its systematic organized wholeness, of which physical theory gives impressive evidence.

IV

Biological Time

Organism and *Durée*

In discussions of time in the physical world it seemed possible and easy to distinguish and separate physical time from the time of consciousness. This is not so in biology, for life and consciousness are intimately linked, are mutually continuous, and cannot be separated. As life is commonly believed to have evolved from nonliving matter, this would provide a further reason for asserting that physical time and the time of our experience are similarly inseparable. Be that as it may, time is inextricably involved in living process in several ways: First, there is metabolism, the complex chemical process peculiar to life, that cannot be accomplished all at once, but inevitably takes time; secondly, there is the time of ontogeny and maturation; thirdly, there is the time of evolution stretching back some millions of years, and then there are the essential rhythms of life, linked to the diurnal and annual rhythms in the physical world and even, perhaps to siderial rhythms, as we may well expect after pondering the demonstration by physicists of the intimate connection between terrestrial and cosmic processes. In this chapter I shall reflect upon the nature and relevance of time in these various respects.

The essential character of a living organism is that it is a coherent system of parts and processes which is self-maintaining and self-reproductive. Where there is no such system there is no life; yet it is remarkable how often scientists overlook this fact when they speculate upon the origin of life, or discuss the mechanisms of evolution. The origin of life is not simply what produces chemical substances of special composition, macromolecules, or polypeptides, though undoubtedly all these will be involved; what has to be produced is a chemical system that is metabolic, that maintains itself in changing and relatively unfavorable circumstances by adapting its own cyclical activity, and also is able to reproduce itself. Without this, it is futile to talk of natural selection or of evolution, for natural selection can operate only upon self-reproducing systems, and what evolves is nothing less than the adaptive versatility of such systems in their methods of self-maintenance.

On the other hand, the organism is a system in dynamic equilibrium with its environment, perpetually exchanging with it energy and matter. While it maintains a persistent form and pattern, as well as a specifically characteristic order of development, it is in constant and unremitting flux.

It follows that time and change are integral and indispensable to life. In a world without change (if that were conceivable) there could be no life. Self-maintenance and self-reproduction would be mere unchanging persistence, the main, though not the necessary, character of the nonliving. Life is essentially a constant adaptation to change. It is, therefore, itself necessarily processual, and it necessarily presupposes an ongoing flux in which and to which it is adaptive. Bergson was consequently right to insist on the reality of time as the necessary condition of life, which he considered to be the nature of all and every reality. Life, he maintained, involves *durée*, which is intuited rather than conceived. It is not what he represents as the intellectually envisaged, spatialized, instantaneous time of physics. Whatever may be true of physical time (and we have already argued that process cannot be altogether eliminated from that), biological time is essentially *durée*; and all the metaphysical puzzles previously noticed apply to it.

But what Bergson seems curiously to have overlooked is that this *durée* is always harnessed by life and subordinated to a dominating and directing organic unity. Nor must we forget that, concomitantly with process, essential to the nature of life is the coherent wholeness, to maintain which is the persistent nisus of its metabolism. Life is the continuance in time, through the process of metabolism, through maturation, reproduction and ontogeny, of a self-maintaining system.

The Emergence of Life

That life originally emerged somehow from the welter of nonliving physicochemical processes is today taken for granted by scientists and laymen alike, almost without exception. But in their speculations and experiments to determine how life originated, biologists have been faced with a dilemma that none have so far been able to escape. As a living entity is a self-maintaining and self-reproducing system, it cannot have emerged from nonliving chemical processes by natural selection for the reason already noted, namely, that natural selection can only act on systems already self-reproducing. They must, moreover, reproduce themselves, not by exact replication but with variations which may or may not give them, *as systems*, survival and reproductive advantages over the non-variant. Any such system is already alive, so it could not have originated through the effects of natural selection, for which it was a precondition.

The alternative is to assume that life arose from chemically complex coacervates (that is, precipitates held in suspension) in a primordial liquid sea or "soup." Through the synthesis of the required protein substances by some accidental occurrence, be it an electrical discharge or whatever, it is assumed that such a coacervate becomes self-reproductive. It could do so, however, only by means of the activity of enzymes of special complication, which have hitherto not been known to synthesize independently of living metabolism, and which probably could not be synthesized in any other way, because the process of synthesis involves the absorption of energy released in small instalments, which, if made available all at once, would disrupt the compound, so that it requires the complex cyclical chemical activity of numerous other enzymes systemically interrelated, which is precisely the metabolism of a living organism. It is clear, therefore, that whatever the original source of life may have been, it can neither have been by the natural selection of nonliving chemical processes, nor by purely accidental and random synthesis of proteins, that it arose. It seems that there must be some principle of unity, creating and maintaining coherent wholes, already inherent in the process of the world from which life originally emerged. This has been found immanent in the physical system prior to life, so the problem should not, in principle, be insoluble.

Evolution

As soon as organisms have come into being, the process of self-maintenance, which typifies them as living, ensures that they will reproduce in order to counteract the natural onset of waste, decay, and degeneration necessitated by the inevitable increase in entropy involved in physicochemical processes. One definition of life, popular among contemporary scientists, is that it is a system for increasing information, or one in which order is conserved and entropy, if not decreased, at least held steady. Reproduction is just one of the ways in which this is ensured. Further, as a self-maintaining system, an organism must modify its internal process and external behavior so as to adapt to changes in its environment. If—and so far as—it fails to do this, it dies. It follows that, as it reproduces itself, modifications of its structure and functioning which favor its survival will persist, while any that prove unfavorable will succumb to hostile conditions. In short, the progeny of the original phenotype will evolve, and the "mechanism" of evolution will be variation and natural selection.

The current neo-Darwinian doctrine is that variation occurs by chance and is completely random, and that natural selection operates by eliminating unfavorable mutations, allowing the favorable ones to proliferate; but, as natural selection is a purely negative influence, simply eliminating the unfit, it is never the source of favorable characteristics, and they must, therefore, according to current theory, be the result of purely chance mutations. The comparatively short time since the origin of life on earth, or even the estimated span of existence for the entire physical world, and the minutely intricate and marvellously functional complexity of modern higher species, makes this account of evolution incredible, especially considering that the vast majority of random mutations are unfavorable and even lethal. Evolution inevitably takes time, but the probability that organisms of the versatility and intricate complexity which exist today could have evolved purely in consequence of a series of chance mutations requires far more time than has been available. For the higher the improbability of the result, the longer must be the time allowed for it to occur by pure chance.

It is not simply (for it is not the case) that there has been insufficient time for the occurrence of vast numbers of diverse mutations to occur. The prodigious proliferation of living forms might well give ample opportunity for that. The point is that current Darwinism tacitly assumes that the evolutionary process is additive, a mere accumulation over time of favorable mutations, and to this all the evidence runs counter. There must be—and biologists have produced convincing evidence that there is—in living things, a nisus towards wholeness and integration exerting a positive influence on how mutations are integrated into the living system, whether they are produced by chance or in some other way.

Arguments supporting this conclusion were set out at length in a book I wrote some twenty-three years ago.[1] To my knowledge, nobody has as yet even attempted to refute them, so I may assume that they still stand. Here I shall give only a brief and summary extract.

1. Organs like the mammalian and molusc eye are not only highly complex and exquisitely functional, but, in order to be so they require accompanying cooperative organs, such as tear glands to secrete lubricant, lids to wipe the conjuctiva clean and keep vision clear, muscles automatically to adjust and focus the lens, and yet other muscles to turn the eyeball reflexly, keeping the object in the line of sight. Add to all this the neural structure needed to control and regulate these functions. Whether it is at all possible that mutations producing all these delicately coordinated features should occur at the same time, that they should do so by pure chance is stupendously improbable. If they were to occur seriatim they must do so in the right order to be advantageous, and if each occurred by itself in the wrong order it would have negative survival value and so would be bred out. We must bear in mind that the improbability of the occurrence of a series of improbable events in an improbable order increases exponentially with the number of events in the series. So the probability that the necessary mutations should occur either together or in succession so as to produce a functional eye which at every stage would have survival value is incalculably small. That eyes have developed in the course of evolution is obvious, and all available evidence suggests that it has been through mutation and natural selection; but it is incredible that the mutations should all have been purely accidental without any further integrating influence.

2. Protective coloration notoriously results from mutation and natural selection; but there are many instances in which protective coloration is effective only if the creature habitually orients itself so as to fit in with the background. Dark-colored moths selected for melanism in smoke-blackened cities instinctively move, after alighting, from lighter to darker surfaces. Many insects adjust their position on a leaf so that the stripes on their wings (or wing cases) align themselves with the veins

of the leaf. They do this immediately and instinctively on alighting. Is it credible that mutations have occurred by pure chance, coordinating both suitably protective coloration and the necessary behavior pattern to make it properly effective, either simultaneously or in the right order?

3. In some cases the protective coloring, to be advantageous, requires even more complicated behavior, not only on the part of one individual but of several; as in the case of the Ceylon black-backed pied shrike (*Hemipus picatus leggei*), which selects material for its nest to match the bare bark of the tree on which it builds, and whose young ones adopt postures in the nest so that the whole ensemble resembles a broken stump. Here chance mutations would have to have produced modifications in coloration and behavior in several different individuals together all mutually adjusted so as to have survival value. The behavioral characters must be such as to change during maturation so as to differ suitably in parent and offspring. All this has to occur so that at no stage is any modification disadvantageous for survival, so that the variation will be preserved and not bred out. For once bred out it can never be recovered.

These are only selected examples but should be sufficient to persuade us that pure chance mutation is an inadequate explanation and that something more is needed. But I am not arguing against the theory that mutation and natural selection are the means to evolution. The evidence in favor of that is much too impressive. My point is that evolution is not and cannot be the result of *pure chance*, as it should be according to the current neo-Darwinism. There is no conclusive evidence that all mutations are entirely random, and there is good evidence that even when they are, another factor of major significance is operative. Biologists have discovered that genes do not act independently in determining isolated characters, that they cooperate and their effects depend on their position in the chromosome. The genome, the entire body of genetic material, acts as a whole, organismically, and changes within it can occur spontaneously. When they do occur, whether by crossing over of chromosomes, or by random mutation, or in any other way, they are mutually adjusted. Some which are disadvantageous may remain recessive but may later become dominant and, if they then have survival value, they will persist.

This is hardly surprising, for the organism is by its very nature adaptive and self-maintaining. If it were not, it would not be alive. Evolution, therefore, should be nothing less than the extended process of the intrinsic adaptive character of living things, constantly maintaining, and to that end increasing, their integrative coherence, to become progressively more self-dependent and self-determining in perpetually changing circumstances. In this process the continual passage of time is inexorable and the persistence of change is ineradicable, for the organism, as a dynamic equilibrium in a steady state in the perpetual exchange of matter and energy, is a permanent pattern of becoming.

Evolution and maturation appear to be very closely connected. The primordial organisms were in all probability single cells, descendents of which survive today as protistans. If these were preceded by viruses, structures not unlike them seem to have been taken up and incorporated into the cell as it became self-sustaining. Possibly, in the course of time, to maintain themselves more effectively, single cells collected together in colonies and adjusted their functioning one to another. These colonial creatures subsequently became more organically integrated as multi-cellular individuals with organs functioning mutually as means and ends one to another and each to the whole. Their evolution continued by successive modifications and natural selection, branching out in numerous diverse directions to create the species that we know today. The detemining influence throughout seems to be the organizing impulse of the whole and a persistent nisus to self-maintenance of the system.

In the maturation process much of this is recapitulated. The organism is reproduced first as a single cell, which then divides and proliferates to form a sort of colony, then differentiates to develop separate though mutually adjusted organs and is finally integrated by means of neural and vascular systems to become a fully developed individual. In the embryological process even certain main phases of evolution from one major phylum to another are recapitulated, which is only to be expected, for how else have single cells managed to become the sort of organisms which exist today? Hence, the time process of maturation and that of evolution are not dissociated; rather, they are the same process alternating between individual and specific forms.

Environment and Biological Clocks

The temptation to think of development and evolution as confined to organisms is, however, to be resisted. The organism is in persistent commerce and interchange with its surroundings and is in intimate organic relation to its environment. Evolutionary theory emphasizes its adaptation and fitness, but it must not be forgotten that the environment too has to be adapted and especially suited to the generation and survival of life. In 1913, there appeared a book entitled *The Fitness of the Environment*, by L. J. Henderson. It was much neglected at the time, despite its perspicacity, but the topic was taken up again in 1955 by Harold F. Blum. These authors show that terrestrial conditions are uniquely adapted for supporting life and are themselves an extraordinarily improbable combination of circumstances precisely appropriate to its emergence. Blum has described these interdependent and indispensable conditions in considerable detail.[2] Some few points may be mentioned, though it is difficult in a short space to give an adequate idea of the intricacy and close-knit interdependence of the listed factors.

The state of the earth depends almost wholly on absorption of energy radiated from the sun. The atmosphere acts as a mediating film, its ozone layer protecting the surface from excessive ultraviolet radiation and exercising a "greenhouse" effect just sufficient to maintain an equable temperature. This is produced by comparatively large percentages of water vapor and of carbon dioxide in the air. The earth's rotation on its axis (unlike that of the moon and some other celestial bodies) prevents one side getting intolerably hot while the other suffers desperate frigidity; and the rate of rotation is just right to maintain the range of temperatures suitable for the survival of living creatures.

That all this (and much more dependent upon it) is special to the earth is shown by the fact that neither Venus nor Mars, both within comparable distance from the sun, have atmospheres at all similar. Neither harbors sufficient quantities of water vapor, carbon dioxide, or oxygen, or seems ever to have maintained conditions suitable to the emergence of life.

Water, in particular, is an exceptional compound particularly necessary to the emergence and survival of life. It is a preponderant and essential constituent of living things. It has a high specific heat, so that it exerts a moderating effect on rapid and extreme changes of temperature. This regulates the temperature of the seas and the atmosphere, and prevents cataclysmic disturbances in ocean currents, or fierce winds and violent storms. Water, likewise, requires a high latent heat for evaporation and condensation, as well as for solidification into ice, and this has similar moderating effect, warming up the colder regions of the earth and cooling down the hotter. The cooling effect of evaporation enables plants and animals to survive under sun temperatures which they could not otherwise tolerate. These properties ensure that the water vapor in the air as well as the liquid water beneath help to buffer the changes of temperature between night and day, while they contribute to the "greenhouse" effect already mentioned. The peculiarity that water attains its highest density at 4°C ensures that it freezes from the upper surface and that the ice floats, preserving a region of safety for living creatures in its depths in periods of extreme cold. Water is, besides, a highly versatile solvent which is of major importance for living metabolism. It was the original and is still the immediate environment, both external and internal, of the great proportion of living species, and it is equally indispensable to the rest. The existence of a hydrosphere is peculiar to this planet. Conditions on Mars and Venus are spectacularly different, although their distances from the sun, their size, and other circumstances, are comparable to those of the earth.

The peculiar and exceptional characteristics of water are, it seems, mainly due to what is known as "the hydrogen bond," a special kind of chemical bridge between elements of high electronegativity, which is found in very few compounds, and of these only water has the necessary physical state at the present temperature of the earth. Hydrogen is another very special element, which, being the lightest, has exceptional and diverse properties, many of which are specially important for life. Being so light, it easily escapes the earth's gravitation, so that much of the hydrogen originally contained among its constituents has probably been lost. But because hydrogen has the capacity to combine with a large number of heavier elements, much of it has also been retained. Its presence in carbohydrates and hydrocarbons integral to living matter is another feature of the fitness of the environment of the planet for the emergence of life.

The other element in these compounds, carbon, moreover, is of paramount significance and is peculiar in that it is able to form over two thousand hydrides, whereas its cognate elements can form only very few, and these hydrides play an immense part in the composition and synthesis of living tissue. Its ability to maintain strong bonds between its own atoms, and so to form long chains and rings, enables it to enter into a large variety of chemical combinations with numerous polymers and diverse properties. Carbon dioxide plays an outstanding and virtually ubiquitous role in living processes, and is unique among the oxides of its cognate elements (e.g., silicon) in being gaseous at normal terrestrial temperatures. In these respects and others, which Blum lists, the conditions of this planet are especially favorable to the presence of life. Blum writes:

> A somewhat different mass or slower rotation could have given the earth
> a different temperature, perhaps one quite incompatible with life as we
> know it. The conditions on our two nearest planet neighbours, Venus and
> Mars, exemplify for us temperature environments that might have
> prevailed on earth under conditions not too different from those that
> exist.[3]

The surface of the earth, its hydrosphere, and its atmosphere have
also had their history. They have undergone changes and still do. They
are in continual flux and motion and the time of their evolution is
interlaced, as are the processes, with that of living species.

The close-knit mesh between life and its inorganic surrounding
gives clear evidence of the unbroken unity of the biosphere with the
physical world; and all temptation must be resisted to treat the organism
and its environment as separable complexes in external relation, or to
think of evolution and development as if they were processes confined to
the former. Evolution is a process common at once to both organism and
environment mutually integrated in intricate interplay. Just as the
physicist describes matter as a singularity in space-time, so we might
describe the living organism as a singularity in the physicochemical
matrix; and as it is sensitive and responsive to stimulation from without,
it registers within it the effects upon it not only of its immediate
surroundings but through them of the entire physical universe, which we
have already found to be a single continuous whole.

In consequence, there is no break between the temporal process of
the physical world and that of life, and the rhythms of the former are
reflected in the behavior and (as it develops) the consciousness of the
latter. We are familiar enough with the changes in living condition and
movement which correspond to the seasons and the alternation of day
and night following the rotation of the earth and its revolution around
the sun. Physical and climatic change with the seasons is reflected in the
behavior of plants and animals. Flowers bloom in the spring, fruit ripens
in the autumn and leaves fall at the onset of winter, animals hibernate
and their activities vary appropriately with the seasons and with the
changing times of day and night. Bodily rhythms are accommodated to
these changes producing biological "clocks" based upon obscure
physiological cycles. The rhythms of sleep and waking are the most
obvious of these, but there are others more mysterious and less

understood. Migrating birds have been found to navigate by relation to the sun and the stars, with an accuracy which is quite astonishing, by means of some obscure kind of internal rhythm or "clock." Sea anemones on the shoreline rocks open when covered with water and close as the tide falls and leaves them exposed to the air; but they have been found to do the same, with the rhythm of the tides, even when kept in a tank. Bees have been observed to adjust their flights to the times when certain flowers, which generate nectar only intermittently, offer their booty. Even coloration is varied in some species (e.g., the fiddler crab), to match the rhythm of night and day. These are only a few examples, and all, or most, of them appear to depend on metabolic processes which are somehow controlled and regulated by physical changes.

It follows that biological time is not different or separable from physical time, providing another argument against those who seek to exclude passage from the latter; for if there were no process in the physical world, there would be none in the biological, which is as much as to say that there would be no biological world, no biosphere, at all.

Behavior

Metabolism in living creatures merges into physiology, and physiology into behavior. In homoiothermic animals, body temperature is maintained at a constant level by the regulation of the basic metabolic rate. This depends on secretions from the thyroid and pituitary glands which are stimulated by temperature change as it is registered through the nervous system and the diencephalon. If heat becomes excessive, perspiration occurs and the temperature is reduced by evaporation from the skin, as also, in some cases, through the respiratory tract (by panting). When the temperature falls too low, the sympathetico-adrenal system is stimulated to produce more blood sugar, to increase the heartbeat, and to initiate shivering to generate heat. As the cold is felt by the animal, it increases its muscular activity to accelerate these processes and, when possible, to move to shelter or a warmer region, as, when it is too hot, it slows down its activity and seeks a cooler spot in which to rest. So metabolism becomes physiological process and that excites overt behavior. This is but one of innumerable examples.

The "structure of behavior" is not that of mere reflex activity. Merleau-Ponty's brilliant book of that title, with its wealth of physiological and psychological evidence, ought, one would have expected, by now to have disposed once and for all of that misconception (if Koffka and the Gestalt psychologists had not).[4] But the stubbornness of Behaviorism in psychology persists, most notably in the work of B. F. Skinner; and the writing of Wittgenstein and Gilbert Ryle bear witness to its seepage into philosophy. Even more recently, Quine has based his theories of logic and language upon it.[5] But the evidence against any reduction of behavior merely to reflex neural activity has been amassed by both neurophysiologists and psychologists so formidably that to marshall new arguments at this stage is hardly warranted.[6]

That behavior has structure, however, the work of a large number of ethologists gives copious evidence.[7] Its structure is that of instinct, which Timbergen has described as

> a hierarchical organized nervous mechanism which is susceptible to certain priming, releasing and directing impulses of internal as well as of external origin, and which responds to these impulses by co-ordinated movements that contribute to the maintenance of the individual and the species.[8]

But this so-called mechanism proves, as he goes on to explain, to be far more than merely neural structure, and is only part of something much more complex, including organized muscular functioning, coordinated endocrine glandular responses, as well as sensory-motor and perceptual activities.

An instinct comprises three main phases of behavior; first, what is called the "innate releasing mechanism," triggered by a "sign-stimulus" (a somewhat infelicitous name for what may be an internal condition of the organism, or a perceived situation, or an object, or all three). This sets in motion a train of appetitive behavior seeking to bring about a new situation in which the animal experiences one or more new sign-stimuli, in response to which it performs a more or less stereotyped "consummatory act" characteristic of the operative instinct (e.g., eating, fighting, copulating, or the like). These three phases occur sequentially always in the same order, and the appetitive behavior, which is the most protracted, may be almost indefinitely varied and variable, often subdivided into subordinate activities, each with a structure comparable to that of the instinct as a whole.

The case most closely studied by Tinbergen is the mating instinct of the stickleback. This is initiated by the rise in temperature with the change of the season and the increase in the duration of daylight. These stimulate motivating agencies in the metabolism and physiology of the fish which in turn excite appetitive behavior while they produce the typical flamboyant color changes in the courting male. He proceeds to seek out a suitable place to build a nest, an urge satisfied by a specific perceptual situation. Here he builds a nest, and is further stimulated to enact defensive and combative behavior on the approach of other males. The appearance of a female releases the courtship ritual—a zigzag ballet—and the subsequent inducement of the female to enter the nest to lay eggs. The male then fertilizes the eggs and proceeds to care for them by aerating the nest, fanning it constantly with the movement of his fins until the eggs hatch out. At that point, the instinctive behavior abruptly ceases. It is not, however, entirely stereotyped and can be relevantly varied with differing circumstances. For instance, when maturing eggs were removed from the nest by an experimenter half way through the process and replaced by fresh eggs, the male stickleback paused in his activity at the point when the eggs should have hatched, but then, as the oxygen content of the water became depleted, resumed fanning.

The instinct as a whole is subdivided into contributory structures of behavior, each set in motion by some appropriate sign-stimulus, each exhibiting an appetitive phase, and each brought to fulfillment by a consummatory act: finding a site, defending the territory, courting the female, fertilizing the eggs, and fanning. Thus, the instinct is a hierarchical structure of behavior sequentially performed as a series of activities governed by a definite principle of order, all of which subserve the organic integrity which maintains the life of the organism and reproduces it to continue the species.

That all this is, like every other living activity, a temporal process is so obvious as to be hardly worth mentioning. Nevertheless, the whole train of instinctive activity is ordered and varied relevantly to a specific need dictated by the persistent drive to maintain the intergrity of the organism (as Tinbergen says, "of the individual and the species"). The principle of organization that determines the animal's organic well-being presides over the order of its behavior and gives its specific character to each of its instincts, while it determines their interrelation and interplay (as, for instance, mating, nest-building, procreation and care of offspring, whether of sticklebacks, birds, or *mutatis mutandis* animals).

Learning is another case in point. It is the modification of appetitive behavior in adjustment to new and unpredictable situations so that the same end is finally accomplished as the instinct (and the maintenance of the individual) requires. It is again a temporal process subserving a principle, the same principle, of organized integrity.

Theories attempting to reduce learning to a mechanical process of conditioned reflex, once again, have been discredited by the bulk of the available evidence. Sufficient testimony has been mustered by the writers and experimenters already cited. The same is true of those who strive to demonstrate that it is simply the result of random activity under the pressure of need, "stamped in" or "reinforced" by the pleasure of satisfaction. These very concepts of need and satisfaction tacitly presuppose the persistent nisus to organic self-maintenance in the creature concerned. W. H. Thorpe has shown that so-called trial and error learning is never purely random but always genuine trial—genuine endeavor to bring about a situation required by the instinctive activity (a specific "innate releasing mechanism"). Exploratory and investigative behavior (e.g., on the part of some insects and of rats) has been shown to be undertaken and to be satisfying for its own sake. Modification of the appetitive behavior, which is always variable in new and sometimes frustrating situations in order to overcome obstacles to satisfaction, Thorpe has also shown, is always directed by some degree of insight, which he rightly defines as the apprehension of relations.[9] Learning is thus simply an extension of the innate capacity of the living organism to adapt and to vary its behavior relevantly to the overriding principle of organic self-maintenance.

Behavior, accordingly, is another example of temporal process regulated and ordered by a principle of structure, which is not itself an event or part of the temporal sequence, and is detectable in the activity and the bodily makeup of the organism itself only as the precipitate (so to speak)—like every bodily organ—of the function performed.

Earlier I stressed the fact that without process and becoming there could be no such thing as life; and we now see that living processes are intimately merged with physical change. It would therefore seem clear that physical time and biological time cannot be divorced, with consequences which will presently become obvious. There can be little doubt that our consciousness of the passage of time derives from the feeling, often quite obscure, of the physiological and metabolic rhythms that I have described, and it is evidently operative in our behavior. To this consciousness the distinction of present, past, and future is indispensable. If it were not also characteristic of the physical world, it is difficult to see how we could ever become conscious of it. My conscious differentiation between now and then must be derived somehow from my feeling of the physiological sequences going on in my body, and these are related to physical changes in the world at large. There must therefore be a physical now and a physical then which corresponds to those of which I am conscious. To the consciousness of time I shall return presently, but before doing so there is another aspect of the unity of organism and environment to which I want to draw attention.

Biocoenoses

Living species sharing a common climatic and geographical zone are intimately interdependent so that they form what ecologists call communities or biocoenoses. The most familiar is probably the domestic aquarium, which if properly aerated and lighted may sustain itself indefinitely, water plants providing carbohydrates and oxygen from photosynthesis, microorganisms feeding on the plants and providing food for the fish, and bacteria which thrive on the fish decomposing dead plant material which again sustains the plants. Likewise, in tropical forests, a single tree may constitute a similar ecosystem. Epiphytic plants such as orchids, which lodge themselves in the notches of the tree's bark, derive nutriment from the humus and debris that collect in the cracks of the bark and weave their roots into webs, often in symbiotic association with fungi which contribute to the collection of plant food. These root meshes are used by ants as nesting sites, and they accumulate material offering a further supply of food to the epiphyte. The ants also give protection to the plant, as well as to the tree itself, by stinging larger animals that they may encounter, while defending their own nest from marauders. Rot-holes and other hollows in the tree collect rain water which becomes a breeding place for insects, the larvae of which feed on the leaves or other plant material, and the nymph forms pollinate the flowers both of the tree itself and of the epiphytes. Birds and small mammals may also make their homes in the tree and prey upon the insects while they help to fertilize the surrounding earth.

Numerous other examples might be given of such biocoenoses. Lakes, rivers, estuaries, coral reefs, and atolls have the same holistic character. Marston Bates writes:

Here on the atoll of Ifaluk, the distinction between land and sea seemed to lose its biological meaning. We could find no logical way of subdividing the environment into a series of discrete biological communities and we came to the conclusion that the meaningful community included the whole atoll situation: land, reef, lagoon and immediately surrounding sea. Everything was all mixed up. The people depended equally on the land and the sea for their food. The hermit crabs that crawled everywhere over the atoll went to sea to lay their eggs, as did the coconut crabs and the land crabs; the sea turtles came out to bury their eggs on land. The influence of the sea was everywhere; it determined what plants and animals were living on the land, because all of these, to get there, had to have some method of crossing the sea, unless they had been purposefully or accidentally brought by man[10]

As the individuals which these systems contain are themselves stable forms in a constant flux of interchange with their environment, so each ecosystem is a dynamic equilibrium of give and take of a second order between individuals and the environment. But no such system is entirely self-contained. Every one is subject to outside influences and is linked with and merges into others. The whole forest constitutes an ecosystem of a still higher order than the tree, as do lakes and rivers and entire geographical regions. For instance, the whole Amazonian basin with its forests and rivers and the mountains that affect its climatic conditions may be regarded as a single ecosystem in which every organism and every contributing factor is dependent upon all the rest. Finally, the biosphere as a whole constitutes one interconnected dynamic equilibrium of living activity, which, if upset, will readjust the internal relations between its constituents to restore the equilibrium. To quote Bates again:

> The biosphere, then, is essentially continuous in space, a single interwoven web of life covering the surface of our planet. But it is far from being a uniform, monotonous web: it is woven into a motley series of patterns and designs.[11]

It is a unity of differences, of ever-changing and flowing diversity, a stable pattern imposed somehow upon a perpetual flux of activity. And it is already apparent that the biosphere is inseparable from the inorganic surrounding, and that again from the rest of the physical world. Just as we have found the physical universe to be a single whole in which we may make distinctions but not divisions, so we now find the organic world to be even more intimately united. And just as we can regard everything from a purely physical point of view, so we can think of the entire universe as one organic whole.

Conclusion

I have made an attempt to indicate the nature of biological time at various levels of comprehensiveness and development. At what we may call the metabolic level, continuous cycles of chemical reactivity are organized in dynamic equilibrium as an integrated individual organism. Function, as it were, precipitates structure to form an organic anatomy, and metabolism merges into physiology. The living activity is ceaseless, but the integrated system constituting the organism is constant. Physiology again merges with behavior and we move to the ecological level. Here we find the organism and its activity intimately linked, not only with its immediate surroundings, but with other organisms and with a wider circle of the inorganic environment, so that the ecosystem remains relatively stable while the interchange of activities among its denizens and between living and nonliving processes continuously proceeds and is indefinitely variable, though always relevantly to a directing principle of order. Ecosystems interlock with ecosystems until the entire biosphere is embraced in a single whole of interchanging processes governed by a presiding principle of balance and mutual adjustment of parts. This cannot be separated from the unity of the physical universe outlined in the previous chapter, so that the whole world can be regarded as one organic totality from a biological point of view.

That the organizing principle dominating this overarching totality is also what determines the course of evolution should now be apparent. For we saw that evolution was not just change and development of the genotype but equally involved the environment, so that it must be a progressive mutual adaptation of living propensities to the conditions within which they are exercised and this will be directed by that same principle of dynamic equilibrium which is effective in the biosphere as a whole.

On all these levels, therefore, we find Spinoza's description valid. The simpler and more primitive entities combine into more complex and more closely integrated individual wholes in hierarchical series until we reach "the face of the whole universe," which embodies a universal principle of structure, constant and unchanging, that directs all the innumerable and unceasing processes which go on within it. This is rightly called the concrete universal which differentiates itself into its own particulars. The processes of life, of metabolism, reproduction and evolution, all mutually continuous, constitute a single indivisible process of self-differentiation of one whole, in effect, a cosmic organism. It is the process of generation of a totality of higher order and significance than the merely physical.

This is what I have been calling biological time, and have now found to be inseparable and indistinguishable from physical time. Thus, there is evidently an eternal principle determining a whole or pattern that does not change, but that is constituted by a perpetually flowing succession of changes, the course of which it directs and regulates. The principle of structure is eternal and the successive changes generate time.

Psychological Time

The Stream of Consciousness

The flow of events in the physical world includes periodicities which are repeated and internalized in the metabolic and physiological activity of living organisms to function as biological clocks, and as this activity reaches a threshold of integrative intensity it takes the form of feeling or sentience. The content of sentience as it is further organized by the activity of attention becomes the object of consciousness, and the general flux of the process of the world is cognized in its rhythmic sequences. In that case, the sentience in the living organism of the cosmic rhythms, and the consequent awareness of time must be continuous with the flux of the external world.

What is sentience? However does it arise in living things? How is it related to the physiological processes upon which it seems to be dependent? These are questions to which neither scientist nor philosopher has ever yet found a satisfactory answer. Aristotle probably came nearest to solving the problem when he said that the soul was the form of the body; and he is followed by Hegel, who contends that soul is feeling (*Empfindung*) the "inwardizing" (*Erinnerung*, or "remembering") of the natural processes registered in the organism.[1]

Throughout nature the pervasive process of activity creates structural wholes, the characterisitic nature and individuality of which is constituted by their form, as are their properties and propensities: for example, atoms, molecules, crystals and living organisms. In the case of the last named, the components of the complex structure are more obviously processes than in the inorganic examples, and their mutual integration is what constitutes the life of the organism. The structural form is no additional constitutent, but is simply the way in which the constituents are organized together. Thus, the atom is a field of force, organizing into a complex structure a group of nucleons with orbiting electrons. Its structural form determines its nature and properties, but it is not an additional constituent (not itself a nucleon or electron). The same is true of a molecule or a crystal. It would not then seem unreasonable to suggest that the form of the highly integrated combination of physiological processes in the organism (in Aristotle's terms, the form of the body) is sentience (what Hegel identified with the soul), that at a certain threshold of intensity this integral activity is felt.[2] If this is so, it also makes sense to say that the physical effects registered within the organism and its reaction to them are "inwardized" as feeling.

Primitive sentience is a single whole, initially containing differences, but differences which are merged and not distinguished by the sentient being. It involves no distinction between subject and object, which, like any other distinction that might be made within the "felt mass" (F. H. Bradley's phrase), must involve the selective and analytic activity of attention.

Sentience is, therefore, while immediately felt, initially not immediately conscious, but it is undoubtedly subconscious, and once attention is directed to it, it becomes a "datum" for consciousness and perception. In this way the world is brought to consciousness, which, in Hegel's phrase, is "the truth of" physical and organic nature. But no perception is ever the mere apprehension of a pure datum. Like the underlying physiological process, it is always an activity of organization. Not only is the minimal percept a *Gestalt*, the elements of which are actively interrelated in the act of attention as a figure distinguished against a background, but what draws attention to particular elements in the sentient field are the organic needs and impulses of the organism, so that the singling out of specific data for conscious apprehension is as much a practical as a cognitive activity.

Living behavior is always "informed" in two senses of that word. It has form or structure, as we noticed in the last chapter, and, at least in its more developed stages, it is the counterpart of, and is directed by, perception. Accordingly, consciousness is an activity constructing—rather than a sort of light suffusing—its objects. The material out of which it constructs them is sentience. It is a continual activity of distinguishing, identifying and interrelating the felt contents of the sensuous field. And as the contents of the sense-field continuously change with the changes of the environment, the activity of perception is obviously sequential. The activity of distinguishing and identifying is inchoate judgement, and there is ample psychological evidence as well as epistemological reason for taking it to be the essential activity of consciousness.

Nobody should be misled by this claim, justified though I believe it to be by the evidence, into thinking that it stresses cognition at the expense of conation and emotion. As has already been intimated, sentience originally encompasses all such feelings, combined and undistinguished, in a single mass. The close association of cognition with impulse and emotive tone is never entirely lost, even in the coldest and driest theoretical speculations of developed consciousness. Nor can cognitive consciousness (i.e. perception) emerge independently of instinctive urges and the drive of biological needs. It is largely this fact that lies behind the appeal and cogency of arguments of existentialists like Heidegger, when he insists on the primacy of such feelings and sentiments as care and anxiety, and their priority to purely cognitive interpretation—often overlooking the converse dependence of these so-called "existentials" on cognition and self-awareness. There will be occasion to return to the implications of this interdependence later. My principal object here is to draw attention to the processive character of psychical states and activities and their continuity, and frequent coincidence, with physical and biological processes.

There is, moreover, another way in which perception is processive. Contrary to common belief, it is never instantaneous. To apprehend an object takes time and requires thought. Much experimental work has shown not only that an object displayed to an observer for a split second is not perceived and that it must be exposed for a minimal period before it is properly grasped (recognition occurring gradually and by stages) but also that this recognition requires and is the product of a process of thinking, which some psychologists have described as forming and confirming (or disconfirming) an hypothesis.[3]

Mere primitive sentience contains numerous qualities and modalities which, as felt, are not distinguished, but are combined, as it were, in one single amalgam of feeling. They are distinguished only when singled out, severally, by attention, identified, and contrasted, each against the ever-present background of the sentient field. Attention itself is a somewhat mysterious agency, and neurophysiologists and psychologists have found some evidence for believing that it is an intensification, or, as it were, a sort of self-enfoldment of feeling, which so structures it as to create a focus of intensity within a series of levels of decreasing definition and clarity. In this way data for perception are created, the different modalities of sensation distinguished, and objects are constructed, interrelated, and projected to constitute the surrounding experienced world.

The process of distinguishing and interrelating by selective attention occurs in early infancy and is therefore not consciously remembered; and it is complex and intricate, involving learning and practice; for perception is a skill requiring training, and the recognition of objects is an achievement which entails interpretation of the emergent data in the light of gradually accumulated and funded knowledge. That this is the case, the experience of corneal graft patients gives evidence. Though they regain their sight after having been congenitally blind, they cannot at first distinguish shapes and objects the knowledge of which they have already acquired through touch.[4] Visual perception has to be learned over a considerable period.

Not only are sensation and perception processes of activity in themselves, but they produce a succession of mental states, some of which register relatively immediately the objects and conditions surrounding the organism, while persistent effects of these linger in the form of memory and imagination. All such mental states, however, have a new and special character, not present at lower levels, which we must presently consider more closely—the character of apprehension, or cognition.

The continuous activity of organizing the sentient field is effected by the imposition upon its contents of schemata, some of them innate and some acquired. These schemata interlock and combine to structure what has been called the life-world, which henceforth forms the background horizon of all perception and thinking. The structure of attention itself is schematic, and other schemata which it creates and imposes on the flow of primitive sentience include the figure-and-ground schema, the body schema and the logically more fundamental spatiotemporal schema, which nevertheless probably all develop concomitantly in the process of maturation and learning, all of them contributing to the distinction between self and other (both animate and inanimate), which is not original but is a product of the continuous process of organization.

The emergence of consciousness and the development of knowledge is thus a process of implicit judgement and inference, becoming explicit as it becomes more self-conscious and reflective. It is a temporal process, but it is, and can only be, recognized as a process in the course of its own development, a circumstance which is the source of a serious metaphysical problem, to which we shall shortly attend. That it should be a temporal process is inevitable in the finite organism whose sensibility results from the continuous transaction between its own internal metabolic and physiological processes and the physiochemical processes of its environing world.

The activity of registering in sense and of organizing what is so registered—in short, of perceiving—the encompassing world, along with its consequences and accompaniments in imagination and memory, is what is known to psychologists as "the stream of consciousness," unceasing in the waking condition and continuing for the most part even during sleep.

If there were no change in the world, there would be no life and no sensibility, and thus no stream of consciousness. The stream of consciousness, therefore, is the way that the organism becomes aware of change as it occurs in its own body as that registers the changes of its immediate and remote environment, and there is no break between physical, biological and psychological time. But if each sensation disappeared completely as the next occurred, no change could ever be cognized, for to be aware of change, we must be aware of the sequential relation of earlier and later, and this is possible only if we have both terms before us together. Accordingly, for awareness of the flux, the passing sensation must be somehow, if only momentarily, arrested. There must be what Husserl called "retention," as also some anticipation of what will follow, what he called "protention." And so we get, once more, the "specious present."

The Specious Present

The numerous and apparently insuperable difficulties involved in the conception of a specious present have been fully and illuminatingly discussed by J. D. Mabbott in the articles to which reference has been made.[5] The psychological doctrine originated in an attempt to discover the basic and unitary origin of our consciousness of time. But the empirical evidence on which it rests is diverse and inconsistent, while results claimed by some investigators could not be repeated by others. The alleged period of the specious present has been variously determined, differing from 12, or even 36, seconds (according to William James) to 0.75 seconds (according to Kollert and Estel). Experiments on sight have arrived at a different value from experiments in sound, so that when, as is usual, vision and hearing operate together the differing specious presents should be discrepant. As the criterion for immediacy was taken as the number of successive sounds which could be recalled without error, Mabbott points out that, for hearing, in the case of the skilled musician, the specious present might span 15 minutes or more; in fact, Mozart claimed to be able to hear a whole symphony in a single apprehension. These inconsistencies alone should make us wary of the doctrine, but there are more difficulties yet.

As analysed by C. D. Broad,[6] it leads (Mabbott shows) to the paradox that the longer the act of sensing takes, the shorter the specious present it can apprehend. The situation is represented thus:

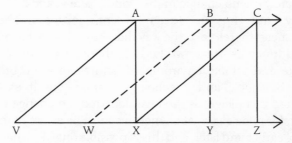

The upper line represents the succession of apprehensions and the lower line their corresponding specious presents, A perceiving V-X, B perceiving W-Y, C perceiving X-Z, and so on. As nothing occurring before W is directly perceived by B, and nothing occurring after X can be perceived by A, an act of sensing lasting from A to B can have no more specious present then W-X; and for an act lasting from A to C, the specious present will be reduced to zero.

This paradox arises because of an implicit inconsistency in the idea of a specious present (one not mentioned by Mabbott) of which Broad and other proponents seem unaware. It is at least tacitly assumed that the apprehension of a brief span of time is momentary—that is, all at once.

But then it is recognized that no act of sensing or perceiving can occur in a single instant. So the problem arises of the time relation between the period of the apprehending process and that of the object apprehended. If they are assumed to be the same the entire doctrine collapses, because no time lapse will then be experienced at any one moment, and the succession of conscious states will coincide with that of the objective events. The attempt to reconcile the two conflicting assumptions—that the apprehension of the specious present is instantaneous and that it must itself take some time—results in the paradox that the longer subjective process correlates with the shorter objective period.

Broad and some others assume that the span apprehended immediately as speciously present is all past at the moment of apprehension (that is why it is said to be "specious"), but others, like James and Husserl (who does not use the phrase) include some anticipation of the future. In either case, yet another difficulty arises of understanding how one specious present succeeds another. It is alleged to be a time span apprehended all at once, combining what has just passed with what is immediately presented, and possibly also what is just about to occur. Thus, it should include at least two, perhaps three, distinguishable events, and these are to be grasped together at one instant. At the following instant another specious succession will be perceived, but, if it is to be continuous with the last, it must include at least one of the previously perceived events. In that case we should continually be perceiving each event at least twice over, possibly even more, depending on how many events we envisage as included in the specious present, and how much we imagine specious presents to overlap. That they should overlap to some extent is inevitable if there is to be any coherent awareness of time; for if each specious present were entirely separate, the very problem would be reenstated that the specious present was supposed to solve, namely, that each immediate presentation would be totally lost before the next arrived.

Let us suppose that events, A, B, and C, occupy the specious present at time t_0, and that at t_1 the events B, C, and D are perceived. Then B and C will be perceived both at t_0 and at t_1 in two different specious presents; that is, they will be perceived twice over. This is certainly not how we perceive the passage of time; yet, if there were no overlap, there would also be no continuity, and so no perception of passage at all. If, on the other hand, one were to contend that continuity could still be maintained without repetition if the second and third events simply remained in view while the first faded out and a new event is included, passage would be introduced into the specious present and immediacy would be sacrificed. At the same time, despite its immediacy and instantaneity, the specious present is supposed to be an apprehension at once of succession (e.g., a series of taps, or a tune, the movement of a bird on a twig, or the like). So there must be passage within the specious present, and its alleged immediacy becomes suspect.

Nevertheless, whatever the difficulties inherent in the idea of the specious present, it does draw attention to and emphasize important aspects of the time sequence. First, it is and can be a sequence only if successive occurrences are grasped together in one cognition as a single series; and, secondly, they must be different and distinguishable events, otherwise they cannot constitute a succession. Thirdly, if there is to be continuity, they must overlap. This is only another way of saying that the essential form of the stream of consciousness is temporal succession, as Kant expressed it, the *a priori* form of inner sense is time.

Time is one of the schematic forms imposed along with others previously mentioned upon the indiscriminate amalgam of primitive sentience, and like every schematic form it is a texture of structural relations. Such textures, although they certainly exist in nature with varying complexity at different levels, are not, prior to the mental level, aware of themselves as structures. This, however, is the peculiar character of consciousness. Not only is it a "stream," but it cognizes itself as such; but it can do so only if the stream somehow is arrested and viewed together as a whole.[7] The notion of the specious present is a somewhat fumbling attempt to envisage this condition, the primary requirements for which were listed in the preceding paragraph. Now, the indispensable condition for all these requirements is that the apprehension of successive presentations be made by a single subject of consciousness, who can grasp them together and relate them as a series in one experience. This is the essential and incontrovertible truth established by Kant,[8] and it carries with it the consequences that time can only be comprehended within a coherent whole of experience, and that every sequence of events can be cognized as a sequence only as an interrelated totality. Yet, again, there can be no such interrelated sequence unless the elements which make it up are mutually distinct, although they cannot be absolutely separable, and to be continuous they must overlap.

The stream of consciousness, therefore, can be cognized as a stream only by a subject which can relate its passing presentations as a sequence, to do which it must itself be outside the stream. It cannot be any one, or any group of the passing presentations, nor can it be itself in passage. In short, it must be the transcendental subject (or *ego*) of Kant, Fichte, and Husserl. The comprehension of the passage of time by such a subject guarantees the unity of the experience which it constitutes, and reminds us once more that the consciousness of time involves both unity and diversity, wholeness and differentiation, eternity as well as evanescence.

The transcendental subject is not to be confused with the natural or empirical self, for the latter is only one element in one of the schemata imposed upon the flux of the primordial sentience. The distinction of self from not-self and their interrelation is a schematic structure the cognition of which presupposes the transcendental *ego* and is effected within the body of its experience. Yet it is the natural self, with its stream of consciousness, that thinks of itself as "I" and claims the experience within which these distinctions are made. The precise relation between the natural and the transcendental subject is the metaphysical problem to which reference was made above and which is implicit in the very fact of cognition.

Time and the Transcendental Subject

Time, we have said, is a texture of structural relations, an order of sequence, of events occurring in succession, related as earlier and later. But such an order is a form of whole, which as such cannot be confined to any one of its own elements, or to any particular group of them. No event, and no group of events taken simply as a collection, can constitute or be identical with the whole; for any such group must be ordered by the structural principle of the whole if it is to constitute either whole or part. Without the principle of organization determining the structure, the principle of order generating the succession, the relations between the terms cannot be established. That principle, therefore, can be neither one of the terms nor any group of them; nor can they be apprehended as terms in relation unless this principle and the structure which it governs, and within which the terms are elements, is grasped as such. Thus, time cannot itself be an event, nor can the conscious subject which apprehends events as related in time; for it must, in order to do so, be cognizant of the series as a whole ordered by this principle.

The stream of consciousness is a succession of mental events, and we now see that the awareness of such a succession would be impossible if it were confined to any one such event. Restricted to a bare now it could not be aware of other nows or of its relation to them. In fact, so restricted, it could not even be now, for the word presupposes the temporal relation of present, past, and future; so any succession and any awareness of succession, or the awareness that it was a member of a series, would be excluded. To be aware of a succession, even if one were a member of it, one must transcend both the flux and the included event with which one identifies oneself and the act of awareness.

Memory provides an illustration of this necessity. To remember an event I must have been aware of it in the past and must now be aware of it as past; and I must be able more or less precisely to assign it to a particular date in my past experience. My remembering is a present mental state, but what it apprehends is past and is apprehended as not occurring now. I may have an image now of the remembered object, but it is not the image which constitutes the object of memory. It is what the image represents, what it images. That is apprehended as occurring, not now, but in the past. I recognize the image as distinct from, but as the image of, the remembered event, so that I can compare the two and relate them as ectype and archetype. Further, to recognize the image as having occurred at a certain date, I must relate it to other dated events in my past experience. To do all this, my remembering cannot be confined either to the present event or to the past but must transcend both, as well as the relation between them. The knowing subject must be able, as it were, to stand back from the whole series of events and comprehend it all at once.

The awareness of temporal passage necessarily involves memory, for we are conscious of events as past in no other way than by being aware that they have passed into our memory. We distinguish past from present as what is remembered in relation to what is immediately perceived. Earlier we had difficulty in identifying the criterion of this distinction, though we acknowledged that it was constantly being made, and we can now see that at least part of the reason for our former embarrassment arises from the fact that the subject who makes the distinction can be identified with neither of the distincta, but must transcend both.

Like every other type of cognition, remembering is essentially judging; that is why it cannot be identified wholly with imaging. If I remember that X occurred in my past experience at a date which I can identify (more or less exactly) in relation to the rest of my experience, I am making a judgement to that effect. But, paradoxical as it may seem, the act of judging defies identification as a psychological event; for judgement is an idea—a complex idea including the relation between ideas—and there is a wealth of psychological evidence to show that psychological events (e.g., images, emotions and the like, although they may never occur apart from ideas) can never be identified with the ideas associated with them. Every attempt made by psychologists to identify idea with image has conclusively failed. Brand Blanshard has demonstrated this with copious examples in *The Nature of Thought*.[9] The same idea can be mediated by several different images (e.g., the idea of a personal friend). Ideas may become clearer as images deteriorate and fade, while images may become more vivid while corresponding ideas become more confused. Spinoza points out, and Hegel persistently protests, that imagery confuses and obscures ideas, that what can be conceived often (if not always) cannot be imagined, that those whose imagination is more prolific are often unable to reason clearly, while the most accurate ratiocination usually dispenses with imagery.[10] For instance, universal ideas defy imagery, and we can form no images of cognitive acts, though, as Berkeley insisted, we have some "notion" of them. Locke found that although we have an idea of substance we cannot form any image of it; and Hume sought, but failed, to find images (in his terminology, "impressions") of identity and of necessary connection, yet unless he had had some conception of them he could hardly have discussed them at such length. Husserl, in his *Logical Investigations* argues voluminously, and has demonstrated cogently, that logical ideas and connections can never be reduced to, or identified with, psychological states, or attributed to psychological causes. Similarly, attempts to identify ideas as mental acts have resulted only in establishing either that no such acts ever occur, or that they are not psychological phenomena and do not appear in the "stream of consciousness."

The upshot of all this is that cognitive acts are not phenomena, but transcend, as they must in order to cognize, the objects and relations which they intend. They are, in fact, performed by the transcendental subject, to which Kant assigned noumenal status (not phenomenal). The reason is that cognizable objects are always structures and are always interlaced within a system of relations in a single organized experience, the subject of which cannot be, if it is to be aware of the objects and their mutual relations, any one term or element within the cognized structure, but must somehow transcend them all and embrace the whole.

Neither the structural whole essential to the temporal ordering of events, nor the subject cognizant of them as temporally ordered, therefore, can be in the temporal process. They must be eternal. They are the universal moments of which the temporally related events are the particulars. Kant and his immediate successors identified this ordering principle as, in the final analysis, the self-conscious *ego*, which is the transcendental condition of any experience whatsoever, and the transcendental subject obviously cannot be a phenomenon in the psychical stream, because it is prior to all experience of temporal objects, and is identifiable with none.

Husserl's account of the phenomenology of inner time conscious-ness provides further illustration, even when he seems to overlook it, of this transcendence of the constituting subject.[11] He distinguishes between the flux of consciousness and the succession of temporal objects, both immanent (to consciousness) and transcendent ("external" to it). This results in a complex of levels of "constitution": that of the transcendent (or external) object, that of the immanent object, and that of the primary flux itself out of which these are constituted. (We must note an ambiguity—not observed by Husserl—in the word "constitute." Something may be constituted out of a sort of material or stuff, but it may also be constituted by an act of structuring which uses, or molds, the stuff into the resulting object. At times it is unclear in which sense Husserl is using the word). At all three levels there is in some sort, temporality. As he puts it:

> It is indeed evident that the perception of a temporal Object itself has temporality, that perception of duration itself presupposes duration of perception, and that perception of any temporal configuration whatsoever itself has its temporal form.[12]

But Husserl distinguishes what he calls "the constitutive flux" as absolutely subjective, containing nothing objective, which "flows exactly as it flows and can flow neither 'more swiftly' nor 'more slowly,' " from that which is constituted out of it. The former, he says, is called a flux only metaphorically.[13]

The constitutive, absolutely subjective, flux is apparently what Husserl elsewhere terms "the hyletic stratum" of consciousness. He is seldom explicit in his description of this level, no doubt because it is, in the nature of the case, indescribable; but it seems to correspond to what

I refer to as primitive sentience, which is pre-predicative and pre-relational, and so not the perception of a series of events at all, although it is the "stuff" within which objects and events are identified and out of which they are constituted. But, for this process, the activity of selective attention is necessary, and its agency must transcend the stream of primary sentience, nor can the agent be wholly immersed in it.

Husserl, however, tells us that, paradoxical as it may appear, the flux of consciousness constitutes its own unity.[14] Yet, in explaining how this is done, he frequently refers to "the regard" (*Blick*), which (he says) "can on occasion be guided by the phases which 'coincide' as intentionalities..." and "can also focus on the flow, on a section of the flow, or on the passage of the flowing consciousness..."[15] Now no such "regard" would be possible, nor could it do what is alleged, if it were itself flowing with the stream. It must obviously be imposed upon the flow from without. Again, in the previous paragraph, Husserl tells us: "In the continuity of modes of running-off we can extract a point..." in which we can find coincidence of modes of running-off. Who, in this process, are "we"?— and, however we are indentified, "we" can clearly not, as we extract a point, be running off in any of the modes that we find. For, if we were, we should not be cognizant of the flow.

Likewise, with reference to the duration of a sounding note, Husserl writes:

> If I orient myself on a sound, I enter attentively into the 'transverse intentionality' .. the enduring tone is present there, ever widening in its duration. If I adapt myself to the 'longitudinal intentionality' and to what is self-constituting in it, then I turn my reflective regard from the sound...to what is new in the primal sensation...etc.[16]

The "I" in this passage obviously cannot be part of, or a point in, the flux. As stated, the "regard" is reflective. The I and its regard must transcend the flux, they must be e-temporal, otherwise they could not be oriented on specific points, or adapted with respect to longitudinal and transverse intentionalities, or turned from one element within the flux to another. The flux itself must become an intentionality for any of these manoeuvres to be possible, and the subject of consciousness by whom it is intended cannot be immersed in it. The cognizant "I," therefore, must be the transcendental subject, which grasps the serial character of the flow as a whole and cannot be in passage with it.

These considerations establish the fact that no consciousness of flow, or of time, is possible, even though it is constituted out of the content of sensuous experience, except for an e-temporal, eternal, subject of consciousness capable of ordering the sensuous elements of primitive experience into a whole, which as such is not in passage.

But now we confront a still more radical problem. This *ego*, which is indispensable to any awareness of process, is I, myself. I claim and experience such awareness. But I am a finite being, aware of myself as a living organism, one among others in a world of objects, subject with them to time and change. Moreover, the acts of cognition and judgement, by which I organize my experience of the perceived world, occur in succession and constitute the life history of which I am cognizant. The flux of my own stream of consciousness comprises my empirical self, of which my awareness enables me, and entitles me, to say "I." Yet, in so doing, I become, and must necessrily claim identity with, the transcendental *ego*.

In his *Cartesian Meditations* Husserl warns us against confusing the natural, or empirical, self with the transcendental subject; and he does so advisedly, for the former is objectified in introspection and in psychological observation, which the latter can never be. Likewise, Kant warned us against the paralogism involved in trying to bring the transcendental *ego* under the categories of the understanding. Indeed, transcendental subjectivity is prior to all introspection and observation. It is all-inclusive and God-like. How then can it be identified with my finite and mortal self? Yet it is fundamental and indispensable to any cognition of the temporal world.

This is really the primary and most radical problem of knowledge, for which the entire world and whatever is conceivable is intended object; yet the claimant of which, the knower, is, and knows him or her self as, a member of that world, transient and perishing, an ephemeral creature of the passing epoch.

The Problem of the Transcendental Ego

Heidegger's doctrine

The so-called transcendental turn has been attacked from several quarters, not least by existentialist writers who followed Husserl. It is, however, questionable whether their arguments are really effective against those summarized above, whether mine, Husserl's, or Kant's.

What, then, are we to make of Heidegger's protests against a worldless subject, or Merleau-Ponty's passionate pleading for a silent, unspoken, primoridal *cogito* lying behind the transcendental *cogito* of Descartes and Husserl? The problem, we have seen, is how experience of a temporal flow in consciousness is possible unless transcendentally constituted while nevertheless claimed by the natural subject. It is in this problem that both Heidegger and Merleau-Ponty are deeply involved.

Heidegger insists that the self is *Dasein*, an existent for whose being that being is itself an issue, and the primary mode of which is "being-in-the-world." It is, moreover, an existence that is not mere cognition, but is primordially prethematic, prepredicative experience, permeated by—or better, whose very form is—*Sorge*, care, interest, concern, felt involvement (just how the word should be translated is somewhat doubtful). This care, again, has many forms and directions, and its ontological *meaning* is temporality. It is "temporalized" as past, present, and future.

Heidegger is certainly right to insist on the priority of being in the world; for *Dasein* is always, and from the beginning, aware of itself as concernedly involved in, and with, its environing *milieu*. Even so, there is some obscurity here. One can hardly escape the impression that "being-in-the-world" is an *awareness*—the awareness of being here (or "there")—*Da-sein*. Yet there is also a strong suggestion that it is precognitive, or as Heidegger would probably say, prethematic; and if this is so it should be preconscious. It would then, presumably, correspond to what Husserl postulates as the *hyletic* stratum of experience, and to what (as we shall presently find) Merleau-Ponty indentifies as "the lived body." In Husserl, the part played by the *hyle* in experience is obscure, and its ontological nature unexplained. There is also an ambiguity in Merleau-Ponty's use of "the lived body" (to which I shall shortly return). But Heidegger simply asserts "being-in-the-world" as the way in which *Dasein* exists, without specifying either the degree of *Daseins* self-awareness, or the cognitive status of being-in-the-world.

It is to original involved concern that Heidegger traces back the temporality, as well as all other existential characteristics, of *Dasein*, who, in reflection on, and interpretation of, its experience (in the sense of *Erlebnis*), both inauthentic and authentic, distinguishes between itself and other *Daseiendes*, between itself and things ready-to-hand (for use in its activity), between itself and things present-at-hand (to be observed). Thus it creates for itself a world of nature, within which it exists (and presumably, in scientific interpretation, it sees itself as a natural product).

Temporality is intrinsic to, and the essential form of *Daseins* being. It is generated from its understanding of its *Seinkönnen* (the possibilities for it of being). These are in its future, seen as "coming towards" it, and among them it chooses what it will make actual. Meanwhile, it exists as "already having been" in its *Geworfenheit* (thrownness). From these immediacies *Dasein* generates its experience of time—inauthentically, when it conceives the temporality (*Innerzeitigkeit*) of itself and of things present at hand as occurring in time, and authentically, when it resolutely accepts its own finitude in the anticipation of death (*Sein zum Tod*).

What Heidegger has done is, in effect, to give a phenomenological existential analysis of the way *Dasein* elaborates out of its own immediate (primitive) sentience, its own world, in and with which it is inextricably involved. That our awareness of ourselves and our world is so generated can hardly be doubted, and that such a phenomenological description is legitimate and instructive is not to be gainsaid, but we must not overlook its intrinsic implications.

The very fact that its own being is an issue for *Dasein* is testimony to its self-awareness, and, as the philosopher himself is *Dasein*, his self-reflectivity is (presumably) no exception. The whole existential analysis, similarly testifies to self-consciousness. Hence, being-in-the-world is, obviously, the apprehension of a relation (however inchoate) between the self and its world, a relation of "being in" (however we interpret "in"), of being surrounded (or environed) by, and of enveloping (or environing), as well as of being involved with. Similarly, *Dasein* must be apprised of the relation to itself of things ready to hand, and of things present at hand. Again, it is aware of itself as "coming towards" itself, and (however inauthentically) of some events as "to come," of others as "having been before," and of things (*Seiendes*) "being alongside," of itself and of one another. All of these are relationships in which it finds itself (and feels, and knows, itself to have) towards (itself? and) other entities. Likewise, it is aware of possibilities (*Seinkönnen*) in "the future," and of being able not to be—of death and its own extinction, to which it is related in *Sein zum Tod*, and so of its own finitude.

None of this is possible except for a self-conscious *Dasein*. Entities (things) being ready to hand, or present at hand, cannot be aware of themselves as related to *Dasein*, or of how they are related to one another. It is not the world in which *Dasein* has its being that is aware of the relation, but *Dasein*; and it is for *Dasein* that its being-in-the-world is an issue, not for the world. Only a self-conscious subject can be aware of relations of entities to one another, or of itself to others (be they things or other persons). The self-conscious *Dasein* is, for Heidegger, the source and origin, as well as the awareness of all these relationships.

So *Dasein* performs the function, in this theory, of the transcendental *ego* in Husserl's theory. But, as Husserl was clearly aware, and (by implication) argued, *Dasein* in its finitude is inadequate to perform this function. To be aware of a relation, the conscious subject cannot be confined to one term of the relation, because it must "hold before itself," or grasp together, both (or all) terms at once. What is finite cannot be aware of its own finitude (as Hegel insisted long ago) unless it has already surpassed the limit that it posits. *Sein zum Tod* implies *Sein überhinaus dem Tod*. My awareness of the limits of my own life (between birth and death) is possible only in terms of my conception of what went before I was born and of what must come after my death. It is possible for me only as transcending both limits in thought. This is true for all the relationships listed, including those involved in temporality and temporalizing—especially for what Heidegger says of the "stretching along" of my being and consequent historicizing.

Heidegger's whole discussion of temporality and temporalizing is infected with the same implication. Expectation (*Erwartung*) and anticipation (*Vorlaufen, Vorgreifen*) necessarily involve a sense and at least incipient awareness of "coming toward"—as Heidegger puts it, "coming toward oneself"—and at the same time "running ahead" and "grasping before." And the "self" towards whom, is a self that "has been" and "is already" there. All this implies an explicit schema, explication of which (*Auslegung*) is inevitably a form of spatialization and involves a sense of movement. Yet in this movement, past, present, and future, though implicit, are still not distinguished by any clear criterion. What is anticipated is anticipated *now* (or it would not be "ante"). What is retained is held back, kept in the present. Both are just as immediate as direct perception. So all three are involved in the here-and-now, just as the now is involved in all three. Thus, on the one hand, the problems from which we began (in Chapter II) have not been solved or evaded, but are still implicitly present; and, on the other hand, relationships are being posited, awareness of which, even though only incipient, requires synthesis of a manifold in the Kantian sense, spontaneous and *a priori*, which can only be attributed to an apperceptive subject logically and ontologically prior to any of the related terms (one of which is *Dasein*).

So we have not escaped the need for a transcendental subject, and so far from avoiding or solving the problem stated above, of relating the transcendental *ego* to the natural self, Heidegger seems merely to have confused the two in *Dasein* in a manner which threatens disastrous consequences.

The relationship of being in the world embraces all others, including that between persons, and it is the form of the being of *Dasein*, who presumably interprets the experience of this relationship (at least in one way) as of an environing nature in which living things exist and evolve to become human. Among these *Dasein* (I myself) must include itself. If this is a misconception due to inauthentic self-understanding, science and the world, conceived as nature, are degraded to the level of phantasmagoria. The world of *Dasein* then transpires as an illusory creation of its own, dependent, as has been shown, on its own self-awareness. On the one hand, *Dasein* is in the world, but at the same time, on the other, there is an important sense in which the world is in *Dasein*. If the conception is authentic, it is a world, membership of which is intrinsic to *Daseins* very being, and within which it recognizes itself as limited by death—as finite. How can both conditions be maintained together: being-in-the-world and being aware of oneself as in the world, being finite and being aware of one's own limitations (impossible unless those limitations have been transcended)? *Dasein* must either be a sort of omniscient god (which cannot be if it is finite), or, not being transcendent beyond the world, it cannot be aware of its own being-in-the-world. So we are driven into a dilemma, or worse, into a position totally foreign and uncongenial to Heidegger's intention—one akin to solipsism: *solis ipse*, with an *ipse* requiring for its individuation relation and contrast to others, and membership of an environing world, the existence of which the *solus* extinguishes.

Merleau-Ponty on Temporality

Merleau-Ponty is acutely aware of the problem of transcendental subjectivity, although he never states it explicitly in the way that I have done. He insists as strongly as Heidegger upon being-in-the-world, and in his *Phenomenology of Perception* he gives his own account of it in terms of what he calls "the lived body." But he is also fully aware of the necessity, for the experience of time, of transcendental apperception:

> Time is thought of by us before its parts, and temporal relations make

possible the events in time. Correspondingly it is necessary for the subject not to be himself situated in it, in order to be present in intention to the past as to the future.[17]

and again:

> We may say that ultimate consciousness is 'timeless' (*zeitlose*) in the sense that it is not intra-temporal. . . Subjectivity is not in time because it takes up or lives through time, and merges with the coherence of a life.[18]

But the ultimate consciousness cannot, he holds, be "an eternal subject perceiving itself in absolute transparency," because no such subject could descend into time, or, in consequence, have anything in common with our experience as we enjoy it.[19]

> The problem is how to make time explicit as it comes into being and makes itself evident, having the *notion* of time at all times underlying it, and being, not an object of our knowledge, but a dimension of our being.[20]

On the one hand, the subject conscious of time cannot be "absorbed into it" and must be "timeless"; on the other, it must recognize itself as in the world, as through and through temporal and finite. So while in some sense he recognizes the transcendental function of subjectivity, Merleau-Ponty refuses to tolerate a transcendental subject apart from and presiding over the flux of temporal experience.

Merleau-Ponty interprets the Cartesian *cogito* as pure thought, transparently its own object and indubitable as no other represented object can be.[21] But, he argues, no thought is pure or wholly explicit in this way. All consciousness has its intentional object, and our awareness of any such object is a reaching out towards it, an orientation of our body in space and a practical "description" (even in geometrical abstraction) of a configuration. It is "the lived body" that underlies and founds all perception, and that again is primary in all cognition. The lived body with its sensory fields and its sensory-motor involvement with the surrounding world provides the pervasive prethematic horizon of everything of which we are conscious, of all perception and all thought. Only in some contextual situation does anything, even language itself, have significance for us, and the meaning of words is nothing but the remembered function they have served in previous situations. The nontemporal is no other than the irredeemable unalterability of the past and its persistent heritage in the present;[22] so we take up and carry forward in our concrete acts a continuity of contact with others which links us with them and with our past selves. Thus, it seems, the activity of the lived body generates temporal (as well as spatial) horizons, both past and future.[23]

We may notice in passing, for it is at best only obliquely relevant to our present discussion, that Merleau-Ponty's critique leaves Descartes's argument unscathed. Descartes does not contend for a pure translucent thought, but for the undeniable and indubitable existence of present consciousness, whatever its object. I cannot doubt or deny my own awareness, however clear or opaque its intentionality, whether or however I may doubt the character or existence of what appears to me. And Merleau-Ponty acknowledges this invincible presence of self-consciousness, admitting it as the source and center of temporality and time-creation (temporalization);[24] but he argues for the indubitability likewise of the external object, because one's awareness of it is one's involvement with it, bodily, even in visual direction towards it, so that its existence is knit up with one's own self-awareness.[25]

His argument is persuasive and often profound, full of rich insights and apt psychological illustrations. It is not necessary nor possible here to go into its detail, either by way of exposition or minute criticism. Suffice it to say that it is for the most part sound. Nevertheless, to be cognizant of the declared relationship of the body and its awareness to its surrounding world of objects, the philosopher must detach himself from both—from his own involvement with the world—in order to view it, himself, and his involvement with it. Thus, he has to become, in some sense, a constituting subject, if only to discover that the constituted object is the world and his own involvement in it.

We shall maintain below that the *cogito* is the self-recognition of the immanent organizing principle of the whole, active in my finite subjectivity—the whole which embraces both me and my world, and brings itself to consciousness, through the dialectical process of development in that world, as my self-consciousness. Consciousness is both finite (and temporal) and transcendent, as became apparent in our discussion above.[26] But Merleau-Ponty tries to resolve the dilemma of this twofold character of the *ego* "existentially," insisting on a prethematic sensory experience which is our primary "alliance with the world," and which underlies all our explicit awareness, providing an inexhaustible horizon for all interpretation. This is the background to temporality;

and that, as it were, is generated and spun out by our own subjective, ongoing activity.

In spite of his eloquence and the richness of his descriptive exposition, Merleau-Ponty never really produces a clear and univocal theory of temporality. He wavers between his persistent conviction of the wholeness of experience (the dependence of significance on context) and his equally insistent belief that consciousness is and can only be in perpetual flux. So he admits that in order to be aware of the relations between the before and after of any point in time the subject "cannot be absorbed into any one of them"—that time requires a synthesis. Yet it is a synthesis that must constantly be repeated, a transitional synthesis that can never be completed; and he maintains that I am aware of time only because I am situated in it and "am already committed to it." But if this is so, surely, the transitional process will itself, to be recognized as such, demand a subsequent synthesis, and the very regress against which Merleau-Ponty inveighs and desperately strives to avoid, reasserts itself. In short, he is at once aware of the indispensability of wholeness and equally of the inevitability of diversity. Our view of time, he says, must be a comprehensive project "which in order to be apparent to itself, and in order to become explicitly what it is implicitly, that is, consciousness, needs to unfold itself into multiplicity" (loc. cit.). This recognition of the mutual implication of wholeness and differentiation, we shall find, holds the key to the solution of at least some of our problems.

There are in Merleau-Ponty's discussion many other deep and telling insights, but also an ominous premonition of a difficulty similar to that already noticed in Heidegger. Merleau-Ponty subjectivizes time and seems to be alleging (like Donald Williams and Grünbaum) that physical time excludes passage. "The objective world," he says, "is too much of a plenum for there to be time." Separated from the finite perspectives which open upon it, it contains only a multiplicity of instances of "now," which are present to nobody, have no temporal character and could not occur in sequence (op. cit., p. 412). And this "objective world" is, it seems, taken to be a construct by the objectivizing intellect (an "inauthentic" awareness) from a more fundamental and primordial consciousness.[27] "Time creation" (temporalization) seems to be an activity of consciousness; the world is "the horizon of life as the primordial unity of all our experiences," and it "remains 'subjective' since its texture and articulations are indicated in the subject's movement of transcendence"; "the *for itself*, the revelation of self to self, is merely the hollow in which time is formed, and. . . the world *in itself* is simply the horizon of my present. . ." Further, the scientific envisagement of a world before human beings evolved is derivative from and presupposes, "our pre-scientific experience of the world" (op. cit., pp. 430-432).

These quotations are taken from passages of great difficulty, in which the argument is complex and unclear, but they suggest a subjectivism that should be as unacceptable to Merleau-Ponty, who claims to have overcome the conflict between Idealism and Realism (cf. op. cit., p. 328f), as it is for us. The suggestion, however, arises out of an ambiguity in the doctrine, which if it could be cleared up, might enable us to see the way out between the horns of the dilemma of transcendental versus natural subject. The ambiguity is in the notion of the "lived body."

For Merleau-Ponty, "the lived body" is the being-in-the-world of which we are primordially conscious. This "lived body" forms, or generates, the horizon of all perception, of which (judging by the way he speaks of it), in its transactions with other things, it is the sensuous subject. It is not the objective body, as studied by the physiologist. That is an objectified abstraction from preobjective (prepredicative) primordial experience—the direct experience of the body in living interaction with other bodies and the world in general spatially arrayed around it. It is of this bodily experience that Merleau-Ponty seeks to give a phenomeno-logical account.

Now the past participle, "lived" (*vécu*), is not really transitive, and properly takes a cognate accusative. In German this is not the case. *Erlebte* is transitive and may be rendered in English as "experienced"— something lived through. But what is thus experienced is subjective, internal to the mind, and its object could well be illusory (e.g., the experience of seeing a ghost, or of poltergeists). Moreover, to speak of experience as "lived" does not exempt it from self-consciousness; rather, it commits one to the recognition that, in being thus existentially aware, we are, as Descartes realized, invincibly apprised of our own existence. The "lived body" (*das erlebte Körper*) is thus the body as experienced, and the way we experience our bodies is in and as bodily feeling. Primordially this is nonobjective; it is a single amalgam of sentience, including undifferentiated sensations of every kind, visceral, distal, kinaesthetic, and emotional. Such sentience is indeed the basis and background of all consciousness. But in its primitive phase it is precognitive, and cognition, in the guise of perception, only emerges from it when the differences in it are distinguished by selective attention to generate objects, the objective body among them, in confrontation with others. It is only after this has occurred that the distinction of self and other is made, and the body in which this sentience is felt, with its sense-fields, is claimed as mine.

Several levels, or phases, of development can be distinguished: (a) the precognitive (or subconscious) level that is neither subjective nor objective; (b) the level of vaguely perceived bodily feeling; (c) the perception of the body as the seat and source of what is felt; and (d) the perception of external objects, of which we are apprised by sensation, and distinguish from our own bodies (although the sensations are of both at the same time). Only the last of these lays claim to full objectivity, and is the projection of what is felt (differentiated as objects) as an external world, of which we perceive ourselves and our felt bodies as members.[28] The second and the third phases are strictly subjective, although the latter develops *pari passu* with the last.

Merleau-Ponty does not distinguish these levels. He speaks of "the phenomenal body," which seems to include the second and the third; but also, from the account he gives of perception, it seems to be involved (as of course it is) in the fourth. At times, however, he strongly suggests that "the lived body" is the first, the purely precognitive, level of sentience; for he repeatedly insists that it is prethematic. In the whole of this theory, therefore, there is an ambiguity between the subjective and the objective, both of which are compounded, if not confused, with the precognitive, which is neither. I have discussed elsewhere the bearing of all this upon the question of perceptual veridicality.[29] Here I am concerned only with time and the transcendental unity of apperception.

The emergence of perceived objects from the background of primitive sentience necessarily requires distinctions between qualities, and relations between distincta, the cognition of which implies a subject able to grasp the terms together and make the kind of syntheses presupposed (as Kant demonstrated) in every experience of objects. This activity of synthesis cannot be lodged in any of the objects so generated, for it is logically and ontologically prior to them all. It cannot, therefore, be attributed to the felt body, so far as it is recognized as such, nor so far as it is precognitive (for then it has not yet occurred). Moreover, it presupposes a totality of experience as a background against which everything within it is distinguished; and that again requires the supposition of a synthesizing subject, which is neither the ground nor the figures distinguished from it. Clearly, the temporalization, so aptly and persuasively described by Merleau-Ponty, involves just this kind of differentiation and relation between objects and events against a horizon of sedimented past experience of such objects. Consequently, it must likewise involve a transcendental synthesis. To allege that the agent of this synthesis is the temporal self (or felt body) at once plunges us into the difficulty already noticed, that the temporal self with its body is one of the entities distinguished in relation to others within the ordered structure that emerges from the sentient manifold; and we are in danger of committing the paralogism of which Kant warned us in the Transcendental Dialectic.[30]

The escape from this embarrassment is to be sought in a dialectical relationship between the subject of experience and the world that becomes the object of its knowledge, a relationship established by way of primitive sentience, as the "inwardization" of natural processes, and the awakened consciousness of the "lived body" and being in the world—the consciousness of a self as a living being evolved and engendered naturally, which through its own metabolism and physiological functioning, sublates the processes of nature in its own sentience, and so brings this totality to consciousness in an experience order by the principle of organization universal to the whole. This universal principle is at once transcendent to the finite contents of the whole that it organizes and immanent in the natural subject of consciousness, so giving it the capacity transcendentally to synthesize and organize its experience. Thus the transcendental subject can become embodied in the natural self, as a phase in the dialectical scale of forms that specifies that concrete universal totality, and is at the same time its objective world.

Solution to the Problem

The ineradicable moment of eternity in all temporality is the universal ordering principle which constitutes the processual flow into a serial structure. As was said earlier, the series as a whole does not change. Its internal relations of earlier and later are fixed and unalterable, even although the terms of the relations are themselves changes. What is eternal is the totality as such, the concrete universality which manifests itself, and exists, only in its particular differentiations. Both aspects are indispensable, for without differentiation there would be no whole, and without the principle of order and specification no serial structure. The temporal process is nothing other than the serial self-specification of the universal principle. For this reason, as in every whole, the universal principle is immanent in each and every particular, so that each is a manifestation (or application) of it in some specific degree; so that it unfolds itself as a scale of forms, through which it actualizes itself progressively in successively more adequate self-manifestations. Each of these, in some specific degree, becoming continually more complete, is thus a microcosm of the macrocosm.

This we have found at every level of being which we have investigated—physical, chemical, biological—and now here at the psychological level we come upon the same form of interrelation. Primitive sentience is a single undifferentiated mass of immediate feeling. In perception, every percept involves a background enclosed within the horizon of the experienced world. This ultimately involves the whole content of consciousness. Every judgement is a stage in the differentiation and articulation of that experienced world. Each mental act, as mine, is an element in an experience to some degree unified and systematized; and the presiding unifying principle is the apperceptive integrity of the *ego*. Our problem is to understand the relation between this *ego*, in its essential transcendental aspect, and the natural self, in its empirical aspect, the self which experiences itself as an organism, born, ageing, and dying—a finite, animate, natural being.

The solution of this problem is to be found in the dialectical-evolutive structure of the world, of which some indication has just been given. The whole, as we have found in previous chapters, and as outlined by Spinoza, consists of a dialectical scale of forms, each relatively self-supporting and each developing out of the preceding less complex and less self-sufficient system. The principle of organization which structures the whole is immanent in each of these forms and determines its nature, its level in the hierarchy, and the order and process of its generation. Each successive form (we have seen throughout our investigation) is a fuller and more characteristic expression of the universal principle which is specifying itself throughout the scale. The earlier and more rudimentary phase is merely physical and specifies itself in physical wholes—atoms, molecules, solar and stellar systems, galaxies, etc.—to constitute the self-contained unity of the physical world. Upon this supervenes the biosphere, similarly self-contained and unified, and similarly diversified into organic wholes from unicellular organisms to mammals, from symbioses to ecosystems, each of which is, in its own way, a microcosm of the whole.

Now we find this biological totality burgeoning out to produce, in the course of its evolution, sentient and conscious animals, the interplay of whose metabolic and physiological processes with their environment is integrated into the sentient registration of their surroundings, in a whole of feeling, that epitomizes the entire natural world. By an activity of self-organization, this sentience is articulated and brings itself to consciousness, and in our minds becomes self-reflective—so that the whole process becomes aware *of itself*. Thus, our consciousness of ourselves is at the same time the consciousness of the world and the world's consciousness of itself; for it has brought itself to consciousness in and through our minds by its own process of self-specification. Because diversity is essential to the unity of this whole, the consciousness of itself achieved in its self-specification is not simply unitary, but, in keeping with the proliferation of its individualized products, is distributed in a multiplicity of centers.

The dialectical process *within* consciousness, through which this is accomplished, moving from sentience to perception and on to understanding and self-reflection, involves, *en route*, the distinction between self and not-self (or other), necessary to locate within the system the organism in and through which the whole has become aware of itself. But this distinction is made *within* the total experience, not between it and some external counterpart. It is within the dialectic of our own experience that we come to recognize ourselves as the developed product of the world-process, and our knowledge as the way in which the world becomes aware of itself in us. *Ego* and world are thus but two aspects of one experience, inseparable and in principle identically the same. Not only is the experience mine, but it is an experienced *world*; not only is it a subjective experience, but it is the sublated development of the entire objective world-process.

The *ego* is therefore transcendental and all-inclusive, just because it *is* the whole bringing itself to consciousness through its own dialectical process. It is the universal principle integrating the whole, which is immanent in the living organism and has now become aware of itself, as "I." Its self-specification throughout the natural scale has been "inwardized" (as Hegel expresses it, *erinnert*, or remembered). As it is registered in the sentience of the organism, in response to the continuing natural process impinging upon it, it becomes the stream of consciousness, in which, through the activity of judging and inferring, it specifies itself into an experienced world. This is at the same time the self-specification of the principle of unity and organization—the unity of apperception active as the self-conscious subject.

This way of presenting the world, and our knowledge of it, is not a return, as some phenomenologists are prone to allege, to "precritical," or "dogmatic" metaphysics. The "critical" or "transcendental" turn (as it has been called) is possible only at a self-reflective level of awareness, which supervenes upon the so-called dogmatic, or "natural attitude" of common sense and empirical science. It is that phase of self-consciousness in which thought makes its own activity at the empirical level its own object and becomes what Hegel terms speculative. It is itself a necessary phase in the dialectical self-development of consciousness, which it presupposes and sublates, and apart from which consciousness itself becomes an impenetrable mystery, and the knowledge of the world a solipsistic illusion.[31] For, unless we recognize the dialectical relation between the mind and the world, as outlined above, being inevitably confined within the limits of our own consciousness, we can discover no ontological basis for any world transcendent to those limits.

It follows that we experience ourselves at once as finite and temporal beings and as eternal (transcendental) subjects. In so far as we are finite organisms, we are the creatures of time and change; and, indeed, we are finite and specific manifestations of the immanent universal, coming into being as a late stage in the process of its self-differentiation. As finite, we are engulfed in the passage of time, we are limited by evanescence and death, towards which inexorable end we are borne by the incessant process of becoming—of coming to be and passing away. But because the universal principle is immanent in us, and because we represent that stage of its self-development at which its activity becomes self-conscious, we become aware of all this, and of ourselves as participants in the process. We reflect upon it and so transcend it. Our consciousness is self-transcendent, because it is the manifestation of the immanent principle of the whole becoming aware of itself. So Spinoza can say with justification that "we feel ourselves to be eternal," and our subjectivity is not only transient but also absolute and transcendent.

As at the levels of physics and biology we found a transcendent and eternal *Gestalt* actualizing itself in a constantly changing flow of particular forms and phenomena, the specific details of which, as well as the order of generation, it determined, so at the psychological level we find a transcendental unifying principle—the self-conscious subject— expressing itself in and regulating an incessant stream of preconscious and conscious mental states, the contents of which it orders and systematizes into a coherently intelligible experience of the world. It does and can do this only because it is, at the level of mind, the active, self-differentiating principle of the whole, now aware of itself as subject, and specifying itself through the activity of thinking, at successive stages, in a fresh scale of forms, ranging from sentience through perception, memory and imagination, to the reflective and self-critical levels of intellect. With the emergence of reason the natural process is trans- formed. Physical reaction and biological instinctive response are converted into self-conscious and responsible action. Physical and biological time are sublated into history.

VI

Historical Time

Res Gestae

Responsible action is essentially the activity of reason, in Spinoza's sense of adequate thinking, and it is possible only for reflective, self-conscious beings, or persons. Irresponsible action is reason corrupted by passion, but it must still be self-conscious, otherwise it would be merely instinctive behavior, which, whether successful or not, is neither responsible nor irresponsible. Personality and self-consciousness, however, develop only in a social setting and are elicited only through communication with other people, recognized equally as rational agents. Responsible action is, therefore, social action, and its performance presupposes social relations and social structures. The study of such action is history, although other social sciences, like sociology and social anthropology, also take it as their object. Their approach and attitude towards it, however, is not that of the historian, even though these sciences are not mutually exclusive, and rationality, in the above sense, is, or ought to be, assumed by all of them as the condition of human action. Claude Lévi-Strauss, for example, admits (as an anthropologist) that "all social life, however elementary, presupposes an intellectual activity in man," although he thinks that "its formal properties cannot...be a reflection of the concrete organization of society."[1]

History, however, is not social anthropology, and still less is it socio-biology (even though it has some relevance to both of these sciences). It is not social anthropology because its concern is not just with the nature and structure of human cultures, but with what the members of these cultures have actually done in the past, in the light of the records they have left. It is not socio-biology because it does not seek to discover how human behavior in general (whether individual or social) has evolved, or how it relates to that of other animal species. The object of history is to discover and record, as well as to explain, the actual deeds of actual persons, individually and collectively, as they have occurred in the past. It is not primarily concerned with generalities, or general laws, but with individual acts and events. Moreover, the subject matter of history is not simply behavior; it is human action, and that is an entirely different category from animal behavior, because it is (in varying degrees) prompted, informed, and directed by self-conscious, reflective and critical thought. R. L. Trivers loses sight of this important distinction, when he writes:

> The chimpanzee and human share 99.5% of their evolutionary history. . . . There exists no objective basis on which to elevate one species above another. . . . It is natural selection we must understand if we are to comprehend our identities.[2]

He overlooks the patent fact that he, as scientist, is able (as is no chimpanzee) to reflect upon his experience, raise questions about what it presents, plan and organize his observations, make inferences from them, and systematize his results. The chimpanzee can, at best, behave on the level of perceptual thinking; but critical reflection elevates perceptual thinking into science and behavior into responsible action, of which only humans are capable, and which requires a new kind of study, different from either psychology or socio-biology.

The deeds of mankind performed in the past are the subject matter of history. Its concern is *res gestae*, things which have been done by human beings. Historical time is thus the time taken by human action. As human beings are natural animals, biological time is obviously presupposed, and as biological processes occur in a physical setting, so also is physical time; but these are not part of the primary object of historical knowledge. So far as the discovery of physical and biological facts are the achievements of scientists they are part of history; but the facts themselves are historical only in as much as they affect or are the concern of human action. Further, the historian's interest is directed only to the past. The present is included only so far as it is continually passing, and the future is no part of history, though the historian may, if he wishes, predict by way of speculation.

If then one is properly to understand historical time, the first question to consider is the nature of human action. The second question, seeing that acts done in the past are no longer available for immediate observation, is how we know what they were. Further, we have to consider the nature of the historical process, to ask whether it is simply a haphazard series of events or if it has any recognizable direction. Is there any legitimate sense in which history has, as Karl Jaspers alleged, an origin and a goal? The full and adequate treatment of these questions would fill a large volume, and what can be covered in one chapter must needs be very sketchy.

Although human action is a development of and is continuous with instinctive behavior, which is purely biological, there is a distinctive difference, in that human action properly so-called is deliberate action, consequent upon conscious choice. Such choice is between alternatives and implies preference, and that again some sort of comparison, and reason for the preference; so that human action is always, at least in some degree, rational. It is the product of a capacity to reflect upon and to organize experience and conduct, and so to conceive ends, to form preferences and to make choices.

The objection that some action is impulsive and is performed without deliberation, need not detain us long. Certainly, we do sometimes act impulsively, even when the action is intentional. We act, as we say, on the spur of the moment, without thinking. But if the behavior evinced is not pure blind instinct, it will be the result of training or social habituation, which was originally initiated by deliberate action. For instance, an adult may impulsively restrain a young child about to dash into a stream of moving traffic in pursuit of a ball. Such an act requires no deliberation; but it is the result of long habituation and training in the ways of road safety and child care, built upon innumerable deliberate actions in the forgotten past.

In order to know what a person is doing, therefore, it is necessary to know how he or she is thinking, to become aware of the agent's purposes and preferences, and to appreciate the way in which the circumstances of the act are perceived by the person acting.

An historical event, therefore, is never simply an external physical or biological change, but always a conscious and rational action; and to know what it is, or was, one must know how the agent was thinking. As the action is past, and the agent may very well not be available for consultation, this can be discovered only by consulting the historical evidence. And even if the agent is still available for questioning, the veracity and reliability of the answers may still be called in question and must be tested against other evidence. By such methods the historian reconstructs in his own mind the thought of the historical agents who created the historical event he is investigating; and unless he does this he cannot genuinely discover what the historical event really was.

Rationality is the capacity to organize, to put things in order; and rational action is therefore organized conduct. Human individuals cannot survive in isolation; they survive only as they live in society, and so human action is always social action. So far as that is rational, social conduct is always organized, and is thus always action within some kind of social order. History, in consequence, even when biographical, is always the history of human society.

Now human society, because it is organized, prescribes an order of conduct for its members, and in the course of time develops a tradition, which is an historical product. Consequently, it is impossible to understand human social behavior apart from the knowledge of the tradition in which it is performed—in short, apart from its history. One cannot understand any society, one's own or any other, without its history; and one cannot understand human conduct, one's own or any other, apart from the social setting in which it takes place. Accordingly, the ancient Greek exhortation to "know thyself" involves historical knowledge; because it requires a knowledge of one's social background and inheritance.

Further, if we bear in mind that history is the knowledge of human action, which is always social, and is essentially rational, deliberate action involving conscious choice, so that to know properly what it is one must know how the agent is (or was) thinking, it is easy to appreciate R. G. Collingwood's definition of history as the self-knowledge of mind.[3] "Man knows himself," wrote Wilhelm Dilthey, "only in history, never through introspection."[4]

The Idea of the Historical Past

But history is the knowledge of the past, and the past is no longer with us. How then do we gain access to it? Our awareness of the passage of time, as we have seen, involves immediate retention, and that extends into memory; but individual memory is often faulty and living memory is short. Recollections are passed down from generation to generation, but again it is notorious that in such inherited traditions much gets left out and much more is variously distorted. Mere memory and tradition, therefore, cannot rank as historical knowledge, because knowledge is by definition true, or at least probable.

No doubt, traditional beliefs and legends enter to some extent into all history, especially into the early history of a nation—like, for instance, the prevalent belief that George Washington confessed, as a boy, to having chopped down a cherry tree. But traditions like these may (or may not) conflict with others. To know what is true, therefore, we must seek evidence, and although traditional legends can themselves serve as evidence of some sort, neither they, nor any other evidence can be accepted at face value. It must all be critically examined and compared.

Apart from current traditions and the direct memory of witnesses, such evidence is always "documentary" in the sense that it consists of artefacts revealing to the perspicacious observer the way in which somebody was acting, to what purpose and with what in mind. Moreover, the evidence and the acts to which it testifies have to be correctly dated so that the continuity of history is maintained, and the relevance of the testimony established. This proves to be a more difficult and complicated task than might appear at first sight, and the efforts of historians throughout the centuries to accomplish it have resulted in what has come to be regarded as the scientific method of history.

Collingwood has maintained that the idea of the historical past is in the Cartesian sense, an "innate idea."[5] "It is not," he claims, "a chance product of psychological causes; it is an idea which every man possesses as part of the furniture of his mind... " Insofar as human beings are rational and social and live in organized communities this must clearly be true. For life in an organized society implies the tacit (or inherent) aware-ness of a traditional mode of conduct rooted in the history of the group. This tradition is learned and is not "innate," but it cannot be learned without some *a priori* concept of historical time.[6] The concept is *a priori* in the sense that it is a principle of order necessary and logically prior to the experience of social action, without which our social consciousness could not be so ordered as to make sense. Social conduct requires the pervasive background consciousness of the society and its expected codes, which is not possible without some, at least tacit, awareness of a tradition that is not a momentary phenomenon but an historical outgrowth.[7]

That the idea of the historical past is *a priori* is not a law or a fact of genetic psychology. Infants are not born with the idea; but, as their minds mature and they become aware of their social milieu and the social determinants of, and restraints upon, their conduct, they are bound to think in terms of a social tradition, the logical presupposition of which is that it is an historical product. Of course, this *a priori* concept of the historical past is connected and associated with our current sense and perception of the passage of time, which has psychological roots; but not even that perception can be a purely psychological function because, as we have already seen, the occurrence of sentient content can only be ordered as a temporal sequence if it is grasped as a serial totality; and that implies an ordering concept and a thinking subject—in Kant's language, an original transcendental *a priori* unity of apperception—prior to all psychological relations, temporal or other.

The concept of the historical past is *a priori* for the further reason that human action is rational, deliberate, and reflective; and it is so because human reason is, of necessity, developed in a social setting. This setting constitutes the background, or horizon, of all practical consciousness. And it is not a static backdrop, but a social process, with a past of which we must be aware in order to act relevantly in a present situation, or prepare for an expected future. Such a conception of an ongoing social process, in which the agent is a conscious participant, is essentially historical; and it is necessarily presupposed in any and every historical act. For this reason, the idea of the historical past is "innate" in the social agent, and is the *a priori* condition of any historical knowledge.

Equipped with this *a priori* concept of the historical past, the historian has to examine evidence in order to discover what in fact happened. But evidence can be accepted only after due criticism and interpretation. If the evidence takes the form of artefacts, as in most archeological investigations, these must be examined to determine their intended employment and the circumstances in which they were used. Nobody can do this on sight, but can decide only in the light of already acquired historical knowledge. If the evidence is in the form of testimony, again it may not be accepted as given. The witness, whether storyteller or former historian, may be lying, or exaggerating, will almost inevitably have omitted much, and have given a slant to the story to suit some limited interest or ulterior purpose. Whether any or all of this is the case may be discoverable by the critical comparison of documents, all of which have alike to be examined and tested. Accordingly, although almost anything whatever may serve as historical evidence if the historian can recognize in it some relevance to the problem with which he or she is dealing (a problem of discovering the historical truth in some specific context), no evidence is a mere given fact. Without interpretation it does not even rank as evidence, and as such all is subject to critical examination.

From the available evidence a connected and consecutive order of events has to be constructed, and as the evidence is always incomplete, and the record always fragmentary, the gaps have to be filled in by the historical imagination. For instance, I may read in some newspaper report of President's Kennedy's assassination that the Vice-President was riding in the motorcade. I next find a report that shortly afterwards he was in Washington, having been installed as the new President. I confidently assume that he must somehow have travelled from Dallas in the intervening time and, in the absence of further evidence, I imagine this to have taken place. I may find evidence to confirm or to contradict what I imagine, so far as that concerns the method of travel; but what I cannot doubt is that the actual journey must have taken place. Where no evidence is available, the links between what are taken as established facts have to be supplied by the historian's imagination; and that is subject to criticism in much the same way as the evidence itself on which he constructs his picture of the historical past. But, quite apart from criticism, the imagination is both necessary and to some extent indubitable, as in the above example the occurrence of the Vice-President's journey cannot be called in question. This is what Collingwood has termed "the *a priori* imagination," *a priori* because it is the indispensable prior condition of constructing any picture whatever of the historical past.

If everything is subject in this way to critical interpretation, the question arises, What serves as the criterion by reference to which the historian decides upon the reliability of the evidence and the truth of the final account of the past which is offered? It cannot be any appeal to so-called fact, because what the historian is endeavoring to discover is just what the fact is, both with respect to the presented evidence, and with respect to that to which it testifies. By what criterion, then, can we judge? There is none, other than the coherence of the imaginative reconstruction of the past which results from historical inquiry. In this sense, the only criterion of historical truth is history itself. There is no perceptible "fact" that can be accepted at face value, and that can serve as an external criterion without critical interpretation. To quote Collingwood at more length:

> It is thus the historian's picture of the past, the product of his own *a priori* imagination, that has to justify the sources used in its construction. These sources are sources, that is to say, credence is given to them, only because they are in this way justified. For any source may be tainted: this writer prejudiced, that misinformed; this inscription misread by a bad epigraphist, that blundered by a careless stonemason; this potsherd placed out of its context by an incompetent excavator, that by a blameless rabbit. The critical historian has to discover and correct all these and many other kinds of falsification. He does it, and can only do it, by considering whether the picture of the past to which the evidence leads him is a coherent and continuous picture, one that makes sense.[8]

The writings of other historians, Marc Bloch and E. H. Carr,[9] corroborate Collingwood's doctrine, and I have nowhere found a convincing refutation of it, nor any satisfactory alternative to it, nor any good reason to reject it. It follows that history is the creation of the historical imagination, not as mere inventive fancy but as a constructive activity interpreting evidence under the guidance of the *a priori* concept of the historical past.

If you object that history is made by human action and not by the imagination, you will be right in the first part of that contention, but, as human action is social action, it is possible only if directed and inspired by historical awareness, which is the product of the constructive imagination, as is here being claimed. It is human action that makes history, but it is the historian's *a priori* imagination that makes it known. Every member of every human society is an historian to the extent that he or she is aware of the historical past; and, devoid of any such awareness, rational social action cannot take place. The professional historian is simply the expert who makes his society more fully and more accurately aware of its own inheritance. Without the historical imagination, then, human conduct would not qualify as rational social action, so it is still true that history is created by the historical imagination.

For this reason, it is not true (*pace* Lévi-Strauss) that "the history men make unconsciously" differs from "history of men consciously made by historians."[10] For the people who make history do so by acting, and action is informed by thinking, which, among rational social beings is implicitly historical thinking. What the professional historian does is to make explicit and scientifically intelligible the history embedded in *res gestae*. There is, in this regard, only one sort of history, and the historical process relates to the science of historiography, as moral observance relates to ethics. The second arises necessarily out of the first as an extension of the reflective thought that makes it possible, and is prompted by the continuing urge toward self-knowledge. Likewise, the philosophy of history is just a subsequent phase of this same self-reflection, in which the historian asks what precisely is being done in the writing of history.

Two questions arise from the contention that history is the product of the historical imagination. The first is how we can distinguish genuine history from historical fiction, which is equally a product of the historial imagination, and equally requires coherence in order to carry conviction. The second is whether there can, on this theory, ever be any such thing as objective historical knowledge. For the historical imagination, as we have admitted, is steeped in social tradition, and must necessarily be molded by the outlook and prejudices of the historical period and the society in which the historian has been nurtured. The historical imagination is as much a product of history as historical knowledge is a product of historical imagination.

The first of these questions is the easier to answer, because the distinction rests simply on the relation of the imaginative construction to the evidence on which it is based. Historical novels, if well written and well researched, are based on good evidence and will contain much genuine history, even if the novelist prefers dramatization to plain narrative (a preference not always renounced by historians). But the novel always contains much that is pure invention and is not supported by evidence. True it is that even scientific history includes some speculation where evidence is lacking; and the novelist can exploit these lacunae for the development of his own characters and his plot. Nevertheless, there is always some overlap between history and fiction. Not only is every novel in some sense historical (even science fiction is a projected future history), but also some genuine history contains elements of fiction. The speeches and dialogues "recorded" by Thucy-dides are a case in point, and so may be the dialogues of Plato. They are fictional yet not deceptive, so far as they do portray the authentic gist of the thought of the historical agents on the appropriate occasions. Only what is adequately supported by evidence, however, is properly historical knowledge, and, as we have seen, the evidence must be as complete as possible and must be woven into a coherent and intelligible pattern.

The second question is more difficult, but a clear answer can be given so long as we keep in mind that the criterion of objectivity is not some external standard independent of the historian's construction, but is its coherence and comprehensiveness. The evidence must, of course, be critically interpreted, and such interpretation is always saturated with social habits of thought. Nor can it ever be freed entirely from contemporary prejudices. But these are not to be disparaged merely as blemishes; they are, as we have said, historical products, and therefore they contribute something to the historical truth, if only as themselves evidence at the disposal of future historians, even if they do tend to bias contemporary inferences. So Gadamer exhorts us not to try to free all interpretation from prejudice and transitional ways of thinking, for no interpretation whatever is possible without them.[11] The bias can be counteracted by expanding the historical purview and critically examining the presented evidence. Bias is really a limitation of outlook and is revealed in lack of coherence. It can be corrected through the detection of internal contradiction, by reinterpretation of the evidence, and by seeking more, in order to remove the inconsistencies. As Collingwood maintained, history has to be rewritten in each succeeding generation. But the final answer to the question about historical objectivity can only be given later, after we have reflected further on the nature of the historical process.

The Historical Process

If the historical process is that of human rational, and therefore social, action, it should reflect the nature and principles of such action. We must not, of course, be misled by this fact into the belief that deliberate action, which must always to some extent be rational, is always, if ever, completely so. Practical thinking is necessarily accompanied by and integrated with emotion and impulse. It is often confused and distorted. But it is so only by reference to rational standards and cannot be pronounced irrational by any other criterion. So far as human beings are nonrational, if they ever are, their behavior is merely instinctive and cannot be castigated as irrational any more than the nest-building of birds. Irrational action is possible only for rational, self-conscious beings. With this caveat, let us continue our reflection upon human social conduct.

The aim of social order is to enhance human welfare (in the widest and deepest sense of this phrase), through cooperation and the interplay of diverse social functions. This is its rational character. The history of societies should then display a continuous trend towards this goal and should be characterized by progress towards it. In modern time, until relatively recently, it was a widespread belief that such progress had always occurred and was more or less inevitable. But neither is this universally accepted today (though often tacitly assumed), nor has it always been believed. Nevertheless, general human welfare always has been the implicit aim of social activity, and has impelled societies to develop from family groupings to tribal and village organizations, and from these to political institutions.

In the modern age, autonomous political organizations have become sovereign nations, and the supremacy of their sovereign governments is premised upon the presupposition that they pursue the national interest, or what is presumed to be the common welfare of the state and the society over which it presides. In the western world, nations have striven, in various ways and with varying degrees of success, to ensure that this should be so by adopting institutions of government representative of the people, in the hope and expectation that their elected representatives will govern with the consent of the governed in pursuit of their best interests. Such institutional forms are commonly described as free governments, and "the inalienable rights to life, liberty, and the pursuit of happiness" are taken to define political freedom. As the ultimate welfare of the individual in society is in principle the aim of rational social action, inasmuch as this is identified with freedom, that is envisaged as the goal or end of history. This is Hegel's contention in his philosophy of world history, and he maintains that the course of history is, in consequence, a dialectical progression directed by reason towards the achievement of political freedom.

Such a doctrine seems to entail the belief in the necessity of human progress, a belief which was strongly reinforced shortly after Hegel's death by the emergence into prominence of the theory of evolution in biology, and its application (legitimate or otherwise) to social theory. Today, the experience of two world wars, the inhumanities of "the gulag archipelago," the horrors of Nazi death camps, the expected cataclysmic effects of nuclear war, and the apparently insuperable world problems by which mankind is faced have made us more sceptical, and there are few who take the idea of progress, except in the case of the natural sciences, seriously. However, as I shall try to show, Hegel's theory does not entail the inevitability of human progress, whether or not Hegel personally believed that it did, but only that history pursues a dialectical course.

If the definition of history and the account of human action we have adopted are correct, Collingwood's assertion that history is the self-knowledge of mind should (in spite of his reservations about Hegel's view) lead to a rapprochement between the thought of these two thinkers. For the mind of which history is the self-knowledge is the rational mind, with its ability to reflect and to set its objects and activities in order, its capacity to "see things together," and to organize itself, its theoretical and its practical world, as a whole. The principle of such organization is always dialectical; so that history ought to unfold as a dialectical progression.

Rational social action, we have seen, aims at the realization of the common welfare of a community. It does so through free and willing collaboration of its members, each performing a specific social function. The common welfare may be defined as the maximum opportunity for the development of the physical, mental, intellectual, and moral capabilities of every individual in the society. Clearly, this objective has never yet been achieved and is still far from being realized; but it remains the aim of all rational human social organization. Only in a community organized for the sake of this end is freedom possible, for whatever frustrates collaboration for this purpose and operates as an obstacle to the common welfare limits the opportunities for development of individual capacities, and is thus a limitation upon freedom. As history is the record of human social activity, it follows that it is the account of the persistent endeavor to achieve freedom. This is Hegel's doctrine.

It clearly does not follow, however, that because freedom is the objective of social activity, the endeavor to achieve it must inevitably succeed. Until now, freedom never has been fully achieved; and the very means used to accomplish the universal aim may frustrate the efforts to reach it. For example, those who believe that it depends on economic equity may seek to ensure this by instituting dictatorships of the proletariate; and others who give priority to civil rights and individual enterprise may be defeated by the inordinate power of accumulated wealth due to inequitable distribution. The use of developments in technology in the endeavor to improve social conditions may have unpredicted side effects which impair the very social conditions they were supposed to benefit; or the pursuit of national security may lead to a nuclear arms race which threatens civilization with extinction. Yet all these eventualities are the results of social action of which the ostensible and professed aim is communal well-being and national interest, the presumed conditions of freedom.

Nevertheless, planned policies seldom run smoothly, without meeting obstacles and opposition. Accidents are always turning awry the intentions of human beings, whether they be reasonable or unreasonable. Contingencies abound, and the art of life may be described as the ability to react effectively to the unexpected.

> ...conduct lies
> In the masterful administration of the unforseen.[12]

But this is not an art universally perfected by mankind, so it is not surprising, perhaps, that some thinkers (like Alexander Herzen) should see history as nothing but "a whirlwind of contingencies." Such a judgement, however, would suggest insufficient reflection.

Dialectical progression is always the process of the self-differentiation of a whole. In the case of history it is that of the active social whole. And the aspect of diversity is as essential to the whole as the element of unity. Where diversity proliferates, distinctions and contrasts, oppositions and conflicts, inevitably arise, due invariably to the finitude and partiality of the distincta (in this case, the limitations and partisanships of the contending parties). This too is the root of all evil, as well as the underlying source of contingency. But in every partial element the principle of organization that constitutes the whole is immanent, and the dynamic process, especially in human affairs, is the continual nisus towards order and rationality (however frustrated by passion and circumstance). Consequently, the chaos and contingency are constantly subject to direction by this urge towards wholeness, towards the reconciliation of conflicts, and the realization of harmony.

For example, the ravages of major wars repeatedly persuade the nations of the need (becoming ever more desperate) for international institutions competent to maintain peace and order. After the Napoleonic wars, five great nations in Europe signed, at Aix-la-Chapelle, an agreement "never to depart, neither among themselves nor in their relations with other states, from the strictest observance of the principles of the Law of Nations." After the first World War, the victors established the League of Nations, and after the second came the United Nations. If each has been, in its way, a spectacular failure, each has led, at the next attempt, to efforts to remedy the defects of its predecessor; and today the peoples of the world are becoming ever more fully aware of the potential reality of a world community and the deepening need to give it effective expression in some form of international organization adequate to common needs.

In such ways historical contingencies are all subject to, and often used by, the perpetual drive, in all historical agents, to improve their lot, and to use their ingenuity, their ability to anticipate eventualities, to organize and plan their lives. In consequence, what Hegel called "the cunning of reason" prevails in the long run to direct contingencies toward desired ends and conduct the course of history in the direction of social objectives, often in ways unintended and unexpected by the persons involved. And if "the best laid plans of mice and men gang oft agley," it is only by reference to such objectives.

Hegel's thesis, like our own, is that social action is rational, and therefore self-reflective and self-critical. Accordingly, in his view it will proceed dialectically; and the Hegelian dialectic gives the impression to the casual observer of driving ineluctably on towards an inexorable absolute, which encompasses human freedom inevitably *en route*. This, however, is a travesty of Hegel, which careful examination and proper interpretation of his writings can dispel. As it is not my main object here to expound Hegel, however, let me approach the problem in my own way.

Because human action properly so-called is always in some degree intelligently informed, all history is the history of thought. As is well known, Collingwood maintained that the historian's task was always to reenact the thought of the historical agents whom he investigated. For this he has been much criticized, but I think wrongly, because the critics have taken him to mean that the historian must have some mysterious capacity to intuit the subjective state of mind of the agent concerned. This Collingwood emphatically denied. What the historian has to do is to reconstruct in his own mind, on the grounds of the presented evidence, the way people saw and understood the situation in which they acted and the purposes they entertained. So stated, the theory is far less controversial; and in any case, we may agree that historical action, as rational, social reflective, and deliberate, is shaped and informed by thinking, so that basically history is intellectual history, not excluding, of course, the accompanying passions and conative impulses; and not forgetting that economic and political activities require the exercise of the intellect as do art, literature, science, and philosophy (even if not always at the same level of intensity). If this is so, one would expect the course of history to follow a route governed by the same principles as that of reason—the self-differentiation (or self-specification) of an ordered system—in short, to be dialectical. But before investigating this implication, I must give some consideration to a contemporary doctrine that denies it, in order to remove from my path what might look like an insuperable obstacle.

Structuralism and Deconstructionism

Today this position is confronted by the structuralist denial that concrete social forms reflect the intellectual activity of the members of the society, an activity they recognize as essential to social conduct. The agents, however, according to this doctrine, are not (and cannot be) aware of the underlying structures that determine their action. It is certainly true that human beings unreflectively going about their day-to-day business are unaware, for the most part, of the overall social structures that their conduct exemplifies, although they cannot be wholly unconscious of the restraints, prohibitions and permissions that these involve. Yet, unless their deliberate actions were informed by some recognition of aims, intentions, plans, and objectives, the social structures would never reveal themselves to the theorist. And unless the theorist (historian or social scientist) can reconstruct in his or her own mind—always, of course, on the basis of valid evidence—the conscious intention (as well as the unconscious promptings) of these actions, the social conduct investigated will simply be misunderstood and the facts will be falsified. In that case the concrete social structures will be obscured and misrepresented, and the resulting theory will be untrue. Moreover, the very fact that the theorist can discover them shows that the concrete social structures are somehow accessible to reflective thought. If human action is to be the object of investigation, therefore, the conscious, deliberate, and critically reflective capacities of the agents may not be neglected or ignored without peril.

On this issue Lévi-Strauss is ambivalent and confused. As a social anthropologist he is emphatic about the need for the scientist to identify with the people he is studying and to appreciate the way they think and the manner in which they assess and interpret their surrounding world. The purport of such thinking, however, he regards as entirely relative to the culture concerned. Likewise, he regards history (written by historians) as biased beyond redemption by the allegiances and viewpoints of the writers; so that it is (apparently) devoid of any legitimate claim to represent the truth. In fact, he denies the existence, and even the possibility of any objective history. Similarly, he impugns (quite implausibly) the validity of all historical dating, regarding the various historical time scales (millenia for prehistory, centuries for modern history, years and even days for biography, etc.) as incommensurable. He seems to argue for some sort of sociology or anthropology of knowledge, as is advocated by Karl Mannheim.[13] At the same time, he commends "dialectical reason," seeming, however, to understand the phrase in a sense peculiar to himself and altogether unlike what I wish to advocate.[14]

Such radical relativism is a disguised form of scepticism, self-refuting and fatal to any theory, be it anthropological, sociological, or philosophical. To the problem of historical objectivity I have already referred and shall presently return. And if what has been said above is true—that social action is dependent upon and continuous with its own history—Lévi-Strauss's submissions would so disintegrate the conception of organized society as to leave no coherent object for the social anthropologist to study. Consequently his own positive doctrine stands in irreconcilable opposition to his critique of historiography.

Nevertheless, there is, especially among contemporary French thinkers, a determined endeavor to disown all deference to meaning and interpretation, and to treat the activity of human beings in society "purely objectively," almost (if not quite) behavioristically. It is just this that Michel Foucault professes to do in his *Archeology of Knowledge*, the more relevant because it is concerned with what has customarily been called "the history of ideas." He claims to examine and analyse only explicit and uninterpreted discourse, to discover the system (for he does, if at times only inadvertently, admit that it is a system) of rules determining the formations into which it becomes organized, and making possible the occurrence and viability of its statements, to distinguish and trace the relations between different discursive formations, to discern the way in which "objects" are identified and distinguished, "concepts" generated and "strategies" deployed. In so doing he professes to renounce any appeal to the common historical concepts of causal connection, tradition, or influence, any appeal to obscure concealed, underlying meanings, or inspiring ideas, to hidden psychological explanations, or to formal and transcendental a prioris. No attempt is made to interpret what is said or written in terms of what is not explicitly stated. Reference to a subject of awareness, although his or her existence is not denied, is eschewed, and even authorship is dismissed as largely irrelevant. Here there is no suggestion of any requirement to rethink the thought of past historical agents—even in the pursuit of "intellectual" history.

Foucault seeks to treat discourse purely as an object in its exteriority, without concern for any attributed meaning or truth value. In the words of Dreyfus and Rabinow, "He contends that, viewed with external neutrality, the discursive practices themselves provide a meaningless space of rule-governed transformations in which statements, subjects, objects, concepts, and so forth are taken by those involved to be meaningful."[15] Meaning and truth are thus given no objective validity but are taken to be merely putative by those engaged in the discourse.

To enter at this point into the detail of Foucault's proposed method of procedure would be inappropriate to our main theme. Foucault, in fact, seems little interested in the nature of historical time. He claims (according to Dreyfus and Rabinow) to be writing the history of the present. He concentrates on the interrelation of discursive formations (or, as he calls them, "positivities"), although he does not neglect their transformations in the course of time. He also, quite rightly, recognizes that these transformations are neither sudden and unheralded nor simple, but are compatible with and accompanied by the persistence and continuity of certain elements (this, in spite of his earlier disparagement of continuity and gradual change). The main defects of Foucault's stance, indeed, are his tacit presumption, and at times almost open admission, of concepts and principles that he has previously emphatically disavowed, and his disregard of the necessary implication, in his very perspicacious account of statement (which is fundamental to his entire conception of discourse), of the very subjectivity that he seeks to eliminate.

Foucault begins by emphasizing an alleged contemporary tendency among historians to adopt a critical attitude towards the forms and centers of unification traditionally revered, to acknowledge discontinuities rather than continuities, and dispersions rather than connectivities.

The new history (he avers) questions themes of convergence and culmination and refuses to seek out obscure and hidden origins. It discounts "influences" and the acknowledgement of a "tradition." It disowns the unity of "the period" and recognizes no "spirit of the age." Consciousness, subjectivity, "lived experience," unconscious psychological compulsions are all to be renounced. Statements are no longer to be treated as "documents," but rather as "monuments," and total history is to be replaced by general history (neither of these having been defined). But in the course of pursuing the proposed new method, stressing dispersions and discontinuities instead of unities, Foucault repeatedly readmits—as it were, by the back door—the very categories he had originally proscribed.

As an example of discontinuity he cites the fact that "literature" and "politics" are recent categories inapplicable, except by retrospective hypothesis, to mediaeval, or even classical, culture. He points out that literature, politics, philosophy, and the sciences did not articulate the field of discourse in the seventeenth and eighteenth centuries as they did in the nineteenth.[16] True though all this may be, and admissible by any sound historian, no historian could become aware of, or affirm, these facts if he (or she) had not traced the continuities (as well, of course, as the transformations) between classical, mediaeval, and renaissance thought, between these and seventeenth- and eighteenth-century culture, and the emergence from it of the nineteenth-century disciplines. And is not this insistence upon divergences a tacit acknowledgement of "periods" and of the differing genius (or "spirit") of each age?—in a sense, no doubt, sufficiently metaphorical to obviate any imaginary presiding ghost. Can discontinuities be recognized apart from a background of continuity? And are not these examples themselves evidence of a tradition that persists even while it changes?

Foucault discounts such concept as "the book," "*oeuvre*," "the novel," and the like. He writes:

> A novel by Stendhal and a novel by Dostoevsky do not have the same relation of individuality as between two novels of Balzac's cycle *La Comedie Humaine*; and the relation between Balzac's novels is not the same as that existing between Joyce's *Ulysses* and the *Odyssey*.

Indeed, we may concur, but here there is the acknowledgement of authorship (previously discounted) and in the last case a clear example of influence (however remote). He continues:

> The frontiers of a book are never clear-cut... it is caught up in a system of references to other books, other texts, other sentences: it is a node within a network. And this network of references is not the same in the case of a mathematical treatise, a textual commentary, a historical account, and an episode in a novel cycle; the unity of the book, even in the sense of a group of relations, cannot be regarded as identical in each case. The book is not simply the object that one holds in one's hands; and it cannot remain within the little parallelepiped that contains it: its unity is variable and relative. As soon as one questions that unity, it loses its self-evidence; it indicates itself, constructs itself, only on the basis of a complex field of discourse.[17]

How true! Whoever (one must wonder) thought a book was "simply the object held in one's hand"? Yet it is admitted that it *has* unity, even if it is not self-evident. It *is* caught up in a *system* of references—and every system is a unitary whole, which (to be a whole) requires the unity to be differentiated. The unity of each individual book, however, is *not* variable, although the unities of different books certainly are. It is, indeed, relative to a complex field of discourse, which is why we identify it differentially, as a mathematical treatise, or a textual commentary, or a historical account, or some other *genre*. Nor should we assume that its author was unaware of all this, or did not, in the majority of cases, deliberately make the references in the network of which the book is said to be a node. This is the essence and the skill of authorship. And without the influence of other writers, other treatises, of a tradition and of current conventions, of trains and continuities of thought and speculation, the references could never have been made nor detected. Whatever unity the book has must have been given it by the intent and artistic, or scientific, vision of its author, without appreciation of which by the reader the complex network of references could never be recognized. Furthermore, this network itself reflects the unity of the integrated and articulated whole that is the social and intellectual system in which alone a book could be produced, and which could only be comprehended by a self-conscious and reflective subject—that of the archeologist (or historian). So the much devalued subjectivity has to be presupposed, whether of author, or reader, or of the theorist (like Foucault) who sees and traces out the network of relationships. Both subject and unity are implied, willy-nilly, in Foucault's own description.

While here Foucault purports to impugn the unity of the "book," later on, when he discusses the materiality of the statement, he admits that, although, in different editions, ink, paper, the placing of the text, and the positioning of signs are none of them the same,

> they are all neutralized in the general element—material, of course, but also institutional and economic—of the 'book': a book, however many copies or editions are made of it, however many different substances it may use, is a locus of exact equivalence for the statement—for them it is the authority that permits repetition without any change of identity.[18]

So, after all, the unity of the book is acknowledged; and how could such "authority" be vindicated apart from the authorship, and the intention and desire of the author to express the intelligible content of the statement made?

Treating of contradictions and oppositions in, or between, positivities, Foucault says that they exercise certain functions, one of which is "to bring about an *additional development* of the enunciative field, to open up sequences of argumentation, experiment, verification and various inferences. . ."[19] and so on. So, here again, continuities are admitted, and it is tacitly (as it should be openly) acknowledged that contradiction can be a spur to further progress. Foucault discourages attempts, in such cases, to discover larger unities in which oppositions may be reconciled; yet, on the very next page, he gives an example of how contradiction may effect just this—induce a reorganization of the discursive field (as he puts it) so that (in the case cited) the opposition of system to method in eighteenth-century natural history resulted in a single form of description giving the method rigor and the system regularity.

Discussing the nature of transformations of discourses one into another, Foucault remarks that several types of transformation may be involved. For instance, in the emergence at the end of the eighteenth century of clinical medicine, variation in the rate of unemployment, labor needs, political decisions concerning guilds and universities, needs and new possibilities of public assistance, etc., were all contributory.[20] If so much is conceded, however, are not some causal connections being acknowledged? And in tracing these connections are we not looking for origins? Moreover, none of these factors are independent of human judgements (e.g., political decisions) and desires, nor can they be detected, appreciated, or properly understood, without them. They must inevitably (if only surreptitiously) be presupposed.

These are only some examples of the way in which what is initially denied or disparaged is later presupposed and tacitly admitted. Throughout his book Foucault repeatedly contradicts, by inadvertency, what he wished to establish and apply. An attempt to detect and list every such case would be tedious and superfluous, but the alert reader will not fail to discern them.

The entire proposal of an "archeology of knowledge" rests upon Foucault's defintion of statement and the account he gives of the enunciative function.[21] For him, a statement is not what it is for those logicians who substitute the term for what others call a proposition. Foucaulty distinguishes clearly and convincingly between a statement, on the one hand, and a logical proposition, or a grammatical sentence, on the other. It is not restricted to either, nor is its relation to what it states the same as that of sign to signified, of proposition to referent, or of sentence to meaning. Neither is a statement the same as a "speech act," which may, and usually does, involve many statements. More important, statement is anterior to all of these linguistic modalities, as well as to their intrinsic and extrinsic relations. It is, says Foucault, "a function that operates vertically in relation to these various units, and which enables one to say of a series of signs whether or not they are present in it." (ibid., p. 86). It is a function that reveals unities and structures of linguistic usage and logical procedures on the basis of which one may decide whether they "make sense," by what rules they are juxtaposed, what they signify, and so forth.

The correlate of a statement, he tells us, is a domain, or group of domains: properly, it has no correlate, but its referential consists of laws of possibility, rules of existence for the objects named or described within it and the relations it affirms or denies. "[I]t defines the possibilities of appearance and delimitation of that which gives meaning to the sentence, a value as truth to the proposition" (ibid., p. 91). Secondly, it has a special relation to a subject, who is not the first person element in a sentence, not necessarily (as in a statement made by a character in a novel) even the "author," and who relates to the statement differently according to the type and character of the discourse and the context in which the statement occurs. The subject, Foucault asserts, is a vacant space that may be filled by different individuals. Thirdly, the function operates on a domain, not an isolated sentence or proposition. It must be associated with an adjacent field which is not simply "context," but which makes context possible and recognizable (e.g., a scientific treatise, a novel, or a travelogue).

The associated field that turns a sentence or series of signs into a statement, and which provides them with a particular context, a specific representative content, forms a complex web. It is made up first of all by the series of other formulations within which the statement appears and forms one element (the network of spoken formulations that make up a conversation, the architecture of a demonstration, bound on the one side by its premises and on the other by its conclusion, the series of affirmations that make up a narrative). The associated field is also made up of all the formulations to which the statement refers (implicitly or not), either by repeating them, modifying them, or adapting them or by opposing them, or by commenting on them; there can be no statement that in one way or another does not reactualize other (ritual elements in a narrative; previously accepted propositions in a demonstration; conventional sentences in a conversation). The associated field is also made up of all the formulations whose subsequent possibility is determined by the statement, and which may follow the statement as its consequence, its natural successor, or its conversational retort. . . Lastly, the associated field is made up of all the formulations whose status the statement in question shares, among which it takes its place without regard to linear order, with which it will fade away, or with which, on the contrary, it will be valued, preserved, sacralized, and offered, as a possible object, to a future discourse (a statement is not dissociable from the status that it may receive as 'literature', or as an unimportant remark that is barely worthy of being forgotton, or as a scientific truth valid for all time, or as prophetic words, etc.). Generally, one can say that a sequence of linguistic elements is a statement only if it is immersed in an enunciative field, in which it then appears as a unique element. (Ibid., pp. 98-99).

Finally, a statement must be embodied in, although it cannot wholly be identified with, a material vehicle: speech, writing, or some other sense-perceptible element, which may be repeated either with or without it, while it may be repeated in other forms (e.g., translations into other languages) and embodied in different media.

What better, or more brilliant exposition could be given of the nature of what idealist logicians used to call the judgement! It should be apparent to any perspicacious reader that this is really what Foucault is describing with such admirable insights. And the enunciative function can clearly be nothing short of thought. It is obvious also, that no statement (or judgement) is possible apart from a conscious, actively thinking subject. Someone must, in anything that could rank as a statement, be, or have been, deliberately (or perhaps inadvertently, yet with intent to convey a meaning), uttering a message, or expressing a feeling; a message that could be understood and appreciated by a hearer, or reader, also cognizant and intelligent. Apart from these no statement could be made. Of this Foucault is well aware, for he declares that to reproduce the letters of the alphabet in the order they appear on a typewriter (or, for that matter, in any other order) is not in itself a statement (compare the futility of the threadbare argument about the monkey playing with a typewriter); although if done with intent to convey the fact that the order presented makes typing easier, it would be.

That in some cases a statement may have a putative or contrived subject who is not its actual author (as in a novel or play) does not remove this condition. Every statement must be the product and expression of active thinking, whether direct, or imputed to another (a fictitious character, or an apparition, or a spectre in a dream), or merely reported anonymously. All statement, then, is the expression by an intelligent subject (or by several) of one or more judgements that are elements in rational discourse; and all such discourse, so long as it is at all intelligible, will proceed and will tend to develop in accordance with rational principles.

Objection might be raised that a judgement may be entertained without ever being expressed, whereas a statement must be embodied in a perceptible vehicle. The distinction, however is specious. Nothing prevents the silent contemplation of a statement unexpressed, although no such silently considered statement can become evidence for the historian until it is uttered. Once made, any and every statement is (at least potentially) such evidence. And none can be a mere monument as opposed to a document (as alleged by Foucault), for the distinction itself is invalid. Every monument, as such, has documentary import, as the inscription on the pedestal testifies, be it only the stark engraving of a name. It stands in evidence of the respect and admiration of a community (or perhaps only a single individual) for some person reputable for noble deeds, or of grief for some loss or disaster, or of the celebration of some victory or achievement. It is a statement made, in the authorization of the erection of the monument, of the esteem, of the sorrow, or of the pride felt by those who erected it and those who do homage before it. The statue of Liberty in New York harbor is no mere pile of stone and metal. It is a silent dialogue between the French donors and the American recipients, expressing joint admiration for, and commitment to, the ideals and aspirations that motivated the American revolution and inspired the Constitution of the United States. It is a complex statement as eloquent after the event as *The Federalist* was before it—not just a spectacle to be viewed, but a document to be interpreted and understood. If it were anything less it would not be a monument at all.

Yet it is the necessary and inescapable subjective aspect of the statement that Foucault persistently suppresses and sedulously conceals in his professed endeavor to treat it as a neutral "discourse-object." Once that is recognized, however, it becomes evident that no genuine or successful historian, or social scientist, can omit the endeavor to recapture the thought of the agent, or author of the discourse, whose actions and statements are being studied, whether simply by way of record, or with the object of relating them systematically and delineating the social structures and discursive formations to which they belong— their categorization and interaction, their transformations, and the discursive practices to which they severally give rise. On this condition—the recognition of the ineradicable cognitive aspect of discourse—what Foucault proposes as "archeology" becomes entirely consonant with what Collingwood declares to be sound scientific historical method. Indeed, to follow out Foucault's recommendations, even if the ideal character of discourse were overlooked, might well lead to useful and informative results; and consequent to his accurate and meticulous description of the statement, it would hardly be surprising if patterns of transformation, rules of organization, and structures of discursive formation turned out in the long run to be dialectical in character. But if the submission is granted that statement is indeed judgement and that the enunciative function is thought, the reflective and systematic study of the history of discourse cannot fail to disclose its dialectic.

Foucault's purpose, however, is very different; and if his determination to neutralize all philosophical and sociological investigation (the study of human beings) is taken seriously, and (in his reaction at once against the phenomenology of Husserl and of Heidegger, the hermeneutics of Dilthey and Gadamer, and the structuralism of such as Lévi-Strauss) his profession to treat discursive practice as a purely external object, discounting its meaning, its truth claims and the validity of its assertions, "archeology" must be seen as an exception, unlike all other discursive practices and exempt from the "historical *a priori*"[22] that conditions them. For they are treated as its objects, about which it makes meaningful statements with positive and definitive truth claims, as they cannot. It will constitute knowledge in the usual sense of that word, while they will be "positivities" revealing only rules of discursive practice (cf. op. cit., p 182). But then Foucault will have committed the epistemologist's fallacy of exempting his own theory and discipline from what it attributes to others. If what he contends were true of discursive formations in general, then critical reflection would be excluded from human discourse, and "archeology," as the reflective study of discursive formations would be impossible. But if it is possible, discourse must be more than a merely neutral object, and the archeological findings must be false.[23]

Or else, his structures, given universal application, would undermine the authority of "archeology" itself, which would then be viewed simply as a pattern of discursive practice obeying anonymous rules. "Meaning" would be imputed to its statements only in accordance with internally generated conventions; the "validity" of its arguments and the "truth" of its conclusions would have no universality or cogency; their scientific value would be dissipated and their command upon our attention nullified. Foucault would then be (and, in effect, indeed is) telling his readers to discount his own asseverations, reducing his own position to that of the sceptic, whose denials and disparagements neutralize his own positive contentions—*ut tandem debeat obmutescere*.[24]

Small wonder that, since writing *The Archeology of Knowledge*, Foucault has turned his attention to other interests. So we may return from what threatens to become a digression, and pursue the theme previously being developed, before the challenge of Post-Structuralism constrained us to interrupt our argument.[25]

Dialectic in History

Historical Thinking

We agreed with Collingwood that history is the self-knowledge of mind, and we did so on the ground that to know oneself is necessarily to be aware of oneself as a social being, and that requires the *a priori* concept of the historical past, the content of which is made explicit by the historical imagination reconstructing past thought on the basis of presented evidence. The past thought, however, which informs the actions reconstructed, is itself in the same way historical. It is also self-conscious thinking by a social being. Historical thinking, in consequence, is a continuously self-reflective self-awareness, of which each successive phase makes the previous phases its object. Accordingly, history is the self-awareness of the civilized mind, its knowledge of its own course of development through successive stages of self-reflection in a dialectical progression in the manner of Hegel's *Phenomenology of Spirit*, a work which is at once history and philosophy of mind.

The process is dialectical because it is a process of rational thinking. Social conduct is always in principle deliberate action to achieve consciously acknowledged or unconsciously directive goals. In the latter case, they are goals originally conceived and deliberately adopted with full awareness, which have since become part of the social tradition and custom; or else instinctive impulses in the process of becoming ordered and rationalized in the social setting. As such, however, and as part of the cooperative effort of a social group, the action motivated is organized, and so rational. Now, it has already been established that self-conscious, rational thought is an implicit whole—an experience united as the intentional object of a unitary subject; and here in addition we have thought determined by the context of the social whole—a system of interlocking social function and institutions.

The growth and development of such a whole is its history; and, like every whole, its deployment in time, constructive or evolutionary, is dialectical. Every genuine whole is a structure of interdependent parts determined in nature and mutual relation by a principle of order that is immanent in each and all of them, so that each implies the others, because the place of each in the whole is determined by its relations to the rest, as dictated by the universal structural principle. If any part is posited in isolation, in implicit denial of the universal principle, it contradicts itself, because its essential nature is constituted by the structure of the whole and its place within it. Consequently, to maintain itself it demands supplementation by its other, with which it must combine in order to fulfil its proper nature. The combination forms a new provisional whole, which better exemplifies the universal organizing principle. But, so far as it is still partial and incomplete, it will again require supplementation, so that the process will repeat itself, generating a series, or scale of forms, each a more or less inadequate expression of the universal principle, yet each more complete and self-sustaining than its predecessor. This process of contradiction, supplementation and coalescence of each form with its opposite is the dialectical process, by which the whole is generated, whether in nature, in practical construction, or in theoretical reflection. It does so through a series of developing structures, each in some sense contradicting its predecessor (by contrast and supersession), yet at the same time complementing it to form a new whole, more fully characteristic of the ordering universal, so that the entire scale is one of progressively increasing degrees of adequacy to that principle.

The development of the social whole is no exception, and this involves a continuous process of conscious rational thought and action, which is historical in character, and which aims at the construction and maintenance of a social system. The knowledge of this process is what we call History, and it is, as we have seen, the product of the historical imagination, constructing from the available evidence a coherent account of the historical past. It does so much in the same way as a scientist pursuing his research, or a detective seeking to discover who committed a crime, by fitting the evidence together into a system of mutually corroborating facts, and so determining a series, or a structure, of historical judgements. These judgements together make up the account of an historical period, or epoch, and so constitute a whole, as the plot of a play or a novel constitutes a whole; and its evolution is dialectical in the manner described.

Our immediate object is to illustrate the fact that the historical process is itself dialectical, and this may be done in several different ways. We may choose a typical example from among many.

Transformation of Conceptual Schemes

Western civilization is so closely bound up with scientific thinking that its history is almost the same thing as the history of science. Some might dismiss this claim as exaggerated, but careful consideration reveals that it is not. Ancient Greek science and philosophy are inseparable and in some respects indistinguishable. In the ancient world, science and religion were (and since then always have been, despite some appearances to the contrary) closely intertwined. Francis Cornford and Bruno Schnell have demonstrated this in detail,[1] and the works of all the great Pre-Socratic philosophers bear witness to it. Even Socrates' professed renunciation of science in Plato's *Phaedo* is largely ironical, because the doctrine he proceeds to unfold is directly derived from Pythagorean science, itself bound up with the religion of Orphism (and his interlocutors in the dialogue are, significantly, Pythagoreans). The influence of both religion and science on Greek art is hardly to be doubted. A significant body of ancient philosophy is written in verse, and the dramatic artistry of Plato's dialogues (especially the *Symposium*) is undeniable.

Mediaeval civilization is frequently held to have been predominantly religious and unscientific. But this is a misconception. Of the so-called Dark Ages we are progressively coming to know more, and are discovering that the scientific and mathematical skill characterizing the practical arts of that period were far more sophisticated than has commonly been supposed. In the later Middle Ages, clerics and scholars were as learned in the science of the day as in theology, but because that science was mainly Aristotelian, popular historians of science have tended to overlook it. At the same time, distinct and important advances were made by such thinkers as Roger Bacon, Jean Buridan, Nicholas of Cusa, and Nicholas Oresme.

Since the seventeenth century, science has invaded every facet of Western civilization. In response to Copernicanism, religion, which was previously theistic, became deistic, God being withdrawn from the physical world as its Supreme Architect rather than its indwelling spirit. Philosophical thought has been permeated by scientific ideas, and even the romantic view of the world absorbed current scientific concepts and images.[2] In the eighteenth century, Western culture became industrialized as the result of developing scientific knowledge and technology, and since then every aspect of practical life has been mechanized and has become irrevocably dependent upon technology. Economic practice and theory have been molded by these developments, and political policies have become permeated by technical and scientific considerations.

There seems little reason then to deny that morals, politics, religion, and art have all been intimately influenced by the scientific thinking of the day at least since the sixth century B.C., and probably even earlier; and from the seventeenth century A.D. onward, scientific thought has undoubtedly been the predominant factor in the shaping of our culture. The structure of the history of modern science, therefore, should give us the clue to the general pattern of the historical process.

This, as several contemporary writers have shown, has been marked by so-called scientific revolutions. In Collingwood's view, these occur when the absolute presuppositions of science change, when the "constellations" of consupponible presuppositions break down under strain.[3] For Thomas Kuhn, a revolution is a change of "paradigm," which scientists are forced to make when the normal process of "puzzle solving" is obstructed by defects in the previous paradigm of the science.[4] Under his influence, the view has become prevalent that scientific theories current in the periods between these revolutions are mutually incommensurable. But this I believe and have tried elsewhere to show, is a mistake.

Neither Collingwood's "constellation" of presuppositions nor Kuhn's "paradigm" is a satisfactory concept; but both recognize the fact that all science operates under the aegis of a conceptual scheme, openly or tacitly acknowledged by the scientist, which prescribes not only the approved methods of research, but also, and more important, the ultimate nature of primary entities. Such a scheme is a systematic structure of ideas, and so, obviously a conceptual whole. It is, in effect, a metaphysical theory concerning the basal structure and the fundamental character of the world. In general, this scheme for Greek science was couched in terms of matter and form, and was summed up in the metaphysics of Aristotle. For seventeenth-century science it was expressed in terms of atomism and mechanism. Today, at least in my view, the underlying ideas are holism and evolution. Each of these epochs in the history of science began with a scientific revolution, about the structure of which Thomas Kuhn writes, and concerning which his insight is broadly right, except that he has entirely missed what is the true logic of transition from each conceptual scheme to the next.

Revolutionary though the new theories may be, they always develop continuously out of the old ones and preserve some elements from them. Each new hypothesis is a modification of the one which had been current before it. Copernicus revived the ancient hypothesis of Aristarchus, which had developed continuously from the Pythagorean belief in the central fire. He also retained the circular orbits of Ptolemy and Aristotle, from which Kepler, by a series of intermediate hypotheses, discovered that the true orbits were elliptical, the circle being a special case of the ellipse. The atomism of modern science developed directly from that of Leucippus and Democritus and was given mathematical and quantitative precision as soon as chemical elements came to be properly understood, a development which was itself continuous with the ancient doctrines through the intermediary of the notorious Phlogiston theory. Relativity theory retains the notion of Galilean inertial systems, and in it the Newtonian laws of motion remain valid in the special case of short distances and low velocities. Thus, continuity is always to some extent preserved.

The reason why revolutions occur is that contradictions are revealed in the conceptual scheme—a term I prefer to both Kuhn's "paradigm" and Collingwood's "constellation of absolute presuppositions"—under which science has hitherto operated. This occurs as scientists proceed with the process of specification and application of the concepts used (what Kuhn calls "normal science"). For instance, the application of Aristotle's theory of motion to projectiles led to contradictions and gave rise first to the thirteenth-century theory of impetus and then by direct continuous development to the theory of inertia. As such contradictions accumulate they become more obtrusive, and obstructive to clear and coherent explanation; so pressure increases for the revision and reformation of the conceptual scheme, and when this is successfully accomplished a revolution in scientific thought has occurred.

What it achieves is a better and more coherent theory with greater and more comprehensive explanatory power. Correspondence between theory and fact has in recent years been abandoned as the criterion of scientific truth, because it has at last become widely recognized that observation of fact is theory-laden, and such correspondence is therefore question-begging. The more generally accepted criterion is now explanatory power, which depends on the systematic and comprehensive coherence of the scientific interpretation of what is observable. Thus, in science no less than in history, coherence proves to be the final criterion of acceptability.

The history of science thus displays itself as a series of epochs, each marked off from its predecessor by a scientific revolution, and by a new conceptual system, progressively increasing in coherence and explanatory power. Each period is dominated by a conceptual scheme which, as it is specified, reveals internal contradictions and so is forced to develop and subsequently to be made self-consistent. As correcting and superseding its predecessor, each theory is opposed to it; but as a continuous development from its predecessor, it is related to it as a higher degree of truth with greater explanatory power. Each successive theory is a new specific form of the science concerned (be it physics, astronomy, or whatever), and what it specifies is a principle of explanation, or organization of the observed facts, constituting a systematic conception of a certain range of experience. Taken together the scientific theories of any one epoch form the world picture characteristic of the period.

The Dialectical Scale

What thus emerges is a scale of forms, each related to the next as opposites, but also as degrees of truth, and at the same time as alternative or specific forms of a universal principle of explanation. Such a scale of forms is a dialectical scale. Its character is expounded in detail by Collingwood in the third chapter of his *Essay on Philosophical Method*[5] and is exemplified by the whole structure of Hegel's philosophical system. What we have found, therefore, is that at least one facet of history does develop through time as a dialectical series of events, because it is a process of development of conceptual schemes, or *Weltanschauungen*. And this is not only peculiar to the history of science but can be recognized in all other branches of the discipline.

In art and painting we have Byzantine, Gothic, Renaissance, Baroque, Roccoco, Romantic, Impressionist, and so on. It is not difficult to see that each of these various styles and art forms, as they succeed one another, develops from the one that precedes, is a reaction against certain features in its predecessor, with which it contrasts, and is a specific case of universal form of art, which it expresses and exemplifies in a higher degree than its forerunners. In short, the history develops as a dialectical scale.

Hegel set out the history of philosophy as just such a scale of forms, and Collingwood has shown how and why the philosophical universal specifies itself in this way. And when we turn to social and political history, the same structure is displayed in different though closely related ways. Hegel, in wide brush strokes, delineated three phases, in terms of liberty, towards which he maintained history moved: despotisms in which only one person was recognized as free, oligarchies in which some were so regarded, and constitutional democracies in which the right to freedom was claimed by all. A similar scale is detectable in Aristotle's classification of constitutions, and he gives besides a quasi-historical scale from the family to the village society and the state. Or, again, we may distinguish the dynastic empire from the city-state, followed by a constitutional city-state (Rome) with a widespeading colonial empire; that leads on to feudalism, succeeded by the modern nation state. All these forms are contrasted opposites, specific examples of states, and degrees of realization of constitutional order. Karl Marx distinguished yet another dialectical scale from primitive communism to feudalism and thence to capitalism and modern socialism.

All these forms have been exemplified in history, they have been dialectically related as we have described, and their professed goal and purpose has been to enhance human welfare. That that goal has been achieved, if at all, only very sparsely does not alter the dialectical character of the progression, nor the concept which has driven it forward. My point is that history can be a dialectical progression towards freedom without the implication that actual success is inevitable. All that the theory commits us to is the belief that wherever there is some degree of rationality, the endeavor of human action is in the direction of liberation, even though it will be frustrated (we may even say inevitably) wherever rationality is perverted and to the extent that irrationality prevails.

The universal concept specifying itself in this scale is that of human social welfare, of which we tendered the definition as the fullest possible development of individual capacities by all the members of the community. To defend and justify that definition would require a volume, yet I think it would be fairly generally admitted that it is at least the ideal and usually the professed aim of social and political organization. The personal realization envisaged involves aesthetic, intellectual, moral, and spiritual satisfaction and so covers the whole range of human action. Obviously it could only, if ever, be actualized in an ordered society and probably more appropriately by such a society as a whole, rather than by any single individual. In fact, no single individual can, in isolation and without the cooperation and support of a community, realize his or her capacities to the full. So the realization of freedom must involve the entire community as a social whole. It is this concept that governs and directs the course of social conduct, even when consciousness of it is so obscure and vague that the aim is temporarily defeated and progress toward it turned awry. In any case, the process of social activity is guided in principle by this conception of a social whole, so organized as to realize to the full the capacities of its members. Once again, therefore, we reach a conclusion in which the course of events— in this case, of history—is a series of changes regulated and directed by an unchanging universal principle of order, the continuous specification through time of a universal whole.

Historical Objectivity

A more complete answer to the question about objectivity can now be offered. Just as scientific and philosophical knowledge advances dialectically towards an ideal system that is all-inclusive and free from internal conflict, so does historical knowledge. The standard of objectivity is this ideal, and approach to it can be judged by tracing the dialectical development of historiography. Collingwood embarked upon this in *The Idea of History*, displaying its progress from narrative history, through "scissors and paste" and critical history to scientific history. Though the work was never properly completed, the criterion of objectivity is set out in the concluding Epilegomena. Objective truth is the generic universal generating itself through the history of the subject, which traces a scale of forms consecutively more adequate to the generic essence. Historical objectivity is itself an historical achievement. It consists in the systematic and coherent comprehensiveness of the theory of its subject matter. But as it depends on evidence, and as evidence is never complete, it is necessarily limited by the finitude of the historian's knowledge.

The Historical Universal

The universal whole towards which the historical process is oriented, however, is more than any one branch of knowledge can comprise. It is the totality of social action pursuing the ideal of complete human freedom as the fullest possible development of the capacities of each and every individual person. The political structure through which, in our day, we strive to actualize this condition is the sovereign nation state.

The sovereign acts of every such state profess to be, and in intention are, directed towards the national interest, or the common welfare of the people; and in any state, the right of the government to the obedience of its subjects can be justified by no other claim than that its laws are made to this end. The power of any government to enforce its authority is lent to it only by the consent and acquiescence of at least a large number of the governed, in the belief that this end is being accomplished. Thus the principle on which the sovereignty of the modern state is founded is that it represents the common good of the nation, the so-called national interest.

But, in the modern world, this principle is violated and the end of political organization is defeated by the fact that the national soverign state is no longer capable of ensuring the common welfare. The reason is that that common welfare now depends on worldwide conditions beyond the jurisdiction of the nation's sovereign authority. These include the control and distribution of the world's population; regulation of the environment of the planet, the ecology of which is being disrupted by uncontrolled use of world resources and unrestricted disposal of industrial waste; they include regulation of world commerce and the equitable distribution of the wealth of the nations; and, most vital of all, the maintenance of world peace, of national security, and the pacific settlement of international disputes.

None of these objectives is the national sovereign state competent to attain, simply *because it is sovereign*, and sovereignty requires that it be subject to no law above its own. But in that case, no higher authority can compel it to keep agreements, and in the knowledge that this is so, no state will ever be able to trust others or to rely on the sanctity of treaties. Despite common professions, treaties are commonly disregarded whenever a state feels strong enough and whenever what is sees as its interests are served by violation. Every government is aware of this fact, and this is why disarmament treaties have never until today been concluded, because among sovereign states armaments and the threat of force are the only way to ensure that the other party to any treaty can be induced to observe its terms. A treaty to limit these means would therefore, in the nature of the case, be self-defeating.

Although a disarmament agreement has at long last been concluded between the United States and the Soviet Union, and although it is a significant sign of released tension, not only does it affect a very small percentage of the opposed arsenals, but it is also no guarantee of future peace. Its signatories are sovereign states which can at any time, if it seems to suit their interests, renounce, revoke, or simply violate any treaty that results; and what their future governments may be like, or what policies they may pursue is unpredictable. The agreement is still just another episode in the continuing process of power politics; and the insistence of the United States administration on its adherence to its strategic defence initiative is evidence that it is not even yet a significant step towards ending the arms race.

For the above reasons, no schemes of arms reduction, arms control, nuclear freeze, or the like, (even though they may have other momentary advantages) can succeed in averting the threat of war. And for the same reason, the prevalent power politics among the nations, inevitable so long as they remain sovereign, results in a persistent effort to maintain the balance of power with the consequent continuing arms race. The evergrowing threat of nuclear holocaust (whether by accident, or by design, or as a result of terrorist activity) that is thus endemic in the contemporary system of international relations, inevitably defeats the very aim and purpose which justifies the existence of the sovereign nation state.

The common interest of the nations lies, therefore, in the remedy of these desperate ills, and there can be no doubt that such common interest exists. It can be served only by the formation of a world community presided over by a world authority with appropriate power to enforce world law and maintain world peace. The ultimate aim of social order nowadays demands the supersession of the nation state in a world federation, and a federal constitution that can embrace the whole of mankind. This is the totality that must be realized in the historical process, to embody the universal principle of human welfare that we have postulated, and to give direction to historical time. If it is not realized within the foreseeable future, there is a high probability of the destruction of all civilization and the extermination of all historical agents, literally bringing history to an end.

Accordingly, if human freedom is the ultimate goal of history (as Hegel believed), towards which its course is a dialectical process, the scale of political forms leading in its direction should tend towards an organized society embracing the whole of mankind. Historical time, therefore, in its political aspect, should display the progressive specification of this institutional whole and the process of its establishment. Independently of whether the goal will ever be achieved, its implication is none the less evident in the course of contemporary history, in the efforts made, the policies pursued, and the social structures that have evolved. Also, it has been made evident in theory ever since the Renaissance by writers like Hugo de Groot, Pufendorf, and Suarez, and later by Immanuel Kant, as well as all those who have advocated some form of world order in the present century. If the goal is not to be achieved, the future of the human race is indeed bleak, if any future at all remains to be contemplated other than total extinction.

Aside from this dismal prospect, however, there is another dimension to history. The human mind is self-reflective, and besides art and science, it seeks by its very nature to unify and comprehend its experience as a single totality. This endeavor with its emotional complement and symbolic expression constitutes its artistic and religious activity, and, in its intellectual phase, its philosophy. In all of these activities its aim is to grasp its experience and its world *sub specie aeternitatis*. In Plato's words, it strives to envisage all time and all eternity; and, experiencing the resulting appropriate emotional exaltation, to direct its practical activity in harmony with its intellectual achievement. In Spinoza's system the final attainment is the perfection of the third kind of knowledge, *scientia intuitiva*, which conceives an adequate idea of things through an adequate idea of God's attributes; that is to say, comprehends everything in the light of the ultimate whole. This is the acme and pinnacle of adequate thinking, which, for Spinoza, is genuine action and true freedom. It is the grasp of the *infinita idea Dei*, which is the source and criterion of all truth, and which, with its accompanying positive emotion, is the *amor intellectualis Dei*. In this intellectual love of God, which is equally God's love for man, the human mind attains blessedness. In it the human spirit finds its ultimate contentment and achieves its highest liberty. "The service of God is perfect freedom."

Infinita idea Dei is the counterpart, as an infinite mode of the attribute of thought, to *facies totius universe* under the attribute of extension. The latter, we saw, was the eternal and unchanging universal that (as Spinoza has it) "compels" the unceasing changes among finite things in the physical world. So, likewise, the infinite idea of God would be the eternal principle determining the process of change within the historical world. For Spinoza, however, God is not only the thinking thing, but is an infinite substance expressing its essence in an infinity of attributes. He must thus be the eternal principle determining all change in the entire world of finites—that eternity of which time, in all its forms, is the moving image.

Our final task must be to consider more closely the conception of this eternal principle and its relation to "the moving image." We have found the temporal process to be dialectical and evolutionary in character, in its physicobiological phase, in its psychological phase, and in its historical phase; and this implies that it tends towards a culminating achievement, which one envisages as the final stage of the process. The dialectical stage proceeds through successive forms exemplifying, in increasing degrees of adequacy, the universal principle of order. The final culmination must then be that universal itself, *in propria persona*. The question immediately arises how this is possible if the ultimate "end" is eternal. How can a world in perpetual change develop towards a totality that is not in process and is not (cannot be) an event in time, or a phase (whether passing or persistent) in the development, but must comprehend the whole? The implication of evolution, as also of historical progress, is that the objective towards which it tends is at least in principle realizable within the process. But if this objective is in principle eternal, the implication would seem to be self-refuting.

In my final chapter I shall give some attention to this problem, and I shall do so by reference, not so much to Spinoza, or to Hegel, but more especially to a modern writer, Pierre Teilhard de Chardin, who thought along similar lines and was himself acutely aware of the problem in its contemporary form. He was not only a theologian and a Jesuit priest, but also no mean scientist, who has, perhaps, done more than any other thinker to reinterpret Catholic religious doctrine so as to reconcile it with the findings of modern science. The special problem with which we are now confronted is discussed in the final chapters of his book, *The Phenomenon of Man*.

VIII

Evolution and Omega

Evolution, Diachronic, and Synchronic

Even before Darwin, the conception of evolution had acquired a significance beyond that assigned to it in biology, which applies it only to the phylogenetic emergence of different species. With the work of Herbert Spencer, if not before, evolution had become a metaphysical concept, determining one's outlook on the universe as a whole. Not only were living species thought of as evolving, but every form of existence was seen as an emergent from other more simple and primitive forms, by what principle of generation was usually left obscure. So conceived, evolution had a double connotation. It implied both the temporal generation of one form from another, but also the permanent, and in some sense timeless, hierarchical interrelation of levels of being, an Aristotelian type of *scala naturae*.

As the concept of evolution became more prevalent in the intellectual outlook of the modern age, the idea that life had emerged by natural development from nonliving matter became commonplace; then notions of the evolution of stars and of galaxies invaded astronomy, and soon physicists developed a theory of the evolution of the universe as a whole. The advance of the sciences to date has presented us with a conception of a universe which is self-contained, or "closed," a finite yet unbounded four-dimensional, hypersphere, constituting a metrical field, in which curvature represents energy, and folds, or singularities in

147

space-time constitute elementary particles (a typical example of what Teilhard de Chardin described by the phrase *enroulement sur soi-même*); these, again combine to produce complex fields of force, forming atoms, while subsequent combinations of homogeneous and heterogeneous atoms constitute molecules, in an increasing complexity, until we reach the so-called aperiodic crystals of which chromosomes are held to be examples, and so to the living forms of cellular structure. From here on, the conventional idea of evolution gives us the development of living species from protozoa to *homo sapiens*, bringing the scale to its present culmination. The whole series is viewed both as a temporal sequence and as a hierarchical structure which implies, and indeed necessarily involves, a final and absolute consummation.

Viewed as a temporal process, evolution seems incontestably to have advanced, if not in a straight line, yet progressively in the direction of increasing complexity and integration, both with respect to the interrelation of orders and species (the biosphere as such) and within the individual organism, increasing its capacity for versatile action and awareness of itself and its world. While this trend is undeniably evident in the temporal process, there seems, on the one hand, to be no guarantee of its inevitable continuance. Rather there are plentiful grounds for trepidation that it will be brought by the folly of men to a premature and disastrous end. On the other hand, if this *denouement* could be averted, there is no clear evidence that the process should not continue indefinitely, as envisaged by Bergson, ceaselessly producing new forms, without ever reaching any assignable termination. In fact, the very nature of experienced time forces us to such an opinion.

Temporal becoming, with its inevitable passage and unceasing evanescence, seems to permit no final resting point. As merely processual, evolution might well be regarded simply as a series of changes brought about by random mutations and natural selection; but only so long as we overlook the fact that it makes no sense to speak of survival unless what survives is a living system maintaining itself as a whole by auturgically adapting its physiology and behavior to the condition in which its survival is determined. Nothing less could ever be "selected" than such an intrinsically self-adaptive system. Besides its serial and processive character, therefore, evolution has to be recognized as a progressive generation of more fully and effectively integrated organic wholes, within the overarching organic whole of the biosphere. And so we are brought back to its second aspect as a graduated scale of forms.

Viewed as an hierarchical scale, the evolving universe presents us with a rather different picture; for each phase, at every level, even within the major divisions, proves to be a more or less self-contained whole with some degree of stable unity, its self-sufficiency proportional to its complexity and internal integration, despite its interdependence with its surrounding environment. Thus, the physical world divides into galaxies, each relatively self-sufficient, and these into stellar systems, each and all composed of atoms and molecules of various complexity, yet each relatively whole and self-complete. At the same time, all these hierarchically ordered systems are mutually interdependent and inseparably determined in their nature and activities by the structure of space-time of and of the physical world as a whole. The same is correspondingly true of the biosphere, with its profuse diversity of organisms and species, its integrated biological communities and its organic integration of organisms and environment.

The world so regarded is a unified system of systems, each relatively whole in itself and self-sustaining, yet each in some measure in mutual commerce with its surroundings so as to integrate with them to form a larger and more self-complete system until the entire universe is included.

Whichever of these two views of the evolutionary scale is taken, the great mass of contemporary scientific evidence confirms Teilhard's insight that at each main level the universe presents itself as a single whole unifying innumerable different elements and processes. Testimony that this is the case in the physical world is given by the major physicists of the age: Einstein, Eddington, Schroedinger, Sciama, Heisenberg, de Broglie, and Bohm,[1] all express their conviction of what Eddington described as "the widespread interconnectedness of things," and they all support the view with impressive evidence. At the biological level the unity of the biosphere is likewise affirmed by the Haldanes (father and son), A.I. Oparin, Joseph Needham, Lewis Thomas, Marston Bates, and Harold Blum;[2] and despite differing views among biologists, it can hardly be denied in the light of the established evidence. The unity in diversity of the noösphere is assured by the conditions of our own experience and follows from the teachings of the great philosophers from Spinoza to Whitehead.

In the evolutionary process there is an evident trend or drive towards progressively increasing complexification and coherence, a trend which, with an ever-increasing degree of improbability, moves towards what some biologists have described as enhanced "information content." It is a tendency which, as Teilhard remarks, rises "upstream against the flow of entropy," creating increasingly coherent and comprehensive wholes, the effect of what he calls "radial energy." Similarly, the hierarchy of forms displays an ascending scale of concrescence (to borrow Whitehead's felicitous term), in which the higher unities incorporate the lower and transform them to subserve their own integrity.

There seems to be a single principle of organization binding the elements at every stage into a whole, as well as connecting the consecutive phases and making them continuous. This manifests itself at the physical level as Pauli's Principle of Exclusion, which operates as an organizing influence in the structure of the atom, and has far reaching consequences, not only in determining such properties as ferromagnetism and optical anisotropy (properties of bodies that their components cannot display in isolation, but which emerge only in collectives), but also in the constitution of chemical bonds, of paramount significance in determining the structure and diversifying properties of macromolecules and polymers indispensable to living processes.

At the level of life, self-maintaining organic systems are generated, reproducing themselves and developing in their degree of self-unification to the point at which the complexity and intensive integrity of their functioning takes the form of sentience and organizes itself further as consciousness. Accordingly, the awareness of self and of other, which finally emerges, is no less than the coming to consciousness of the concrescent principle that has all along been directing the process, revealing itself to itself as the self-conscious *ego*, and revealing to that the entire process by which it has evolved.

Within this scale the two critical points of transition are those which mark off these main levels one from another: that at which life emerges from the non-living, when the first metabolisms ensure the self-maintenance of an organic system, enabling it to register its environment through sentience, and so to become a focus of the entire encompassing world; and that at which this sentience develops to the level of self-conscious thought and becomes self-reflective awareness.

The transitions at both of these critical points are at once expressions and intensifications of the unity and wholeness of the world. The first subordinates and utilizes the entire physicochemical universe and the laws governing the interaction of its elements, by self-adaptation to encompassing conditions, to maintain its own organic integrity, thus becoming a focus or epitome of the whole. The second emerges from this organic whole as the form in which its integrity is felt and its sentience structured, first to become the cognition of a surrounding world, and in that very activity of structuring, engendering a self-awareness, which concurrently distinguishes itself from, and unifies itself with, the cognized world as one self-conscious whole.

The unity of the physical world is ensured by the self-completeness of the metrical space-time field, and that of the biosphere by the metabolism and the sentience of organisms in symbiotic relation. But the most comprehensive unification of the world is effected in the self-reflective awareness of the self-conscious person, in which all these subordinate unities are actualized and made evident. It is an awareness emergent from the biological and physical levels, depending upon them through the living body, through a process that has raised the physiological functions to sentience, and sentience to perception, so that in its reflective phase it brings the whole cosmic scale to consciousness. It is only in the noösphere, in the self-reflective scientific and philosophical knowledge of a society of rational beings, that the wholeness of the world and its evolutionary process come to consciousness; and concomitantly that rational persons become aware of themselves as the evolved product of a natural world, bringing itself to consciousness through them, in and as their knowledge. In this consciousness the world becomes aware of itself in us, and we become aware of ourselves as inhabiting it. Thus Teilhard rightly concludes that

> we see not only thought as participating in evolution as an anomaly or as an epiphenomenon; but evolution as so reducible to and identifiable with a progress towards thought that the movement of our souls expresses and measures the very stages of progress of evolution itself. Man discovers that *he is nothing else than evolution become conscious of itself*, to borrow Julian Huxley's striking expression.[3]

The Features of Wholeness

At each stage of the hierarchical structure, whether physical, biological, or psychological, actuality presents itself as a genuine whole. That is, it is a unity constituted out of parts or elements that are inseparable though distinct, the nature and operation of each of which is determined by its interrelation with all the rest, as the hexagon shape of the cells in a honeycomb is determined by their mutual contiguity, so that while they can be mutually distinguished they cannot be separated. Every such whole is a system structured by a principle of organization, which governs these interrelations, and so is immanent in them; likewise, as they determine the nature and behavior of the various elements, it is equally immanent in the parts. It reveals itself fully, however, only in the totality; and of that we must say that, while it is nothing in addition to its elements (as the honeycomb is nothing in addition to the cells), yet because of its organized form it is more than simply a sum, or collection, of its parts. In short, the principle of structure is both immanent in each and all of the parts, and yet, in the whole is transcendent beyond them.

These characteristics are displayed in almost any example one may select from the hierarchy of forms within Nature. The principles of structure of the physical world manifest themselves fully only in the space-time whole, yet they govern every detail within it. They are not, however, additional items among its components, nor do they reveal themselves in any mere collection of particles or random scattering of celestial bodies. They transcend the simple sum of physical entities. The structure of the atom is determined by Pauli's Principle, which is not an additional electron or proton, and yet is immanent in each of these constituents as well as in the relations between them. The way in which the metabolic and physiological cycles in a living organism are interrelated, and the structure of its organs are both governed by the life of the whole; but that life, while it is immanent in every part and process, is not an additional organ or physiological cycle. It is something over and above the mere component flesh and bones which without it are no more than a corpse. Again, the character of a person, while it manifests itself in every one of his or her traits and actions, is no single one nor any collection of them, but is transcendent beyond each and all of the thoughts, feelings, and sentiments which make it up.

Each whole is a unity, but none is a blank unity; it is, and to be an actual entity, must be, differentiated. Each is a structured whole of interrelated parts, which, in their mutual dependence, diversify and exemplify the structural principle that integrates them into one system. Taken in abstraction from its self-differentiation, this principle is nothing, or at best a mere abstraction. To become actualized it must specify itself into its diverse and intermeshing parts to constitute a genuine and actual whole.

Another feature of wholeness is that, by its very nature, it must be complete. A partial whole is a contradiction in terms. And as every genuine whole is a systematic structure, and every system is necessarily a whole, there can be no "partial system" which does not necessarily imply completion. There can be no arc of a circle if the complete circle is not at least foreshadowed. The diurnal revolution of the earth and the phases of the moon imply the existence of the solar system and the revolution of the planets around the sun, which, with all its consequences for each of them individually, involves, in the last analysis, the rest of the galaxy, and if physicists are to be believed, the rest of the entire universe.[4]

Accordingly, when we consider the temporal process of evolution as generating wholes in hierarchical succession, we must infer that the principle of organization that determines the process of their generation is present from the first, is immanent in whatever is produced and in every finite product. Yet it is also transcendent beyond every finite collection.

Partial wholeness, I have said, is a contradiction in terms. Yet within the range of our experience there is no totality which completely fulfills the requirements of absolute self-sufficiency, and the nisus which is evident throughout the world towards further concrescence and greater integrity prefigures an ultimate wholeness which is finally and totally self-sustaining. It must do so, because every partial element, being integral to the whole that determines its very nature, has immanent in it the universal principle that governs that whole; and the manifest occurrence in the world of holistic forms in an hierarchical scale is itself evidence of the necessary completion. The scale is a series of forms of increasing unity and integrity, tending persistently toward total closure and self-sufficiency. The hierarchy, therefore, implies a consummation and the process requires a final fulfillment. It is this requirement that impels the process onward and is the source of its creativity. Let us first briefly consider the nature of its procedure.

Differentiation and Process

Every whole is a unity of differences. It cannot be a whole unless it unites within itself a multiplicity of diverse elements. As a structural unity, it is dominated by a principle of order regulating the relation between these elements, and for this reason no such whole can be posited all at once in a single point-instant. Its principle of unity must particularize itself by setting out its differences in the proper order; and, as this is determined by that universal principle of structure, which likewise shapes the nature and regulates the behavior of the parts, this self-differentiation of the whole will take the form of a serial unfolding.

Wherever this begins, it can do so only with a finite element. But any limited part of a whole such as has been described is, as we have said, dependent for its intrinsic nature and for its very existence upon its interrelations with the other parts. In its endeavor to maintain itself, or (to use Spinoza's phrase) "to persist in its own being," it must appeal to and draw upon the resources of other elements within the context in which it finds itself. Thus, the elementary particle is a singularity within the field—a wave-packet in the flow of radiant energy. The living organism maintains itself as a dynamic equilibrium within its environment, drawing from it and discharging into it matter and energy in constant exchange with its surround. This interdependence is, of course, governed and directed by the organizing principle of the whole. In every finite part, therefore, there is a persistent drive to unite with its other, fueled by the immanence in it of the principle of structural wholeness.

The result is a continuous process of self-definition, first by exclusion and negation of what is other than the posited element, and next by combination with that other to form a larger, more self-contained and more sustainable whole. This is the process which Teilhard describes as *enroulement sur soi-même* impelled by what he hypothesizes as "radial energy" and what I have here identified as the immanence of the universal structural principle. The result is the unfolding of a scale of forms, of which each, so far as it is finite, defining itself by exclusion and negation of its other, while claiming, nevertheless, to be self-sufficient, is in contradiction with itself, because it omits (in its finitude) what is essential to its own being and intrinsic character. To resolve this contradiction, it must be supplemented by that which it lacks, and when this occurs it more adequately exemplifies the universal principle of wholeness. Consequently, the scale is one in which the successive forms relate to one another first as opposites, then as examples or specifications of the generic principle of the whole, and thirdly as degrees of adequacy in the expression or manifestation of that principle. I have previously called a scale of forms so interrelated a dialectical scale. It is evolutionary or developmental, and this is precisely what we find revealed by the conception of the world of Nature presented by the contemporary sciences.

Certain corollaries follow from the argument so far developed. The first is that the most recent phase of the scale, being the most complete and comprehensive to date, will express the nature of the universal organizing principle better, and will be a more adequate realization of it, than any prior phase. It will therefore be the key to understanding the nature of its predecessors and of the scale as a whole, as well as the most reliable indication of the ultimate culmination. So Teilhard is persuaded that the course of evolution can be understood as the process of hominization issuing in what he terms noögenesis, the human mind and its knowledge serving as the explanatory principle of the entire prior evolutionary sequence.

Secondly, the inevitably serial structure of the scale will give it a temporal character. Its phases will come into being and pass away; yet each successive stage will not simply presuppose those that have passed but will also incorporate, or encapsulate, everything in its predecessors which has produced it as the successor. Thirdly, despite this evanescent appearance of every phase and entity in the series—because it consists of a sequence of forms (each to some extent structured), which, as it continues, progressively increase in coherent integrity—it cannot continue indefinitely, but necessarily prefigures a consummation; so it gives persistent evidence of the reality of the completed system which its phases portend.

This completed system will have to be at once the absolute whole and the total actualization of the universal principle of order. It must encompass the entire process, in which it is immanent from beginning to end, and which is altogether impossible without its perennial reality. The process is, after all, nothing other than the self-specification, the self-development of the totality, which is its final culmination. Just as each phase incorporates its predecessors; therefore, the whole process must somehow be included in its final outcome. While it is, in a very definite sense, the bourne of the whole evolutionary drive, it cannot be merely the end of the series, a final temporal phase. As we shall presently see, it cannot be an event in time at all.

That the whole process must be contained in its result, and the culmination must comprehend the entire gamut of forms in the scale, is confirmed by the fact that each phase contains and sublates in itself all of its predecessors in realizing their potentialities. Further, the outcome of biological evolution is an organic body, embracing in its own nature the chemistry and physics of the lower levels, as well as the traces of prior phases of its own biological development. It is, moreover, an organism conscious of its surrounding world, and encompassing in its developed knowledge the awareness of the process of its own development. Thus it comprehends within its own nature the whole in which it is still but one part, and the entire scale of which it is the latest product. As such, and especially in its conscious thinking activity, it exemplifies the universal ordering principle of the world better than any less developed form. Yet because the human being is but a finite organism and no more than a part of the whole—only a denizen within the world which it inhabits—it cannot be the final consummation of the cosmic scale, which, as we have said, implies and prefigures an ultimate and absolute final fulfillment.

This ultimate end, which the whole course of evolution fore-shadows, is what Teilhard designates "Omega." But it is just as much and as essentially Alpha, for it is the indispensable presupposition of any finite existence, of any beginning and of any process. My next task will be to try to indicate how we may conceive its nature, if only in vague forecast or premonition.

The Clue to "Omega"

I have said that the most recent outcome of the evolutionary scale to date will be the most reliable guide to the nature of the universal principle of order. Human self-consciousness, therefore, is what must give us our best clue. The organizing principle here is reason—not the merely formal analytical reason of computation, but the Platonic synoptical reason (*epistēmē*), which sees all things together and is "the spectator of all time and all existence." The universal principle of organization and the ubiquitous *conatus* in finite things towards complete wholeness, the activity (whatever it is) of the so-called radial energy, throughout the course of evolution, is one of organizing and integrating. It continuously develops until it emerges as the activity of thought, aware of itself in deliberate action and self-conscious reflection. This then must be the nearest analogue we can conceive of the activity of Omega.

In both cases we have a self-specifying universal constituting a concrete whole (or world), with which it is at once identical, yet also opposite (as universal to particulars); and, as no whole, in the last resort, can be grasped as such except in a consciousness able to synthesize its elements (as interrelated and ordered), the actual world, the specifying scale, necessitates a corresponding universal subject that projects its own self-particularization as object and becomes aware of it as itself—its own self-differentiation.

The human mind is a whole of feeling which is differentiated and organized by the activity of judging (the discrimination by attention of figure from ground, of "this" from "that"). So its contents become the objects of consciousness, mutually distinguished and related as an environing world. Such is human experience, and (as Kant showed) only as cognized by a unitary subject of consciousness is it possible. No representation occurs apart from the spontaneous synthesizing activity of the *ego*. Every presentation, even of the simplest object, to perception is an organized configuration that must be held together under unifying principles by this activity of synthesis, which at the same time is an activity of distinguishing, relating and ordering—in short, the activity of thought. All observation (as contemporary philosophers of science have come to recognize) is theory-laden i.e., is organized and interpretive on structural principles. The whole of our experience of the world, therefore, commonsensical as well as scientific, reveals itself on reflection as the self-specification of the principle of unity inherent in the knowing subject. In this way the human *ego* specifies itself in its experience, which it projects as a world of objects, and then recognizes this world as itself; and this in two ways, first as the content of its own mind, and secondly, as the evolutionary process of its own generation—the active principle throughout the process being one of concrescence and integration, which transpires as its own self-conscious thought.

Omega, the ultimate concrete universal principle, in the same way, differentiates itself as (i.e., creates) a world, which, through the very activity of its genesis, through the process of evolution, becomes aware of itself as a mind reflecting in itself the process of its own generation (the world), and of the world as the self-differentiation of the universal creative and ordering principle—that is, it becomes aware of itself as the reflex of its eternal Other. So Omega, though it is not the physical world, not any physical entity, not the biosphere, nor any living organism, not the historical nöosphere, not any finite human personality, is immanent in all of these, yet transcends them all, projecting them as a real world, just as the human *ego* projects its experience as the knowledge of that world. Omega is thus the creative principle of the world, which generates man as (among creatures so far evolved) the highest and most adequate expression of the generic principle of the whole.

Omega and Time

It must further be evident that the universal principle, though as Alpha it is immanent in all finite and temporal being, as Omega cannot itself be in time. Just as we learn from Kant that the apprehension of the temporal series in human experience is possible only for a transcendental *ego*, which cannot be brought under the categories, or presented as a phenomenon, so Omega, the universal principle of all order, cannot be identified with any of its own products, with any evolutionary or historical event, or with any system, however large, of finite entities. It transcends the temporal deployment of its own self-differentiation, in which it is nevertheless immanent, and cannot itself be in time. But we can now see that time is nothing else than the process of the self-specification of the universal, which gives it its content and makes it truly whole and concrete.

The questions remain. If the temporal process is the actual concrete content of the absolute whole, and if it unfolds as a dialectical scale, that scale must have a culmination, which is in some sense a final phase; yet now we find that this culmination must transcend time. How is this possible? How can time be brought to an end? How can what transcends time be the final phase in a temporal process?

The answer to these difficult questions is to be found, once again, by seeking the clue in human self-consciousness. That is the contemporary outcome of the process; but while in its sentient, appetitive, and practical activity it is necessarily temporal, in its conceptual grasp of its own nature and of the necessary implications of its temporal experience, it apprehends the eternal. "Time itself, in its concept," says Hegel, "is eternal."[5] Moreover, in the highest grade of our reflective thinking, in art, religion, and philosophy, we become aware of the transcendent and identify with it. Thus, the temporal evolutionary process, in self-reflection ultimately transcends itself and seeks atonement with the infinite. This is why the transition from the merely organic and biological phase to the self-reflective is so critical and so essential. Hegel expresses this position unerringly when he writes:

> Time is the Concept [the Universal] itself in present existence (*der da ist*) and presents itself to consciousness as empty intuition; therefore the mind appears necessarily in time, and it appears in time just so long as it *does not apprehend* its concept, that is, does not extinguish time.[6]

and Teilhard presents the same truth thus:

Yet we must be careful to note that under this evolutive facet Omega still only reveals *half of itself*. While being the last term of its series, it is also *outside all series.*.. If by its very nature it did not escape from the time and space which it gathers together, it would not be Omega.[7]

The end towards which the temporal process tends, therefore, is not a temporal end, or termination, but is "end" in the sense of aim or aspiration. That is a condition which action aims to bring about, but it is a continuing condition, not a termination. It is a continuing state of activity, generated and sustained by the temporal processes, but informed and inspired by a transcendent concept of the whole, which is not temporal, and, as Hegel says, extinguishes time.[8] Thus, the final phase of the evolutionary process is a temporally continuing activity of living directed by conscious identification with and devotion to a transcendent Idea—it is Aristotle's *energeia*.

Omega and Deity

So far I have spoken of Omega as the universal principle of order, though we have seen it to be a dynamic principle of self-differentiation and creativity, and have observed that it issues in the activity of self-conscious and reflective thought. But I have also maintained that it is the absolute whole, and the mutual compatibility of these two aspects has yet to be made apparent. It cannot be a merely abstract logical (or even ontological) principle, for that is not, as such, a whole. As Hegel proclaimed, "The truth is the whole, but the whole is only the essential reality fulfilling itself through its development."[9] The outcome of that development is a concrete unity, of which any abstract principle must fall far short. The current issue of evolution is human personality, so Omega cannot be *less* than that. An impersonal principle is abstract and Omega is essentially a concrete reality, the most concrete conceivable. An abstract principle can attain concreteness only in a completely self-specified whole, an actually existent system. Once more, our guiding thread is the human mind, of which the active organizing principle is rational thought; but the concrete actualization of that principle is a varied practical and theoretical experience—a total personality. The ultimate principle can actualize itself in nothing less, or lower. And as personality must be self-conscious, what transcends that can be nothing short of a whole that is at once both real and ideal.

From what has already been affirmed, it follows that the explanation of all finite existences and all process cannot be sought through reductionism, and cannot be found by reversion to its more primitive forms. It can be found only in its result, by projection beyond its temporal achievements. This result has transpired in the course of natural development as human personality, which is manifestly not the final consummation. That, however, cannot be less than personal, and must be at least self-conscious. In fact, true wholeness is only achieved in self-consciousness, which can grasp together, and in mutual relation, the different elements of its objective experience, as one systematic whole. So it is as personality and in the interrelation of persons, and in nothing short of this, that the nature of Omega is to be sought.

Human personality, lodged as it is in a natural 'organism, is inevitably finite and temporal. Its experience unfolds through time and in the medium of the stream of consciousness. But consciousness is in its very nature self-transcendent, and at the personal and reflective level, especially, it transcends itself in the awareness of its own finitude. For to be aware of a limit is already to have passed beyond it, and to recognize one's own finitude is to be apprised of a standard by which it is judged as finite; that is, to conceive of an infinite. It is this self-transcendence that points towards and gives premonition of the infinitude of Omega.

This is the source of all genuine religious feeling and belief, which identifies what Teilhard calls Omega with God (the Alpha and the Omega); and religion, like art or philosophy, is one of the ways in which human personality transcends itself and finds fulfillment by immersing itself in the revelation of the infinite in its experience. Religion, of course, takes many forms, some more and some less pictorial and symbolic, some more and some less "mystical." In these forms the conception of Deity varies accordingly. In some it is clearly inadequate to the infinite nature of Omega, in others it is more perspicacious. From the position so far reached, we can go on to maintain without much risk of serious cavil that there is a rational basis for belief in an absolute principle that may with good reason be identified with what religion reveres as God, and that there are grounds for belief that the true nature of Deity is such as some religions (notably Christianity) adumbrate. If God is identified as the concrete universal principle of order evident in the unity of the physical and biological world, and if His nature is revealed in the outcome of its evolutionary process, it is no mere fantasy to see God as the Alpha and the Omega, no simple mythology to say that God creates the world, and man in his own image, and that He is revealed to the human mind through its own reflective contemplation of reality as a whole. If it has often been said in derision that man creates God in his own image, it should now be apparent that the jibe has a more sober justification.

Because of its finitude, however, human personality can realize itself as a self-conscious being only in relation to an object, primarily and essentially another self-conscious person, but also a world of objects both inorganic and organic. Nevertheless, in its self-consciousness, it transcends (in Hegel's term *übergreifft*) this objective world, in both its natural and in its social manifestations. The individual subject identifies itself with (as well as distinguishing itself from) its object (in ways we have already noted) and, to quote Hegel again, "finds itself at home in its other."

In infancy it is only through elicitation by other persons that one's own self-awareness emerges, and only concomitantly, and with the help of others, does the consciousness of inanimate objects, of the distinction of self from other, and generally of a surrounding world, progressively develop. Consequently, self-consciousness is always at the same time the consciousness of others, and personality is always corporate or social. Our clue to Omega thus dictates that it must be, at the very least a self-conscious personality, not merely singular but corporate.

The essentially social character of human personality is actualized through the institution of organized society, in which the activities of individuals are interwoven so that they cooperate to attain ends sought in common by the members of the community. Despite what many philosophers have argued to the contrary, it seems to me clear that such communities do have communal minds and wills. They are expressed and realized in practice only through the activities of the individual members; nevertheless, no individual alone can possess in full detail what can rightly be described as the knowledge of the community (for instance, of a scientific community), or privately and without consultation come to a decision that requires a consensus, or single-handed carry out policy which involves cooperative and coordinated action by several differently skilled agents. In all these corporate actions each member of the community is aware of (and is activated by) the purpose and guided by the knowledge and the skill of all. Compare, for instance, the concerted action of musicians playing together in a quartet, or in a symphony, or the group effort of a corps de ballet, or of a football team.

The mind ultimately at work in such cases is not just that of the single individual but of the whole corporate society. Taking human society as our clue to Omega, therefore, we should postulate something like what the Bible refers to as "the Kingdom of God," or what the Church has defined as the body of Christ, of which He is the head and the communion of saints the members.

Another important characteristic of any self-conscious whole is that, while its unifying principle is the self-identical subject, it realizes itself only in its self-specifying activity, in a dynamic structure of cognitive and practical dispositions, traits, sentiments, and talents—in the exercise of its capabilities. So Omega, as the unifying principle of the ultimate whole realizes itself only in its deployment as the serial and hierarchical scale of the temporal evolutionary process. This issues in human mentality with its intellectual and moral capacities, implying an ideal of personal perfection exemplified in such historical persons as Jesus and Gautama, who are revered as divine. Thus the human ideal and the Deity merge into one and are seen as the expression of a single holy spirit. Jesus exhorts his followers, "Be ye perfect, as your Father in Heaven is perfect." The suprapersonal being which is Omega, accordingly, will be a triune personality—at once divine, human, and the immanent spirit of all being and all blessedness. This gives further significance to the religious assertions that man is created in the image of God, and that the Holy Spirit works in and through the community of worshippers.

Finally, the pervading and consolidating sentiment that alone can bind together the members of any society, more especially and essentially a holy community, and which must necessarily be reciprocal between the body and its Head, is love—not a sensuous or sentimental love, but a genuine felt concern for the true welfare of its object. In any community whatsoever that can maintain itself as a society, there must be some degree of mutual reliance and trust. Even among thieves there must, if they are to depend on mutual assistance and effort, be some sort of loyalty and honor. Distrust and suspicion result only from the expectation by some members of a group of self-interested action on the part of others. But where mutual love is universal, distrust is disarmed and excluded in the very nature of the case. So the only unfailing bond of union in any and every society is the mutual love of its members.

There is a sense in which love pervades the entire universe, as that universal tendency towards unity and coherent harmony previously stressed. Teilhard refers to it as "the radial zone of spiritual attractions."[10] At the biological level it surfaces as sexual attraction, parental tenderness, and filial dependence, as well as in the gregariousness of many species. But these are only the precursors of human love, in which they become transformed by self-reflection into something more than mere sentiment. While the emotional and conative aspects are not lost, love now becomes rational. It is genuine concern for the welfare of each and every individual, it is the universal respect for persons, that treats each as an end and none merely as a means. And because every individual is a social being, it is a concern for the welfare of the entire community, in which all are integrated and on which all depend. Nor can that welfare, for which this rational love is concerned, be confined to any one local or national community, because the welfare of every community depends, like that of each individual, upon the welfare of all.

Genuine rational love, therefore, must extend to the entire human race. It is the love for which, in St. Paul's words,

> there is neither Greek nor Jew, circumcision nor uncircumcision, Barbarian, Scythian, bond nor free: but Christ is all in all.[11]

As human rational activity is socially organized and embodied in political institutions, love comprehends and transcends all political and social virtues. It is the emotional and sentimental counterpart and expression of the unity of the perfected human community—referred to as "the Kingdom of God." Thus, it is precisely in and as love that Omega reveals itself to us.

Such love is experienced in many different ways besides that between individual persons in communities. It is felt as joy in the contemplation of a landscape, or of the majesty and power of the sea, the yearning for unity with nature, and as aesthetic ecstacy of all kinds. But as the emotional counterpart of the comprehension of the universal whole, and the self-identification, or atonement, with it, it is the love of God— *amor intellectualis Dei.*

Love of God and love of one's neighbor, however, coincide; for, as Christ says:

> Inasmuch as ye have done it unto one of the least of these my brethren, ye have done it unto me.[12]

Love of neighbor, in the full sense, transpires as the love of the entire community and devotion to the ideal Kingdom of Ends. It is an unreserved devotion to that ideal—Christ's love, through which, by his service and sacrifice for the salvation of mankind, God is revealed; and in which again human and divine are united. It is the love and comfort of the Holy Spirit; in short, it is the love of God. Love of one's neighbor and love of God are therefore one and the same.

As the living organism is presided over by an all coordinating brain, by which it is maintained in balance and organic health; while and because the brain itself is served by those very organs and physiological cycles that it coordinates—so the corporate suprapersonality of Omega maintains itself by and in the mutual love of its component personalities. This love they can sustain in its proper strength and purity only through their devotion to the sovereign principle of unity. Its immanence in and operation through them is the Grace by which it gives them power to love one another. So Spinoza contends that man's intellectual love of God is identical with God's love for man.[13]

While each individual, in love, identifies with all and with every other, there can be no question of their several individualities being obliterated in a common merger, or being absorbed into and vanishing in some ultimate Nirvana. Any such extinction of the members would equally destroy the whole, which, as we have seen throughout, is and can be a genuine whole only in and through its self-differentiation. Its wholeness and concretion is actualized only in its self-diremption, in its self-utterance and self-giving. It can be concretely absolute only as the union of its diverse members, its own self-specifications, apart from which it remains a mere abstraction, "a dance of bloodless categories," or worse, an empty formula. That, as we have seen, cannot be Omega, which, while it transcends each and any of its finite self-manifestations, must yet be immanent in them all and unite all in its own encompassing embrace.

This then is Omega, a transcendent suprapersonality uniting in itself all other persons, while maintaining their several individualities in mutual interdependence and love, and bringing to final fruition its own self-manifestation in a world as an evolving hierarchical scale of physical, biological, psychological, intelligent, moral, and spiritual forms. Only through such evolutionary processes is its inner diversity properly actualized; and the process of actualization involves continuous change and so generates time, in the forms I have reviewed in the previous chapters. The appearance of passage is common and inescapable in all of them, but it is not, and cannot be, simply a form of physical motion, and its precise nature remains enigmatical. That time is real is established by the inevitability of the evolutive dialectical process required for the inner complexity of absolute wholeness. For without it, Omega could not be Omega, and there would be no world. No real or genuine whole is undifferentiated, nor could there be any such without consciousness of itself as a totality. As conscious of itself, it must make itself an object, which is *ipso facto* to differentiate itself, and so to generate a world as a scale of forms, in each and all of which it is immanent, so that they display degrees of adequacy in the exemplification of the generic principle of organization, thus bringing the entire gamut progressively to consciousness of itself as an infinite totality in which all time is absorbed, sublated, and (as it were) congealed. This is true of self-consciousness even at the human level; but in the final outcome the scale culminates in the absolute self-knowledge that is Omega—the complete and absolute union of world and idea, of self and other. For this reason, all time and all process imply, and exist only within, a nontemporal totality. Because the universal principle of organization is immanent in all finite things, and the existence of all finite things is temporal, in its passage, time is always an image, a progressive manifestation, of eternity.

"Mysticism"

This conclusion has been reached through reasoning as close and careful as I can make it. It is a philosophical (or metaphysical) conclusion based on established evidence gathered from all the major sciences. Though it claims to be in agreement with religious beliefs, often expressed in symbolic images and allegorical forms, it is not therefore to be rejected as fanciful or "mystical." For it emerges from a serious endeavor to interpret and "see together" the results of the empirical sciences, as they have been advocated and cogently defended by their most reputable savants.

I have not attempted to expound or defend Teilhard's own position in any detail, and have not discussed his doctrine of convergence; I have merely borrowed his terminology and have quoted him with approval. He has been attacked, sometimes viciously and, in my opinion, unfairly,[14] as "mystical" and visionary; but the scientific evidence that he uses to make his case is always sound and well established. If my own conclusions are in harmony with his and give support to religious doctrine, they may not be rejected as unwarranted unless fault can be found with the argument, and only if that can be demonstrated may the conclusion legitimately be impugned. Distaste and prejudice are not philosophically relevant. I have sought to avoid vagueness, and I deplore mystification as much as any. I have asserted only what seems to me to have a basis at least in probable reasoning. Any to whom it may not appeal as sensible are under obligation to say why.

Moreover, what is meant by "mystical" in this context needs to be clarified. There is a level of thought for which any speculative reasoning appears mystifying and irrational. Those who employ analysis without synthesis, and insist on a bogus "precision," are incapable of comprehending systematic holism. But the type of reason described by Plato as "Dialectic" and by Aristotle as *noesis noeseos*, the speculative thinking of Schelling and Hegel, grasps the whole as the essential product of reason.[15] If this is "mysticism," it is not mystery-mongering, and certainly not the kind of "flitting and gibbering" rightly condemned by Collingwood, which is the legitimate object of criticism.

Notes

Chapter I
The Nature and Vindication of Metaphysics

1. Cf. *Formal, Transcendental, and Dialectical Thinking* (Albany, N.Y.: State University of New York Press, 1987).

2. Cf. *Nature, Mind, and Modern Science* (1954) and *Hypothesis and Perception* (1970) (London: George Allen and Unwin).

3. Sir Karl Popper, *The Logic of Scientific Discovery* (London, 1959).

4. Thomas Kuhn, *The Structure of Scientific Revolutions* (Chcago, IL.: Chicago University Press, 1962, 1970).

5. Cf. Paul Feyerabend, "Consolations for the Specialist" in *Criticism and the Growth of Knowledge*, I. Lakatos and A. Musgrave, eds. (Cambridge: Cambridge University Press, 1970).

6. Cf. Edmund Husserl, *Die Krisis in der europäischen Wissenschaften und die transcendentale Philosophie*, herausgegeben von E. Ströker, Felix Meiner Verlag, Hamburg, 1977 (translated by David Carr: *The Crisis of the European Sciences and Transcendental Phenomenology*, Evanston: Northwestern University Press, 1970).

7. Cf. Martin Heidegger, *"Die Zeit des Weltbildes"* in *Holzwege*, Frankfurt,

1950; and Edmund Husserl, *The crisis of European Sciences and Transcendental Phenomenology*, trans. David Carr (Evanston: Northwestern University Press, 1970).

8. That Engels and Lenin adopted this position is well known; it is sometimes denied that Marx did so. But cf. *The Holy Family* in *Writings of the Young Marx on Philosophy and Society*, ed. and trans. Lloyd D. Easton and Kurt H. Guddat (Garden City, N.Y.: Doubleday, 1967), pp. 419-420 and *passim*.

9. Cf. Constantin Brunner, *Science, Spirit, Superstitution*, Trans. Abraham Suhl, ed. Walter Bernard (London: George Allen and Unwin, 1968), Part II, B, Chap. III; and Hans Goetz, *Denken ist Leben* (Frankfurt-am-Main: Athenäum Verlag, 1987), pp. 89-90, 97-102.

10. Cf. Maurice Natanson, *Edmund Husserl: Philosopher of Infinite Tasks* (Evanston, IL.; Northwestern University Press, 1973), p. 43.

11. Hubert L. Dreyfus and Paul Rabinow, *Michel Foucault: Beyond Structuralism and Hermeneutics* (Chicago: University of Chicago Press, 1982, 1983), 2nd. ed., p. xix.

12. Jean Piaget, *Structuralism*, trans. Chaninah Maschler (New York: Basic Books, 1970).

13. See Chaps. VI and VII below.

14. Cf. *Process and Reality*, (Cambridge: Cambridge University Press, 1929), p. 3.

15. Cf. *Kritik der reinen Vernunft*, A 97.

16. Cf. *Republic*, VII, 537c.

17. Cf. André de Muralt, *L'idée de la Phénoménologie, l'exemplarisme husserlien* (trans. Garry L. Breckon: *The Idea of Phenomenology, Husserlian Exemplarism* [Evanston: Northwestern University Press, 1974]).

18. Cf. Martin Heidegger, *Einführung in die Metaphysik*, Tübingen, 1953 (trans. Ralph Manheim: *Introduction to Metaphysics* [New Haven, Yale University Press, 1959]).

19. Cf. Hans-Georg Gadamer, *Philosophical Hermeneutics*, trans. D. E. Linge (Berkeley: University of California Press, 1976); and *Wahrheit und Methode* (Tübingen, 1960).

20. Oxford University Press, 1940.

21. Heidegger gives expression to similar ideas in the third section of the first Introduction to *Sein und Zeit* (Tübingen, 1967), p. 9: "*Die eigentliche 'Bewegung' der Wissenschaften spielt sich ab in der mehr oder minder radikalen und ihr*

selbst durchsichtigen Revision der Grundbegriffe. Das Niveau einer Wissenschaft bestimmt sich daraus wie weit sie einer Krisis ihrer Grundbegriffe fähig ist." ("The real 'movement' of the sciences takes place when their basic concepts undergo a more or less radical revision which is transparent to itself. The level which a science has reached is determined by how far it is *capable* of a crisis in its basic concepts." (John Macquarrie and Edward Robinson's translation [London: SCM Press, 1962], p. 29). Heidegger also relates investigation into these "basic concepts" to the ultimate ontological investigation properly called metaphysics, although he reserves that term for the traditional metaphysic, the attitude and approach of which he castigates as misguided. Also he distinguishes (as Collingwood does somewhat differently) between the "ontic" concerns of the sciences and the "ontological" interests of philosophy (or phenomenology).

22. Oxford University Press, 1933.

Chapter II
Metaphysical Problems of Time

1. Cf. *Confessions*, Bk. XI, xiv.

2. This point was made by Plotinus in the Seventh Tractatus (Sects. 7-13) of Ennead III.

3. Cf. op. cit., XI, xv ff.

4. Cf. "The Myth of Passage," *The Journal of Philosophy*, Vol. 48, 1951, reprinted in *Principles of Empirical Realism*, Springfield, Ill., 1986, and in *The Philosophy of Time*, ed. Richard M. Gale (Garden City, N.J.: Anchor Books, Doubleday, 1967; London, 1969).

5. Cf. *The Nature of Existence*, vol. 2 (Cambridge, 1927), chap. XXXIII. (Excerpted in Gale, *The Philosophy of Time*).

6. The same applies, perhaps more obviously, to the days of the week and the months of the year.

7. Cf. *The Phenomenology of Perception*, trans. Colin Smith (London: Routledge and Kegan Paul, 1962-1965), p. 424.

8. See "The Status of Temporal Becoming" in *The Philosophy of Time*, ed. Richard M. Gale (a reprinted version of the Louis Clark Vanuxem Lecture, delivered at Princeton University, March 2, 1967, being a revision of chap. I of *Modern Science and Zeno's Paradoxes* [London 1968]).

9. Cf. *The Concept of Nature* (Cambridge, 1926), p. 57.

10. Cf. J. D. Mabbott, "Our Direct Experience of Time," *Mind*, LX, 1951

(Reprinted in Gale, *The Philosophy of Time*); and "The Specious Present," *Mind*, LXIV, 1955. Merleau-Ponty voices the same opinion: "A past and a future spring forth when I reach out towards them. I am not, for myself, at this very moment, I am also at this morning, or at the night which will soon be here, and though my present is, if we wish so the consider it, this instant, it is equally this day, this year, or my whole life." (*The Phenomenology of Perception*, Pt. III, chap. 2, p. 421. Colin Smith's translation).

11. Could this, perhaps, or something like it, be what Heidegger means when he writes: *"Die Gewesenheit entspringt der Zukunft, so zwar, dass die gewesene (besser gewesende) Zukunft die Gegenwart aus sich entlässt."* (*Sein und Zeit* [Tübingen, 1976], p. 326). "The character of 'having been' arises from the future, and in such a way that the future which 'has been' (or better, which 'is in the process of having been') releases from itself the present." (Macquarrie and Robinson's translation.)

12. Cf. Heidegger, op cit., Sect. 65, pp. 325f, and Sect. 68, pp. 336ff.

13. Op. cit., p. 325.

14. New York, Evanston, and London: Harper and Row, 1970, p. 188.

15. Cf. below, Chapter V. Heidegger, of course, denies the existence of any transcendental (worldless) *ego*.

16. Cf. *An Examination of McTaggart's Philosophy*, vol. 2, part I (Cambridge, 1938)).

17. Compare Cratylus and Hume.

18. See *Critique of Pure Reason*, A187, B230.

19. *Sophist*, 245D.

20. I have argued this more at length elsewhere: cf. "Time and Eternity," *Review of Metaphysics*, Vol. XXIX,3, 1976.

21. *Enzyklopädie*, Sect. 258 and *Zusatz*. Cf. also Josiah Royce's argument in *The World and the Individual*, Series I, Lecture IX, and Series II, Lecture III, where this position is defended at length.

22. In numbering Spinoza's *Epistolae*, I follow van Vloten en Land, and A. Wolf, who gives a table showing the correlation of present numbering with that of editions prior to 1882. See *The Correspondence of Spinoza* (London, 1928, 1966), p. 19.

Chapter III
Physical Time

1. E. Meyerson, *Identity and Reality*, trans. K. Loewnberg (London, 1930), p. 238. Quoted by G. J. Whitrow, *The Natural Philosophy of Time* (London and Edinburgh, 1961), p. 4.

2. Cf. Adolf Grünbaum. op. cit.

3. J. J. C. Smart, "Spatialising Time," *Mind*, Vol. 64, 1955. (Reprinted in Gale, op. cit.)

4. Cf. *Albert Einstein, Philosopher-Scientist*, ed. Paul Schlipp (Evanston, IL., 1949), pp. 52-53.

5. Cf. E. A. Milne, "Fundamental Concepts of Natural Philosophy" in *Proceedings of the Royal Society of Edinburgh*, Sect. A, Vol. 62, 1943-44, Part I.

6. Ibid.

7. A different conception of chaos is associated with turbulence, recent investigations of which, with the help of computer graphics, have revealed that it involves hitherto unsuspected forms of order, mathematically generated fractal patterns of immense intricacy and entrancing beauty. These developments further support the thesis I am advocating in this chapter and throughout this book. Cf, James Gleick, *Chaos* (New York, Viking, 1987), and H.O. Peitgen, P.H. Richter, et al, *Schoenheit im Chaos: Frontiers of Chaos* (Bremen, Mapart, Universität Bremen, 1985).

8. Cf. Bertrand Russell, *Principles of Mathematics* (London, 1937), pp. 347ff.

9. Cf. G. J. Whitrow, op. cit., p. 136.

10. Cf. Grünbaum, op. cit., Sects, 2-3, p. 425ff.

11. Cf. G. W. F. Hegel, *Enzyklopädie der Philosophischen Wissenschaften*, Sect. 100, *Wissenschaft der Logik*, I, pp. 211ff. (Suhrkamp edition), *The Science of Logic*, trans. A. V. Miller (London, 1959), pp. 199ff., and E. E. Harris, *An Interpretation of the Logic of Hegel*, (Lanham, New York, London, 1983), pp. 126ff. Here the word "moments" is not used in the temporal sense, but it refers to dialectical opposites, on the analogy of weights in the opposite scales of a balance.

12. Cf. E. A. Milne, op. cit. Eddington writes: "A region outside the field of action of matter could have no geodesics, and consequently no intervals. All the potentials would then necessarily be zero.... Now if all intervals vanished space-time would shrink to a point. Then there would be no space, no time, no inertia, no anything. Thus a cause which creates intervals and geodesics must,

so to speak, extend the world." (*Space, Time and Gravitation*, Cambridge University Press, 1950, p. 157f). Milne suggested that this cause is the spreading light wave. Cf. also, Milič Čapec, *The Philosophical Impact of Contemporary Physics* (New York, 1961), chap XI.

13. Eddington, *The Expanding Universe*, (Cambridge University Press, Cambridge, 1933), p. 73.

14. K. Gödel, in *Albert Einstein, Philosopher-Scientist*, ed. Paul Schlipp (Evanston, 1959), p. 560.

15. David Park, *The Image of Eternity* (Amherst, MA.: University of Massachusetts Press, 1980), p. 94.

16. Ibid., p. 92.

17. Cf. O. M. Bilaniuk, S. L. Brown, B. De Witt, W. A. Necomb, M. Sachs, E. C. G. Sudarshan, S. Yoshikawa, "More about Tachyons," *Physics Today*, Vol. 22, No 12, 1969; O. M. Bilaniuk and E. C. G. Sudarshan, "Particles Beyond the Light Barrier," *Physics Today*, May 1969, pp. 43-52; Paul Fitzgerald, "Tachyons, Backward Causation and Freedom," *Boston Studies in the Philosophy of Science*, Vol. VIII, eds., R. S. Buck and R. S. Cohen, (Reidel, Dordrecht [Holland], Boston, London, 1970); T. Chapman, *Time: A Philosophical Analysis* (Reidel, Dordrecht [Holland], Boston, London, 1982), chap I and II.

18. Cf. A. Einstein, B. Podolsky, and N. Rosen, "Can Quantum-theory description of physical reality be considered complete?" *Physical Review*, 47, 1935, pp. 777-780. D. Bohm and Y Aharonov, "Discussion of experimental proof for the paradox of Einstein, Podolsky and Rosen", *Physical Review*, 103, 1957, pp. 1070-1076.

19. Cf. Henry P. Stapp, "Are Faster-than-light Influences Necessary," *Quantum Mechanics versus Local Realism—The Einstein, Podolsky, and Rosen Paradox*, ed. F. Salleri, Plenum Press, 1987; "Quantum Mechanics and the Physicists' Conception of Nature: Philosophical Implications of Bell's Theorem," *The World View of Contemporary Physics: Is there a Need for a New Metaphysics?*" ed. R. Kitchener (Albany, N.Y.: SUNY Press, 1988)

20. Cf. Sir Arthur Eddington, *The Philosophy of Physical Science* (Cambridge University Press, 1939).

21. D. W. Sciama, *The Unity of the Universe*, (New York, 1961), p. 87.

22. E. A. Milne, op cit.

23. Sciama, op. cit., Pt. II, Introd.

24. Cf. Werner Heisenberg, *The Physicist's Conception of Nature* (London,

1958), and *Physics and Philosophy*, (London, 1959).

25. D. Bohm, *Wholeness and the Implicate Order* (London and Boston, 1980, 1983), p. 172.

26. F. Capra, *The Tao of Physics* (London 1975, 1983).

27. P. Davies, *God and the New Physics* (London, 1983; Harmondsworth, 1986).

28. Cf. Samuel Alexander, *Space, Time and Deity* (London, 1929). Bk. III, chap. II, p. 38.

29. Cf. *Formal, Transcendental and Dialectical Thinking* (Albany, N.Y.: SUNY Press, 1987).

Chapter IV
Biological Time

1. Cf. *The Foundations of Metaphysics in Science*, chap. XII, sects. 3 and 4.

2. Cf. *Time's Arrow and Evolution* (Princeton, New Jersey, 1955), chaps. IV, V, and VI.

3. Op cit., p. 64f.

4. Cf. Merleau-Ponty, *The Structure of Behavior*, trans. A. L. Fisher (Boston, 1963); K. Koffka, *Principles of Gestalt Psychology* (London, 1955), pp. 310ff., and *The Growth of the Mind* (London, 1928), chap III.

5. Cf. L. Wittenstein, *Philosophical Investigations*, trans. G. E. M. Anscombe (New York, 1958); Gilbert Ryle, *The Concept of Mind* (London, 1969); W. van O. Quine, *Word and Object* (Cambridge, Mass.), 1960.

6. Cf. Le Gros Clark, "The Anatomical Perspective" in *Perspectives in Neuropsychiatry*, (ed. D. Richter (London, 1950); R. B. Livingston, "Central Control of Afferent Activity," ibid.; K. S. Lashley, *Brain Mechanisms and Intelligence* (Chicago, 1929); K. Lewin, *Psychol. Forsch.*, 7, pp. 3-40; *Koffka*, op. cit.; N. Tinbergen, *A Study of Instinct* (Oxford, 1952), p. 2; W. H. Thorpe, *Learning and Instinct in Animals* (London, 1963), p. 81.

7. Cf. W. H. Thorpe, op. cit.

8. N. Tinbergen, *A Study of Instinct*, p. 112.

9. Cf. W. H. Thorpe, op. cit., p. 118.

10. *The Forest and the Sea* (New York, 1960), p. 31.

11. Ibid. These interdependencies have more recently been freshly

emphasized in two books by eminent scientists. Lewis Thomas, in *The Lives of a Cell* (New York, 1974), has compared the earth as a whole, with its atmospheric mantle, to a single cell; and James Lovelock has insisted that this is to be taken seriously as a scientific hypothesis, the "Gaia hypothesis," in his book, *Gaia: A New Look at Life on Earth* (Oxford University Press, 1979).

Chapter V
Psychological Time

1. Cf. Hegel, *Enzyklopädie*, section 401.

2. Cf. E. E. Harris, *The Foundations of Metaphysics in Science*, (London, 1965) chap. XVI; and Susanne Langer, *Philosophical Sketches*, I, (1962) and *Mind: An Essay on Human Feeling*, vol. I, (Baltimore, Johns Hopkins Press, 1967), chap. I.

3. Cf. Sir Frederick Bartlett, *Remembering* (Cambridge University Press, 1961), chap. II; R. R. Blake and G. V. Ramsey, eds., *Perception—An Approach to Personality* (New York, 1957), chap. 5; J. H. Rohrer and M. Sherif, eds., *Social Psychology at the Crossroads* (New York, 1951), chap 10.

4. Cf. M. von Senden, *Raum und Gestaltauffassung bei operierten Blindgeborenen vor und nach der Operation* (Leipzig, 1932); *Space and Sight* (London, 1960); I. London, "A Russian Report on Post-operative newly seeing," *Amer.J. of Psychology*, 1960, 73, pp. 478-482; A. H. Riesen, "The development of visual perception in Man and Chimpanzee," *Science*, 106, 1947.

5. See above, Chap. II, note 8. The arguments of C. K. Mundle responding to Mabbott (*Mind*, LXIII, 1954) do not escape the suppressed contradiction (discussed below) between the assumed instantaneity and the actual duration of the apprehending act.

6. Cf. C. D. Broad, *Scientific Thought*, and *An Examination of McTaggart's Philosophy*, and *Mind and its Place in Nature*.

7. Cf. Josiah Royce, op. cit.

8. Cf. *Critique of Pure Reason*, A106-108, B132-140.

9. Brand Blanshard, *The Nature of Thought*, (London: G. Allen and Unwin, 1939, 1948), book II, chap. VII.

10. Cf. Spinoza, *Ethics* II, Prop. lxix, Schol., *Epp.* XII and XXXVII, *Tractatus Theologico-Politicus*, chap II; Hegel, op. cit., sect. 20 and *passim*.

11. Edmund Husserl, *The Phenomenology of Internal Time Consciousness*, ed. Martin Heidegger, trans. J. S. Churchill (Bloomington and London: Indiana University Press, 1964, 1973).

12. Ibid., p. 42.

13. Ibid., pp. 99-100.

14. Ibid., P. 106.

15. Ibid.

16. Ibid.

17. Op. cit., p. 414.

18. Op. cit., p. 422.

19. Op. cit., p. 424.

20. Op. cit., p. 415.

21. Op. cit., pt. III, chap I.

22. Op. cit., p. 392.

23. Op. cit., p. 414.

24. Op. cit., pp. 371-372.

25. Op. cit., p. 424.

26. To be transcendental is to be the prior condition (logical or ontological) of the possibility of empirical experience. To be transcendent is to lie beyond the limits of empirical experience.

27. Cf. F. H. Bradley's account of Nature in *Appearance and Reality* (Clarendon Press, Oxford, England, 1897, 1951).

28. These stages are not identical with, but they run parallel to, those distinguished by Piaget in the development in early childhood of the concept of an object. He lists six stages: (i) reflex action; (ii) formation of early habits (e.g., of grasping and sucking); (iii) secondary circular reaction; involving prolongation of movements of accommodation; (iv) searching for objects that have disappeared; (v) objects seen as permanent individual things; (vi) formation of images of absent objects and their displacements. Piaget maintains that similar and parallel stages are distinguishable in the development of the child's awareness of objective time. But for him the nature of objective time is simply assumed as commonly understood, and he regards it as a sort of projection upon the world of the inner experience of passage, which he does little to explain or even to describe. He simply takes for granted our general familiarity with it. Psychologically, his experimentation and discussion are of outstanding importance and of fascinating interest, but their direct contribution to the philosophical understanding of temporality is not great. Cf. Jean Piaget, *The Construction of Reality in the Child*, trans. Margaret Cook (New York: Basic Books, 1954), chaps. I-IV.

29. Cf. E. E. Harris, *Perceptual Assurance and the Reality of the World*, (Worcester, MA.: Clark University Press, 1974).

30. The urge to eliminate the transcendental subject continues in the work of the structuralists and post-structuralists. Michel Foucault firmly renounces any approach towards transcendentalism. But this renunciation only conceals, and does not abolish the activity of a subject in human discourse. As his primary concern is with the historical study of human action and knowledge, I have deferred discussion of his views to the next chapter.

31. Cf. E. E. Harris, "The Problem of Self-constitution in Idealism and Phenomenology," *Idealistic Studies*, VII, No. 1, 1977.

Chapter VI
Historical Time

1. Cf. Claude Lévi-Strauss, *Totemism* (Boston: Beacon Press, 1963), p. 96.

2. Quoted by Harold J. Morowitz in *Mayonnaise and the Origins of Life* (New York: Schribners, 1985), p. 20.

3. Cf. R. G. Collingwood, *The Idea of History* (Oxford University Press, 1946, 1956, 1961), pp. 10, 12, 217ff.

4. W. Dilthey, *Gesammelte Schriften*, VII, p. 279. Cf. also, Martin Heidegger, *Sein und Zeit*, Einführung, II, sect. 6.

5. Op. cit., pp. 247-248. Again Heidegger may be cited in support: "*Die existenziale entwurf der Geschichtlichkeit des Daseins bringt nur zur Enthüllung, was eingehüllt in der Zeitlichkeit schon liegt.*" ("The existential projection of Dasein's historicality merely reveals what already lies enveloped in the temporalizing of temporality." And again: "...*dieses Seinde nicht 'zeitlich' weil es 'in der Geschichte steht,' sondern... umgekehrt geschichtlich nur existiert und existieren kann, weil es im Grunde seines Seins zeitlich ist.*" ("Dasein is not 'temporal' because it 'stands in history,' but it exists historically, and can so exist, because it is temporal in the very basis of its being"). *Sein und Zeit*, Erstes Teil, Zweites Abschnitt, Kap. V, sect. 72. (Macquarrie and Robinson's translation).

6. The *a priori* idea of the historical past must not be confused with what Michel Foucault calls "the historical *a priori.*" That is something empirically ascertained, and is historical in the sense that it is, as it were, historically sedimented. It is the field defined by a "positivity" of discourse, in which formal identities, thematic continuities, translations of concepts and polemical interchanges may be deployed—i.e., the condition of reality for statements. Cf. *The Archeology of Knowledge*, trans. A. M. Sheridan Smith (London and New York:

Tavistock Publications, 1974), p. 127.

7. Cf. Heidegger, *Being and Time*, Introd. chap. II, sect. 6, where he maintains that self-analysis of *Dasein* involves its tradition, and so is historical. While he considers knowledge of tradition necessary, Heidegger believes that traditional thinking is apt to obscure its authentic nature. But what he himself says later, in Division II, Chap. V, makes it clear that authentic self-awareness is essentially historical, and that what makes anything historical is its embodiment in the interests, concerns and purposes of human agents in the past. Cf. sects. 72 and 78.

8. Op. cit., p. 245.

9. Cf. Marc Bloch, *The Historian's Craft*, (New York, 1953); E. H. Carr, *What is History?* (Cambridge, 1961; New York, 1972).

10. Cf. Claude Lévi-Strauss, *The Savage Mind* (Chicago and London, 1968), chap. 9, p. 250f.

11. See above, Chap. I, note 8.

12. Robert Bridges, *The Testament of Beauty*.

13. Cf. Karl Mannheim, *Ideology and Utopia* (London: Kegan Paul; New York: Harcourt Brace, 1936, 1946; London: Routledge and Kegan Paul, 1949).

14. Cf. Lévi-Strauss, loc. cit.

15. Cf. Hubert L. Dreyfus and Paul Rabinow, *Michel Foucault: Beyond Structuralism and Hermeneutics,* 2nd ed. (Chicago University Press, 1982, 1983), p. 79.

16. Cf. Michel Foucault, *The Archeology of Knowledge*, p. 22.

17. Op. cit., p. 23.

18. Op. cit., p. 102.

19. Op. cit., p. 154.

20. Op. cit., p. 172.

21. Cf. op. cit., Pt. III, chaps. 1, 2, and 3.

22. See note 6, above.

23. Cf. Dreyfus and Rabinow, op. cit., pp 87ff.

24. Spinoza, *Tractatus de Intellectus Emendatione*.

25. For a detailed and even more devasting critique, set against a historical background, cf. Gillian Rose, *Hegel contra Sociology* (London: Athlone Press; New

Jersey: Humanities Press, 1981), and *Dialectic of Nihilism: Post-Structuralism and Law* (Oxford and New York: Basil Blackwell, 1984).

Chapter VII
Dialectic in History

1. Cf. Francis Cornford, *From Religion to Philosophy* (London: E. Arnold, 1912; New York, 1957); Bruno Schnell, *The Discovery of the Mind: The Greek Origins of European Thought* (Harvard University Press, 1953).

2. Cf. A. N. Whitehead, *Science and the Modern World* (Cambridge University Press, 1926, 1930), chap. V.

3. Cf. *An Essay on Metaphysics* (Oxford, 1939).

4. Cf. *The Structure of Scientific Revolutions* (Chicago, 1970).

5. Oxford University Press, 1933, 1956.

Chapter VIII
Evolution and Omega

1. Cf. A. Einstein, *Relativity, The Special and General Theory* (London, 1954), *The Meaning of Relativity* (London, 1956); A. Einstein and L. Infeld, *The Evolution of Physics* (New York, 1954); E. Schroedinger, *Space-time Structure* (Cambridge University Press, 1950); Sir A. Eddington, *The Expanding Universe* (Cambridge University Press, 1933); *The Philosophy of Physical Science* (Cambridge University Press, 1939); W. D. Sciama, *The Unity of the Universe* (New York, 1959); W. Heisenberg, *The Physicist's Conception of Nature* (London, 1958), *Physics and Philosophy* (London, 1959); L. de Broglie, *The Revolution in Physics* (London, 1954); David Bohm, *Wholeness and the Implicate Order* (London, 1980-1983); Paul Davies, *God and the New Physics* (London, 1983; Harmondsworth, 1986); Fritjof Capra, *The Tao of Physics* (London 1975, 1983). See Chap. III, above.

2. Cf. J. S. Haldane, *Organism and Environment* (New Haven. Conn.: Yale University Press, 1917); Lewis Thomas, *The Lives of a Cell* (New York: Viking Press, 1974; Harmondsworth: Penguin Books, 1978); Marston Bates, *The Forest and the Sea* (New York, 1960); Harold Blum, *Time's Arrow and Evolution* (Princeton, New Jersey, 1955); J. Needham, *Time, the Refreshing River* (London: Allen and Unwin, 1944; A. I. Oparin, *The Origin of Life* (London, 1957). To these may now be added: Rupert Sheldrake, *A New Science of Life* (London: Paladin, 1987), and John Lovelock, *Gaia, A New Look at Life on Earth* (Oxford University Press, 1979).

3. Pierre Teilhard de Chardin, *Le Phénomène Humaine* (Paris: Edition Seuil,

1955). Translated by Bernard Wall as *The Phenomenon of Man* (London: Collins; New York: Harper and Row, 1959; revised translation, 1965), p. 221.

4. Cf. E. A. Milne, op. cit., W. D. Sciama, op. cit., Sir A. Eddington, op. cit., and other authors cited above.

5. Cf. G. W. F. Hegel, *Enzyklopädie*, Sect. 258, *Zusatz*.

6. G. W. F. Hegel, *Phänomenologie des Geistes*, chap. VIII, *Werke*, vol. III (Suhrkamp), p. 584. Baillie's translation, p. 800; A. V. Miller's translation, p. 487.

7. Cf. Teilhard, op. cit., p. 270f.

8. What the concept extinguishes is not the actual process in nature but transition in thought between opposite moments in the dialectic. The absolute idea, the Concept in its fulfillment, is the whole immediately conscious of itself in full explication.

9. G. W. F. Hegel, *Phänomenologie*, Preface, Miller's translation, p. 11; Baillie, p. 81f.

10. Teilhard, op. cit., p. 265.

11. Colossians, 3:11.

12. Matt. 25:40.

13. Spinoza, *Ethics*, Pt. V, Prop. XXXVI, Cor. and Schol.

14. Cf. P. B. Medawar, *Mind* LXX, 277, January 1961, and my defense of Teilhard, *The Foundations of Metaphysics in Science*, (New York, London: Lanham, 1965, 1983), pp. 150ff.

15. Cf. William Earle, *Mystical Reason* (Chicago: Regnery, 1980).

Select Bibliography

Alexander, S., *Space, Time and Deity* (London: Macmillan, 1929).
_____, *Spinoza and Time* (London: G. Allen and Unwin, 1921).

Allport, Floyd H., *Theories of Perception and the Concept of Structure* (New York: Wiley, 1955).

Aristotle, *Physics*, trans. Edward Hassey (Oxford [England]: The Charendon Press; New York: Oxford University Press, 1983). P. H. Wickstead and F. Cornford (London: Heinemann, 1929, 1934).
_____, *Metaphysics*, trans. W. D. Ross (Oxford [England]: Clarendon Press, 1924).
_____, *De Generatione et Corruptione*, trans. C. J. F. Williams (Oxford [England]: Clarendon Press; New York: Oxford University Press, 1982).
_____, *Basic Works*, ed. R. McKeon (New York: Random House, 1984)
_____, *Works*, ed. W. D. Ross (Oxford [England]: Clarendon Press, 1928, 1963).

Augustine, Saint, *Confessions*, ed. John Gibb and W. Montgomery (New York: Garland Press, 1980). Trans. E. B. Pusey (Chicago: Encyclopedia Britannica, 1955).
Reprinted in Gale, R. M. (ed.), *The Philosophy of Time*, (Garden City, N.J.: Anchor Books, Doubleday, 1967; London, 1969).

Bartlett, Sir Frederick, *Remembering* (Cambridge [England]: Cambridge University Press, 1961).

Bates, M., *The Forest and The Sea*, (New York: Random House, 1960; Vintage Press, 1965).

Bilaniuk, O. M. S., L. Brown, B. De Witt, W. A. Necomb, M. Sachs, E. C. G. Sudarshan, and S. Yoshikawa, "More about Tachyons," *Physics Today*, Vol. 22, No. 12, 1969.

Bilaniuk, O. M., and E. C. G. Sudarshan, "Particles beyond the Light Barrier," *Physics Today*, May 1969.

Blake, R. R., and G. V. Ramsey (eds.), *Perception: An approach to Personality* (New York: Ronald Press Co., 1951).

Blanshard, B., *The Nature of Thought* (London: George Allen and Unwin, 1939).
————, *Reason and Analysis* (La Salle, IL.: Open Court, 1962).

Bloch, M., *The Historian's Craft*, trans. P. Putnam (New York: Knopp, 1953).

Blum, H., *Times's Arrow and Evolution* (Princeton, N.J., 1955).

Bohm, David, *Fragmentation and Wholeness* (Jerusalem: van Leer Foundation Series, 1976).
————, *Wholeness and the Implicate Order* (London: Routledge and Kegan Paul; Boston, 1980, 1983).

Bohm, D., and Y. Aharanov, "Discussion of experimental proof for the paradox of Einstein, Podolsky and Rosen," *Physical Review*, 103, 1957.

Bohm, D., and J. Krishnamurti, *The Ending of Time* (San Francisco, Ca.: Harper and Row, 1985).

Bradley, F. H., *Appearance and Reality* (Oxford [England]: Clarendon Press, 1897, 1930).
————, *Ethical Studies* (Oxford [England]: Clarendon Press, 1927).
————, *The Principles of Logic* (Oxford [England]: Clarendon Press, 1922).

Brain, Sir W. Russell, *Mind, Perception and Science* (Oxford [England]: Blackwell; Springfield, IL., 1951).

Bauer, O. D., *Dialektik der Zeit: Untersuchungen zu Hegels Metaphysik der Weltgeschichte* (Stuttgart: Bad-Constatt, Fromann-Holtzboog, 1982).

Broad, C. D., *Examination of McTaggart's Philosophy* (Cambridge [England], Cambridge University Press, 1933-1938).
————, *Mind and its Place in Nature* (London: Kegan Paul, Trench; New York: Harcourt Brace, 1925).
————, *Scientific Thought* (London: Kegan Paul, Trench, 1923; Atlantic Highlands, N.J.: Humanities Press, 1952).

Brunner, Constantin, *Science, Spirit, Superstitution*, trans. by Abraham Suhl, ed., Walter Bernhard (London: G. Allen and Unwin, 1965).

Campbell, C. A., "The Mind's Involvement in 'Objects,' An Essay in Idealist Epistemology" in *Theories of the Mind* (J. Scher, ed.) (Free Press of Gencoe, IL.; London: Macmillan, 1962).

Capra, Fritjof, *The Tao of Physics* (London: Wildwood House; New York: Random House, 1975, 1983).

—————, "The role of Physics in the Current Change of Paradigm," in *The World View of Contemporary Physics: Is there a Need for a New Metaphysics?* Richard Kitchener, ed. (Albany, N.Y.: State University of New York Press, 1988).

Čapek, M., *Bergson and Modern Physics. A reinterpretation and reevaluation* (Dordrecht [Holland]: Reidel, 1971).

—————, *The Philosophical Impact of Contemporary Physics*, (Princeton, N.J.: van Nostrand, 1961).

Carr, E. H., *What is History?* (Cambridge [England]: Cambridge University Press, 1961; New York: Random House, 1972).

Cohen, R., and M. Wartoffsky (eds.), *Hegel and the Sciences* (Boston Studies in the Philosophy of Science, Vol. 64; Dordrecht [Holland]: Reidel; Boston and London, 1984).

Collingwood, R. G., *An Essay on Metaphysics* (Oxford [England]: Oxford University Press, 1934, 1965).

—————, *An Essay on Philosophical Method* (Oxford [England]: Oxford University Press, 1934, 1965).

—————, *The New Leviathan* (Oxford [England]: Oxford University Press, 1942).

—————, *The Idea of Nature* (Oxford [England]: Oxford University Press, 1945).

—————, *The Idea of History* (Oxford [England]: Oxford University Press, 1946, 1956).

—————, *Essays in the Philosophy of History* ed. W. Debbins (Austin, TX: University of Texas Press, 1965).

Copernicus, *De Revolutionibus Orbium Coelestium*, (Bruxelles: Culture et Civilization, 1966).

Cornford, F., *From Religion to Philosophy, A Study in the Origins of Western Speculation* (London: Arnold; New York: Longmans Green, 1912).

Cottle, T. J., *Perceiving time: a psychological investigation with men and women* (New York: Wiley, 1976).

d'Abro, A., *The Evolution of Scientific Thought from Newton to Einstein* (New York: Boni and Liveright, 1927; 2nd. ed., revised and enlarged, New York: Dover,

1950)

————, *The Rise of the New Physics*, 2 vols. (New York: Dover, 1951).

Davies, Paul, *God and the New Physics* (London, 1983; Harmonsworth [England]: Penguin Books, 1984, 1986).

de Broglie, L., *The Revolution in Physics: A non-Mathematical survey of Quanta*, trans. R. W. Wiemeyer (London: Routledge and Kegan Paul, 1954; New York: Noonday Press, 1953).

de Muralt, A., *l'Idée de la Phénoménologie:l'Exemplarisme Husserlien* (Paris: Presses Universitaires de France, 1958). Translation by G. L. Breckon. *The Idea of Phenomenology: Husserlian Exemplarism* (Evanston: Northwestern University Press, 1974).

Dilthey, W., *Gesammelte Schriften* (Stuttgart: Trübner; Göttingen: Van den Hoek & Ruprecht, 1914-1972; Leipzig, Berlin, 1929).

————, *Selected Works*, trans. and ed., R. Makkreel and F. Rodi (Princeton, N.J., 1985-).

Dreyfus, H., and Rabinow, *Michel Foucault: Beyond Structuralism and Hermeneutics* (Chicago, IL.: University of Chicago Press, 1982, 1983).

Earle, W., *Mystical Reason* (Chicago, IL.: Regnery, 1980).

Eddington, Sir Arthur, *New Pathways in Science* (Cambridge [England]: Cambridge University Press, 1935).

————, *Space, Time and Gravitation*, (Cambridge [England]: Cambridge University Press, 1950).

————, *The Expanding Universe* (Cambridge [England]: Cambridge University Press, 1933).

————, *The Nature of the Physical World* (Cambridge [England]: Cambridge University Press, 1928).

————, *The Philosophy of Physical Science* (Cambridge [England]: Cambridge University Press, 1939).

Einstein, A., *Relativity, the Special and General Theories*, trans.R. W. Lawson (London: Methuen, 1954).

————, *The Meaning of Relativity* (London: Methuen, 1956).

Einstein, A., and L. Infeld, *The Evolution of Physics* (New York: Simon and Schuster, 1954).

Einstein, Podolsky, and Rosen, "Can Quantum-Theory description of physical reality be considered complete?" *Physical Review*, 47, 1935.

Feyerabend, P., "Consolation for the Specialist" in *Criticism and the Growth of Knowledge* eds. I. Lakatos and A. Musgrave (Cambridge [England]:

Cambridge University Press, 1970).

Fichte, J. G., *Grundlage der Gesamten Wissenschaftslehre*, in *Sämtliche Werke* (Leopzig: Mayer und Muller, 1845-46).
———, *Science of Knowledge*, trans. Peter Heath and John Lachs (New York: Cambridge University Press, 1982).

Fitzgerald, P., "Tachyons, Backward Causation, and Freedom," *Boston Studies in the philosophy of Science*, Vol. VIII, eds., R. S. Buck and R. S. Cohen (Dordrecht [Holland]: Reidel; Boston and London, 1982).

Foucault, M. *l'Archéologie du savoir* (Paris: Editions Gallimard, 1969). Translated by A. M. Sheridan Smith, *The Archeology of Knowledge* (London and New York: Tavistock Publications, 1972, 1974).
———, *Birth of the Clinic* (London: Tavistock Publications, 1973).
———, *Histoire de folie á l'âge classique* (Paris: Union Général d'Editions, 1964).
———, *Les mots et les chose* (Paris: Gillimards, 1966).
———, *Madness and Civilization* (London: Tavistock Publications, 1967).
———, *Naissance de la clinique* (Paris: Gillimards, 1973).
———, *Power/Knowledge, selected Interviews and Other Writings, 1972-1977*, ed. Colin Gordon, trans., Colin Gordon, Leo Marshall, John Mepham, Kate Soper (New York: Pantheon Books, Random House, 1972-1980).
———, *The Order of Things* (London: Tavistock Publications, 1970).

Flood, R., and M. Lockwood, *The Nature of Time* (Oxford [England]: Blackwell, 1986).

Gadamer, Hans-Georg, *Philosophical Hermeneutics*, Trans., D. E. Linge (Berkeley, CA.: University of California Press, 1976).
———, *Wahrheit und Methode* (Tübingen, 1960).

Gale, R. M. (ed.), *The Philosophy of Time* (Garden City, N.J.: Anchor Books, Doubleday, 1967; London: 1969).

Galilei, Galileo, *Dialogue Concerning the Two Chief World Systems*, trans. Stillman Drake (Berkeley, CA.: University of California Press, 1962).

Gelven, M., *Commentary on Heidegger's Being and Time* (New York, Evanston, London: Harper and Row, 1970).

Gibson, J. J., *Perception and the Visual World*, (Boston: Houghton Miflin, 1950).

Gleick, J., *Chaos: Making a New Science* (New York and Harmondsworth [England]: Viking, Penguin, 1987).

Goetz, H., *Denken ist Leben* (Frankfurt-am-Main: Athenäum Verlag, 1987).

Gödel, K., "A Remark about the relationship between Relativity Theory and

Idealistic Philosophy" in *Albert Einstein, Philosopher-Scientist*, ed., P. Schilpp (Evanston: Library of Living Philosophers, Northwestern University Press, 1949; New York: Harper, 1959).
———, *Collected Works*, Solomon Feferman et al. (eds.) (New York: Oxford University Press; Oxford [England]: Clarendon Press, 1986).

Haldane, J. S., *Organism and Environment*, the Terry Lectures (New Haven, CT.: Yale University Press, 1917).

Hanson, N. R., *Patterns of Discovery* (Cambridge [England]: Cambridge University Press, 1958).

Harris, E. E., *An Interpretation of the Logic of Hegel* (Lanham, MD., New York, and London: University Press of America, 1983).
———, *Annihilation and Utopia* (London: George Allen and Unwin, 1966).
———, "Dialectic and Scientific Method," *Idealistic Studies*, Vol. III, No. 1, 1973.
———, "Epicyclic Popperism," *The British Journal for the Philosophy of Science* Vol. 23, 1972.
———, *Formal, Transcendental and Dialectical Thinking* (Albany, N.Y.: State University of New York Press, 1987).
———, *Hypothesis and Perception, The Roots of Scientific Method* (London: George Allen and Unwin, 1970).
———, *Nature, Mind and Modern Science* (London: George Allen and Unwin, 1954).
———, *Perceptual Assurance and the Reality of the World* (New York: Clark University Press, 1974).
———, *Salvation from Despair, A Reappraisal of Spinoza's Philosophy*, (The Hague: Martinus Nijhoff, 1973).
———, "Teleonomy and Mechanism," *Proceedings of the XVth. International Congress of Philosophy*, 1973.
———, *The Foundations of Metaphysics in Science* (London: George Allen and Unwin, 1965. Reprinted by The University Press of America, [Lanham, MD., New York, London] 1983.
———, *The Survival of Political Man* (Johannesburg: Witwatersrand University Press, 1950).
———, "The Problem of Self-constitution in Idealism and Phenomenology," *Idealistic Studies*, VII, 1, 1977.
———, "Time and Change," *Mind*, LXVI, 1957.
———, "Time and Eternity," *Review of Metaphysics*, XXIX, 3, 1976.

Harrison, Edward, *Masks of the Universe*, (New York and London: Collier, Macmillan, 1985).

Hegel, G. W. F., *Gesammelte Werke*, F. Hogemann and W. Jaeschke (eds.) (Hamburg: Felix Meiner Verlag, 1981-).

—————, *Enzyklopädie der Philosophischen Wissenschaften, Werke* (vols. VI-VIII) (Frankfurt-am-Main: Suhrkamp Verlag: 1971-1978).

—————, *Encyclopaedia of Philosophical Sciences: Logic*, trans. W. Wallace (Oxford [England]: Clarendon Press, 1892; revised by A. V. Miller, with Foreward by J. N. Findlay, 1975).

—————, *Phänomenologie des Geistes, Werke*, (vol. III) (Frankfurt-an-Main: Suhrkamp Verlag, 1971-1978).

—————, *Phenomenology of Mind*, trans. J. Baillie (London: G. Allen and Unwin, 1910; revised 1931, reprinted, 1955, 1966).

—————, *Phenomenology of Spirit*, trans. A. V. Miller (Oxford [England]: Oxford University Press, 1977).

Heidegger, Martin, *Holzwege* (Frankfurt-am-Main, 1952).

—————, *Einführung in der Metaphysik* (Tübingen, 1953). Translated by Ralph Manheim, *Introduction to Metaphysics* (New Haven, CT.: Yale University Press, 1959).

—————, *Sein und Zeit* (M. Wiemeyer, Tübingen, 1967). Translated by J. Macquarrie and E. Robinson, *Being and Time* (London: S. C. M. Press, 1962).

Heisenberg, W., *Das Naturbild der heutigen Physik* (Rowalt, 1955). Translated by J. Pomerans, *The Physicist's Conception of Nature* (New York: Harcourt Brace, 1958; Westport, CT.: Greenwood Press, 1970).

—————, *Philosophical Problems of Nuclear Science* (London: Faber & Faber, 1952).

—————, *Physics and Philosophy: The Revolution in Modern Science* (New York: Harper and Row, 1959, 1962).

—————, *Wandelungen im den Grundlagen der Naturwissenschaft* (Leipzig: S. Hirzel, 1945).

Hofstadter, D. R., *Gödel, Escher, Bach* (New York: Vintage Books, 1980).

Hume, David, *Treatise of Human Nature*, Selby-Bigge (ed.) (Oxford at the Clarendon Press; New York: Oxford University Press, 1978; London: Dutton, 1911).

Husserl, E., *Die Krisis der europäischen Wissenschaften und die transcendentale Philosophie*, herausgegeben von E. Ströker, (Hamburg: Felix Meiner Verlag, 1977).

—————, *Erfahrung und Urteil*, (Hamburg: Felix Meiner Verlag, 1972).

—————, *Husserliana. Gesammelte Werke* (The Hague: Martinus Nijhoff, 1950-).

—————, *Formale und Transcendentale Logik, Husserliana*, Band, XVIII. (The Hague: Maratinus Nijoff, 1950-).

—————, *Ideen zu einer Phänomenologie und phänomenologische Philosophie* (The Hague: Martinus Nijhoff, 1982).

—————, *Logische Untersuchungen* (Tübingen: M. Niemeyer, 1968).

————, *Experience and Judgment*, trans. J. S. Churchill and K. Ameriks (Evanston: Northwestern University Press, 1973).

————, *Formal and Transcendental Logic*, trans., Dorian Cairns (The Hague: Martin Nijhoff, 1969).

————, *Ideas*, Trans., W. Boyce Gibson (London: George Allen and Unwin, 1931, 1956).

————, *Logical Investigations*, trans., John Findlay (London: Routledge and Kegan Paul, 1970).

————, *Phenomenology of Internal Time Consciousness*, ed. Martin Heidegger, trans. J. S. Churchill (Bloomington and London: Indiana University Press, 1964, 1973).

————, *The Crisis of the European Sciences*, trans., David Carr (Evanston: Northwestern University Press, 1970).

Ittleson, H. W., "Size as a Cue to Distance: Static Localization," *American Journal of Psychology*, vol. 64, 1951.

Ittleson, H. W., and H. Cantril, *Perception, a Transcendental Approach* (Garden City, N.J.: Doubleday, 1954).

Ittleson, H. W., and F. P. Kilpatrick, "Experiments in Perception," *Scientific American*, 185, no 2, 1951.

Jasper, H. H. (ed.), *The Reticular Formation of the Brain* (Henry Ford Hospital International Symposium, 1958).

Jeans, Sir James, *Physics and Philosophy* (Cambridge [England]: Cambridge University Press, 1942).

Jonas, H., *The Phenomenon of Life* (New York: Harper and Row, 1966).
————, *Philosophical Essays* (Englewood Cliffs, N.J., 1974).

Kant, Immanuel, *Kritik der reinen Vernunft* herausgegeben von G. Hartenstein (Leipzig: Leopold Voss, 1953); Raymond Schmidt, hrs., Leipzig: Felix Meiner Verlag, 1926, 1930).
————, *Critique of Pure Reason* trans., Kemp Smith, (London: Macmillan, 1929).

Koffka, K., *Principles of Gestalt Psychology* (London: Routledge and Kegan Paul New York: Harcourt Brace, 1935).
————, *The Growth of the Mind*, (London: Kegan Paul, Trench, 1928).

Kuhn, T., *The Structure of Scientific Revolutions* (Chicago: Chicago University Press, 1962, 1970).

Lakatos, I., and A. Musgrave, *Criticism and the Growth of Knowledge* (Cambridge [England]: Cambridge University Press, 1970).

Landsberg, P. T., *The Enigma of Time* (Bristol [England]: Hilger, 1982).

Langer, S., *Mind: An Essay on Human Feeling.* (Baltimore, MD.: Johns Hopkins University Press, 1967-1983).

———, *Philosophical Sketches* (Baltimore, MD.: Johns Hopkins University Press, 1962).

Lashley, K. S., *Brain Mechanisms and Intelligence* (Chicago: Chicago University Press, 1929).

Lavoisier, A. L., *Traité elementaire de Chimie* (Paris, 1789; Brussels, 1965).

Levi-Strauss, C., *Le Pensée Sauvage* (Paris: Libraire Plon, 1962). Translated as *The Savage Mind* (London: George Weidenfeld & Nicholson, Ltd., Chicago: University of Chicago Press, 1966, 1968).

———, *Totemism* (Boston: Beacon Press, 1963).

London, I., "A Russian Report on Post-operative Newly-seeing," *American Journal of Psychology,* 73, 1960.

Lovelock, J., *Gaia, A New Look at Life on Earth* (Oxford [England]: Oxford University Press, 1979).

MacIntyre, A. (ed.), *Hegel* (Notre Dame, Ind., London, New York: University of Notre Dame Press, 1972).

McTaggart, J. E., *The Nature of Existence* (Cambridge [England]: Cambridge University Press, 1927).

Mabbott, J. D., "Our Direct Experience of Time," *Mind,* LX, 1951.

———, "The Specious Present," *Mind,* LXIV, 1955.

Mannheim, K., *Ideology and Utopia* (London: Kegan Paul, Trench, 1936; New York: Harcourt Brace, 1936; London: Routledge and Kegan Paul, 1949).

Margenau, H., *The Nature of Physical Reality,* (New York: McGraw Hill, 1950).

Marsden, D., *The Philosophy of Time* (Oxford: Holywell Press, 1955).

Marx, K., *The Holy Family* in *Writings of the Young Marx on Philosophy and Society* ed. and trans. Lloyd D. Easton and Kurt H. Guddat (Garden City, N.J.: Doubleday, 1967).

Medawar, Sir P. B., "Critical Notice on the *Phenomenon of Man* by Pierre Teilhard de Chardin," *Mind,* LXX, 277, Jan. 1961.

Merleau-Ponty, M., *The Phenomenology of Perception,* trans., C. Smith (London: Routledge and Kegan Paul, 1962).

———, *The Structure of Behavior,* trans. A. L. Fisher (Boston, 1963).

Milne, E. A., "Fundamental Concepts of Natural Philosophy," *Proceedings of the Royal Society of Edinburgh,* Sec. A, vol. 62, 1943-44, Part I.

————, *Relativity, Gravitation and World Structure* (Oxford [England]: Oxford University Press, 1935).

Miller, I., *Husserl, Perception and Temporal Awareness* (Cambridge, MA.: M.I.T. Press, 1984).

Minkowski, E., *Lived Time: Phenomenological and Psychological Studies*, trans. with Introd. by Nancy Metzel (Evanston: Northwestern University Press, 1970).

Morowitz, J. H., *Mayonnaise and the Origins of Life* (New York: , Schribners, 1985).

Monod, J., *Le hazard et la necessité* (Paris, 1970).
————, *Chance and Necessity*, trans., A. Wainhouse (New York, 1970).

Mundle, C. K., "How Specious is the Specious Present," *Mind*, LXIII, 1954.

Muralt, A. de, *L'Idée de la Phénoménologie: l'exemparisme husserlien* (Paris: Presses Universitaires de France, 1958). Translated by G. L. Breckon, *The Idea of Phenomenology: Husserlian Exemplarism* (Evanston: Northwestern University Press, 1974).

Mure, G. R., *Aristotle* (London: Benn, 1932).
————, *Introduction to Hegel* (Oxford [England]: Oxford University Press, 1940).
————, *A Study of Hegel's Logic* (Oxford [England]: Oxford University Press, 1950).

Natanson, M.A., *Edmund Husserl, Philosopher of Infinite Tasks* (Evanston: Northwestern University Press, 1973).

Needham, J. *Time, the Refreshing River* (London: G. Allen and Unwin, 1944).

Newton, Sir Issac, *Philosophiae Naturalis Principia Mathematica*, 3rd. ed., Alexander Koyrè and Bernard Cohen (eds.) (Cambridge [England]: Cambridge University Press, 1972).
————, *Mathematical Principles of Natural Philosophy*, ed. and trans. F. Cajori, trans. Motte (Los Angeles, CA.: University of California Press, 1966).
————, *Opticks* (New York: Dover Publications, 1952).

Newton-Smith, W. H., *The Structure of Time* (London: Routledge and Kegan Paul, 1980).

Oaklander, L. N., *Temporal relations and Temporal becoming: A defence of a Russellian Theory of Time* (Lanham, MD., New York and London: University Press of America, 1984).

Oparin, A. I., *The Origin of Life* (London: Oliver & Boyd, 1957).

Park, D., *The Image of Eternity* (Amherst, MA.: University of Massachusetts Press, 1980).

Piaget, J., *Le Structuralisme* (Paris: Presses Universitaires de France, 1968). Translated by Chaninah Maschler, *Structuralism* (New York: Basic Books, 1970).

————, *The Psychology of Intelligence* (London: Routledge and Kegan Paul, 1950).

————, *The Constitution of Reality in the Child*, trans. Margaret Cook (New York: Basic Books, 1954).

Planck, M., *The Philosophy of Physics* (London: G. Allen and Unwin, 1936; New York: Norton & Co., 1936).

————, *The Universe in the Light of Modern Physics* (London: G. Allen and Unwin, 1937; New York: Norton & Co., 1951).

Plato, *Dialogues of Plato*, trans., Benjamin Jowett (Oxford [England]: Clarendon Press, 1953).

————, *The Works of Plato*, Edith Hamilton and Huntington Cairns (eds.) (Princeton, N.J.: 1963).

————, *Plato's Theory of Knowledge; Theaetetus and Sophist*, trans., F. Cornford (London: Routledge and Kegan Paul, 1935).

————, *Plato's Cosmology; Timeaus*, trans., F. Cornford (London: Routledge and Kegan Paul, 1937, 1957).

Poincaré, H., *Science and Hypothesis* (New York: Dover Publications, 1952).

Popper, Sir Karl, *Conjectures and Refutations* (New York and London: Basic Books, 1962, 1963).

————, *Objective Knowledge; An Evolutionary Approach* (Oxford [England]: Clarendon Press, 1979).

————, *The Logic of Scientific Discovery* (London: Hutchinson, 1959).

————, *The Open Society and its Enemies* (Princeton, N.J.: Princeton University Press; London, 1950, 1966).

Price, H. H., "Appearing and Appearance," *American Philosophical Quarterly*, Vol. I, 1964.

————, *Perception* (London: Methuen, 1950).

Reitmaster, L. A., *The Philosophy of Time* (New York: Citadel, 1962; Westport, CT.: Greenwood Press, 1974).

Richter, D. (ed.), *Perspectives in Neurosychiatry*, London: H. K. Lewis, 1950).

Riesen, A. H., "The Development of Visual Perception in Man and Chimpanzee," *Science*, 106, 1947.

Rohrer, J. H., and M. Sherif (eds.), *Social Psychology at the Cross-roads* (New York: Harper, 1951).

Rose, G., *Hegel contra Sociology* (London: Athlone Press; New Jersey: Humanities Press, 1981).

————, *Dialectic of Nihilism: Post-Structuralism and Law* (Oxford and New York: Blackwell, 1984).

Ross, Sir David, *Aristotle* (London: Methuen, 1937, 1949).

Russell, Bertrand, *Human Knowledge, its Scope and Limits* (London: George Allen and Unwin, 1948).
————, "Logical Atomism," *Contemporary British Philosophy*, Series I, (London: George Allen and Unwin, 1924).
————, *Our Knowledge of the External World* (New York: Norton, 1929).
————, New York: *The Philosophy of Logical Atomism* (Minneapolis, Minnesota: University of Minnesota Press, 1959).
————, *The Principles of Mathematics* (New York: G. Allen and Unwin, 1937).

Russell, B. and Whitehead, A. N., *Principia Mathematica* (Cambridge [England]: Cambridge University Press, 1927; reprinted 1973).

Schelling, F. W. J., *System des Transcendentalen Idialismus* (Tübingen: Klett Cotta, 1800; Leipzig, Felix Meiner Verlag, 1957).
————, *System of Transcendental Idealism*, trans. Peter Heath (Charlottesville, VA.: University of Virginia Press, 1978).

Scher, J. (ed.), *Theories of the Mind* (Free Press of Glencoe, New York, 1962).

Schlipp, P. A. (ed.), *The Philosophy of A. N. Whitehead* (Evanston: Northwestern University Press, 1941).
————, *Albert Einstein, Philosopher, Scientist* (Evanston: Northwestern University Press, 1949).

Schroedinger, E., *Space-Time Structure* (Cambridge [England]: Cambridge University Press, 1950).
————, *Science and Humanism* (Cambridge [England]: Cambridge University Press, 1952).

Sciama, D. W., *The Unity of the Universe* (Garden City, N.J.: Doubleday, 1959, 1961; London: Faber and Faber, 1959).

Sheldrake, R., *A New Science of Life* (London: Paladin, 1987).

Sherover, C. M., *Heidegger, Kant, and Time* (Bloomington: Indiana University Press, 1971).

Snell, B., *The Discovery of the Mind, The Greek Origins of European Thought* (Oxford: Blackwell, 1953).

Spinoza, B., *Collected Works*, trans. and ed. E. Curley (Princeton, N.J.: Princeton University Press, 1985-).
————, *Ethics*, trans. A. Boyle (London: M. Dent, 1910).

————, *Ethics, and Selected Letters*, trans. S. Shirley (Indianapolis, Indiana: Hackett, 1982).

————, *Opera quotquot reperta sunt*, van Vloten en Land (eds.) (The Hague: Martinus Nijoff, 1913-1914).

Stapp, H. P., "Are Faster-than-light Influences Necessary," in *Quantum Mechanics versus Local Realism—The Einstein, Podolsky and Rosen Paradox*, ed. F. Salleri (New York: Plenum Press, 1987).

————, "Quantum Mechanics and the Physicist's Conception of Nature: Philosophical Implications of Bell's Theorem," in *The World View of Contemporary Physics: Is there a Need for a New Metaphysics?* ed. R. Kitchener (Albany, N.Y.: State University of New York Press, 1988).

Stonier, T., *Nuclear Disaster* (Harmondsworth [England]: Penguin Books, 1963).

Teilhard de Chardin, P., *Le Phénomène humain* (Paris: Editions du Seuil, 1955).

————, *The Phenomenon of Man* trans. B. Wall, Introduction by Julian Huxley (London: Collins; New York: Harper and Row, 1959).

Thirring, W., "Urbausteine der Materie," *Almanach der Osterreichischen Akademie der Wissenschaften*, Band, 118, 1968 (Imp. 1969).

Thomas, L., *The Lives of a Cell* (New York: Viking Press, 1974; Harmondsworth [England]: Penguin Books, 1987).

Thorpe, H., *Learning and Instinct in Animals* (London: Methuen, 1956, 1963, 1964-1966).

Tinbergen, N., *A Study of Instinct* (Oxford [England]: Oxford University Press, 1952).

United States Atomic Energy Commission, *The Effects of Nuclear Weapons* (Washington, D.C., 1964).

United States Congress, The Holifield Committee Hearings on Radiation, 1959.

Verene, D. P. (ed.), *Hegel's Social and Political Thought* (Atlantic Highlands, N.J.: Humanities Press, 1980).

Vernon, M. D., *Experiments in Visual Perception* (Harmondsworth [England]: Penguin Books, 1966).

————, *The Psychology of Perception* (Harmondsworth [England]: Penguin Books, 1969).

von Senden, M., *Raum und Gestalt auffassung bei operierten Blindgeborenen vor und nach der Operation* (Leipzig, 1932).

————, *Space and Sight* (Free Press of Glencoe, IL., 1960).

von Wright, G. H., *The Logical Problem of Induction* (Oxford [England]: Blackwell, 1957).

Whitehead, A. N., *Adventures of Ideas* (Cambridge [England]: Cambridge University Press; New York: Macmillan, 1933).

————, *An Enquiry into the Principles of Natural Knowledge* (Cambridge [England]: Cambridge University Press, 1919, 1925; New York, Dover 1982).

————, *Process and Reality,* D. R. Griffin and D. W. Sherburn (eds.) (Cambridge [England]: Cambridge University Press, 1929; New York: Free Press, 1978).

————, *Science and the Modern World* (Cambridge [England]: Cambridge University Press, 1926; New York: Macmillan, 1925, 1948; New York: New American Library, 1953).

————, *The Concept of Nature* (Cambridge [England]: Cambridge University Press, 1920, 1971).

Whitehead, A. N., and B. Russell, *Principia Mathematica* (Cambridge [England]: Cambridge University Press, 1927; reprinted 1973).

Whitrow, J. G., "On Synthetic Aspects of Mathematics," *Philosophy*, vol. XXV, no. 95, 1950.

————, *The Natural Philosophy of Time* (London and Edinburgh: Nelson, 1961; New York and Evanston: Harper, Torchbooks, 1963).

Whittaker, Sir Edmund, *From Euclid to Eddington* (Cambridge [England]: Cambridge University Press, 1949).

Williams, D., *The Ground of Induction* (Cambridge, MA.: Harvard University Press, 1947).

————, "The Myth of Passage," *Journal of Philosophy*, V, 48, 1951; reprinted in *Principles of Empirical Realism* (Springfield, IL., 1966), and in R. Gale (ed.), *The Philosophy of Time* (New York: Anchor Books, Doubleday, 1967; London, 1969).

Wittgenstein, L., *On Certainty* (Oxford [England]: Blackwell, 1969).

————, *Philosophical Investigations* (London: Routledge and Kegal Paul, 1967).

————, *Tractatus Logico-Philosophicus* (London: Routledge and Kegan Paul, 1960).

INDEX